Comparative
Human Rights Law

Carolina Academic Press
Comparative Law Series

Michael Louis Corrado
Series Editor

Comparative Constitutional Review
Cases and Materials
Michael Louis Corrado

Comparative Law: An Introduction
Vivian Grosswald Curran

Comparative Consumer Bankruptcy
Jason Kilborn

Comparative Law of Contracts
Alain Levasseur

Comparative Criminal Procedure, Second Edition
Stephen C. Thaman

Comparative Human Rights Law, Vol. 1:
Expression, Association, Religion
Arthur Mark Weisburd

Comparative Human Rights Law, Vol. 2:
Detention, Prosecution, Capital Punishment
Arthur Mark Weisburd

Comparative
Human Rights Law

Detention, Prosecution, Capital Punishment

Volume 2

A. Mark Weisburd

MARTHA M. BRANDIS PROFESSOR OF LAW
UNIVERSITY OF NORTH CAROLINA AT CHAPEL HILL

CAROLINA ACADEMIC PRESS
Durham, North Carolina

Library of Congress Cataloging-in-Publication Data

Weisburd, A. Mark (Arthur Mark), 1948-
  Comparative human rights law : detention, prosecution, capital punishment
/ by Arthur Mark Weisburd.
      p. cm.
  Includes bibliographical references and index.
  ISBN 13: 978-1-59460-441-6   ISBN 10: 1-59460-441-X (alk. paper)
  1. Criminal procedure. 2. Detention of persons. 3. Human rights. I. Title.
  K5401.W45 2008
  341.4'8--dc22
                                      2007049902

CAROLINA ACADEMIC PRESS
700 Kent Street
Durham, North Carolina 27701
Telephone (919) 489-7486
Fax (919) 493-5668
www.cap-press.com

Printed in the United States of America

To My Wife

Contents

Table of Authorities

Japan

Cases

Constitution

European Human Rights System

Official Reports

Council of Europe, *Implementation of judgments of the European Court of Human Rights: Court Judgments Pending Before the Committee of Ministers for Control of Execution for More than Five Years, or Otherwise Raising Important Issues, AS/Jur (2005) 32, 9 June 2005*, 13

Council of Europe, *Implementation of judgments of the European Court of Human Rights: Supplementary Introductory Memorandum (Revised), AS/Jur (2005) 55, 20 December 2005*, 13

India

Cases

Constitution

Statutes

Code of Criminal Procedure

Evidence Act

United States

Miscellaneous

_____, *Pleas of the Crown* (1736), 132, 133, 137

Hawkins, William, *Pleas of the Crown* (T. Leach 6th ed. 1787), 133

Holdsworth, Sir William, *History of English Law* (3d ed. 1944), 132

Howell, Thomas Bayly, *A Complete Collection of State Trials and Proceedings: from the Earliest Period to the Year 1783 and Continued from the Year 1783 to the Present Time* (1816–1828), 132, 133, 141

Jardine, David, *Criminal Trials* (1832), 132, 137

Langbein, John H., *Prosecuting Crime in the Renaissance* (1974), 132, 137

Oppler, Alfred C., *Legal Reform in Occupied Japan: A Participant Looks Back* (1976), 5

Perry, Richard L. and John C. Cooper (eds.), *Sources of Our Liberties* (1959), 134

Schwartz, Bernard, *The Bill of Rights: A Documentary History* (1971), 134, 135

Stephen, Sir James. F., *History of the Criminal Law of England* (1883), 132, 137

Wigmore on Evidence (2d ed. 1923), 131, 133, 136, 138

Wigmore on Evidence (McNaughton rev. 1961), 112

Wroth, L. Kinvin and Hiller B. Zobel (eds.), *Legal Papers of John Adams* (1965), 134

Articles and Book Chapters

Beer, Lawrence W., "Constitutional Revolution in Japanese Law, Society and Politics," 16 *Modern Asian Studies* 33 (1982), 3

Herrmann, Frank R., S.J. and Brownlow Speer, "Facing the Accuser: Ancient and Medieval Precursors of the Confrontation Clause," 34 *Virginia Journal of International Law* 481 (1994), 131

Kirst, Roger W., "Appellate Court Answers to the Confrontation Questions in *Lilly v. Virginia*," 53 *Syracuse Law Review* 87 (2003), 142

Okudaira, Y., "Forty Years of the Constitution and Its Various Influences: Japanese, American and European," at *Japanese Constituitonal Law* 20 (Percy R. Luney and Kazuyuki Takahashi eds. 1976), 5

Pollitt, Daniel H., "The Right of Confrontation: Its History and Modern Dress," 8 *Journal of Public Law* 381 (1959), 134

Preface

The Aim of This Book

This book is intended to introduce American law students to variations in approaches to human rights in several of the more important legal systems of the world. The key word in the previous sentence is "introduce." The subject is so vast, and the range of relevant law so great, that a comprehensive discussion of the subject would require many volumes. Nonetheless, it is possible even in a relatively brief work to provide a sense of the ways different societies provide legal protections for their members.

This work is intended to permit comparisons, but its brevity required focusing its coverage. Therefore, the cases in this work are drawn from only four legal systems; the hope is that the possibility of gaining some overall sense of the workings of each of these systems compensates for the narrowness of this approach. Selection was dictated by three factors. First, there seemed to be no point in considering cases from countries where the courts are either ignored or lacking in independence. Second, allowing for the first consideration, it was crucial to examine a variety of legal systems. Finally, it was necessary to focus on systems from which case reports were available in English. Accordingly, the legal systems addressed in this work are the Japanese system, showing the approach of a developed, non-Western country; the European human rights system, illustrating rights thinking in a system sharing with the United States many values regarding the relationship between individuals and society; the Indian system, interesting because it reflects the work of an active and fairly effective court system operating in a developing, non-Western country; and, finally, the United States' system, with which students are likely to be most familiar and which can provide a benchmark.

Again, to facilitate comparison, only a limited number of rights are addressed, even taking into account the companion volume to this one. All are so-called first generation rights, addressing civil and political protections; all were chosen from among those that seem so basic as to be essential to any system of rights protection.

This volume addresses the right to the writ of habeas corpus, various rights relating to criminal procedure, and the death penalty. Habeas corpus is part of the foundation of government by law. So long as an individual can force government to demonstrate a legal basis for confinement, arbitrary detention can be controlled. The procedures governments must follow in order to impose criminal penalties on individuals are also fundamental protections of freedom. The range of issues which could be addressed under this heading is vast. The discussion in this volume has focused on three issues which bear heavily on protection of individuals: the nature of the right to counsel in a given system, the extent of the right against self-incrimination, and—what is essentially the obverse of the foregoing issue—the limitations the police are obliged to observe in interrogating criminal suspects. Finally, this volume addresses the different attitudes toward the death penalty taken in the different legal systems discussed in this volume. Given the intensity of opinions on this subject, it seemed useful to provide an indication of the range of views regarding capital punishment taken in different parts of the world.

The first chapter of this book provides introductions to the legal system of Japan, to the European human rights system, and to India's legal system. These brief discussions are aimed at explaining to students the structure of each of those systems, and the importance of judicial opinions in them. The following chapters address the rights listed above.

It should be noted that, while all cases from the European Court of Human Rights and the Supreme Courts of India and the United States are available from English-language data bases, decisions of the Supreme Court of Japan are available in English only in a limited selection on that Court's website and also from translations made for various purposes and published, the cases being selected for translation according to the translator's criteria. Since the editor does not read Japanese, it is possible that significant Japanese cases do not appear in this work; nonetheless, the discussion is believed to be reasonably complete.

The Book's Structure

This book includes a relatively small number of lightly-edited—and therefore, in many cases, lengthy—excerpts from judicial decisions, a limited number of notes providing information regarding particular legal systems' treatment of issues not adequately addressed in any decision, and an appendix of legal instruments relevant to decisions making up the book. It therefore differs from many casebooks in its lack of textual material, its omission of questions intended to provoke thought, and in the necessarily limited scope of the issues raised by the decisions set out. It may be useful to explain why the book was structured in this way.

The series of which this book is a part aims at providing relatively short books which may be used to focus discussion in comparative law classes on particular topics. Since books in this series cannot be lengthy, editors do not have the luxury of resolving doubts by including material not deemed to be essential. That fact, in turn, forces editors to decide what exactly is essential in the context of particular works.

The subject of this book is comparative human rights, so it is obviously essential to present cases addressing a range of rights from a range of different legal systems. While, as noted above, the length of the book limits both the number of rights and the number of legal systems which may be addressed, one possible way of dealing with this circumstance would have been to include much shorter excerpts from a greater number of cases, as well as explanatory textual material. That approach, however, would have worked against what seemed to be a second essential element of the book.

That element relates to the purposes of the study of comparative law. While one such purpose is of course to convey to students the differences in substantive law between systems, there are others which are also important. One of those additional purposes is to permit students to get a sense of the styles of legal reasoning used in different legal systems. What sorts of arguments are legitimate? What counts as a conclusive argument? Yet another purpose is to permit students to reflect upon the unarticulated assumptions underlying each legal system—ideas about how the world works seen as so fundamental in each system that they do not require explanation, or indeed, as so very basic that it would never occur to judges that there was any other way to think about legal issues. These latter aims cannot be achieved if students are provided only with snippets of decisions setting out rules of law, but omitting either a description of the facts different courts saw as crucial to their decisions or the way those courts' own explanation of their reasoning about the facts. While textual materials and leading questions following cases might provide information to students on those subjects, that approach would seem to defeat the purpose of a casebook—that is, to force students themselves to read cases carefully in order to understand all that each case can teach. But if a short book is to present excerpts from cases long enough to permit students to see how different courts reason about difficult human rights issues, and to include as well the language of the legal instruments with which those courts must work, it cannot include many cases. And, while this means that coverage cannot be very great, that is inevitable anyway if human rights issues from a number of countries are to be addressed in a work of approximately 200 pages. (This is clear if one considers how long a casebook would have to be to comprehensively address all matters relevant only to the Bill of Rights and Reconstruction Amendments in the United States Constitution.) When all of these factors are taken into account, what has resulted is this casebook. It is hoped that this reasoning makes sense.

Usage Conventions

To permit readers to avoid having to adjust to different arrangements of material in different cases, it seemed helpful to make some rules of usage. They are:

First, where the original documents reproduced here employed British rather than American spelling, the spelling has *not* been altered.

Second, bracketed material has been inserted by the editor, generally to summarize important but lengthy portions of a document, occasionally to add explanatory material too important to be left to footnotes.

Third, regarding footnotes, please note that most of those in the documents reproduced in this work have been omitted. Those footnotes which have been retained are numbered consecutively in each document, without regard to their original numbering. Footnotes by the editor are indicated by lower case letters.

Fourth, please note that case naming conventions and citation formats necessarily vary from jurisdiction to jurisdiction. Japanese cases are, when possible, named according to the label attached to them on the website of the Supreme Court of Japan, and are cited by case number, date of decision and reporter in which they appeared (except when the website does not name that reporter). Cases not taken from the Supreme Court's website are named and cited as they were in the source from which they were taken. Cases from the European Court of Human Rights are cited to the official reports of that court; earlier decisions are therefore cited by their number within Series A of that court's publications and by date of decisions; later cases, appearing in the volumes entitled *European Human Rights Cases*, are cited to those volumes, which are abbreviated E.C.H.R. Cases from the Supreme Court of India are, when possible, cited to the Supreme Court Reports, abbreviated S.C.R., and to the Supreme Court sections of the All-India Reporter, abbreviated A.I.R.(S.C.). Occasionally, however, Indian citations are to the All-India Reporter Supreme Court Weekly, abbreviated A.I.R.(S.C.W.), or the Supreme Court Journal, abbreviated S.C.J. There is also one citation to the Federal Court Reports, abbreviated F.C.R., reporting decisions of the highest court of pre-independence India.

It was necessary to decide how to deal with the texts of legal instruments discussed in the book. The basic approach taken was to reproduce only the sections/articles of the various Constitutions/statutes/treaties relevant to the cases decided, instead of attempting to present the entirety of each instrument; where cases refer to an entire instrument but not to any of its component sections/articles, e.g. "The ABC Statute of 2006" instead of "Section 28 of the ABC Statute of 2006," nothing is reproduced. Where a case cites a section/article itself having little to do with human rights and the thrust of which is clear from the discussion, that section/article is not reproduced; such sections/articles are marked with an asterisk(*) the first time they are cited in each case or other discussion, but not especially designated otherwise. Finally, where a section or article is not reproduced in the appendix, but is quoted verbatim in the case or other discussion which refers to it, that section or article is marked with two asterisks (**) the first time it appears, and not otherwise marked. All other sections/articles mentioned in the discussions which follow appear in the Appendix.

Translations

The translators of Japanese cases taken from the website of the Japanese Supreme Court are indicated to the extent that information is provided on the website. The translators of Japanese cases taken from copyrighted works are indicated to the extent that information is provided in those works. Some of the separate opinions from European Court of Human Rights decisions are described on that court's website as translations, but that website does not provide the name of the translator; since the translations appear on that website, however, they are presumably official.

Acknowledgments

The Editor wishes to acknowledge, with gratitude:

Cavendish Publishing Limited, for permission to reprint material from Meryll Dean, *Japanese Legal System*, Second Edition, 2002.

The University of Washington Press, for permission to reprint material from John M. Maki, *Court and Constitution in Japan: Selected Supreme Court Decisions, 1948–1960*, with translations by Ikeda Masaaki, David C.S. Sissons, and Kurt Steiner, 1964.

The University of North Carolina Law Foundation, for its support of this project.

Comparative
Human Rights Law

Chapter One

Non-United States Legal Systems

A. Introduction

The following sections provide brief introductions to the non-American legal systems from which this volumes draw cases. While the cases are probably comprehensible without these discussions, it seemed useful to provide at least some background for American students unlikely to be familiar with foreign legal structures.

B. Japan

(Taken from Meryll Dean, *Japanese Legal System*, Second Edition, 2002, pages 445–456, 345, 353–354, 129–131.)

The Constitutional Framework

The recent constitutional history of Japan can be divided into two main periods, the modern and the contemporary. The modern spans the period of monarchical constitutionalism from the mid-19th century to the Second World War, including the Meiji Restoration and the introduction of a Western inspired constitution in 1889. The contemporary is from the promulgation of the 'new' constitution in 1946 to the present and has been a period of constitutional democracy. Both periods have been characterised by a leading commentator as "constitutional revolutions" and were "assimilative reactions to Western legal traditions" rather than responses to internal growth and organic development.[1]

---

1. Lawrence W. Beer, *Constitutional Revolution in Japanese Law, Society and Politics*, 16 Mod. Asian Studies 33 (1982).

Although introducing Western ideas, the Meiji Constitution preserved many of the hierarchical and societal norms embodied in a system of monarchical constitutionalism. In short, it was "nothing less than the transplantation of a Western legal heart into the Japanese body."[2] However, during the early 20th century, as a result of a complex interplay of sociological and political forces within that "body", there was a growing awareness of new norms and ideas, although not the development of a coherent tradition....

The Meiji Constitution had been a bridge between the semi-feudal Tokugawa heritage and the new, centralized authoritarian government. Heavily influenced by Western thinking, it nevertheless retained the Emperor as the embodiment of national identity, thus linking traditional legitimacy to the new state authority. In a similar manner the 1946 Constitution could not divest itself completely of the Meiji heritage; instead, inspired in the main by the American Occupation reformers, the old apparatus of state authority was transformed and a foundation for a new democratic constitutionalism established. The link between the two was Article 73* of the Meiji Constitution which enabled the reformers to present the new constitution as an amendment to the old one. Furthermore, albeit of necessity, the Emperor was preserved as a symbol of the state who could reign but not rule, thus providing a certain and, at the time, essential continuity between monarchical constitutionalism and constitutional democracy.

Thus, one of the important features of the second "revolution" was to convert the Emperor's subjects from objects of the constitution to citizens of a new democratic order. Inherent in this process was the notion of democracy and accountability in government and the law, as well as the protection of the individual through the creation of fundamental rights....

In pursuance of these objectives and following the redesignation of the Emperor as symbol and instrument of constitutional government in Chapter 1 of the 1946 Constitution, the next chapter consists of Article 9* alone, the renunciation of war clause. Next comes Chapter 3 which sets out the 'Rights and Duties of the People' and only after these provisions are the institutions of democratic government, parliamentary democracy and justice dealt with....

The three pillars of the present constitutional framework, popular sovereignty, pacifism and protection of fundamental human rights, are based upon the foundation of respect for the rule of law and are guaranteed by the Supreme Court through the use of judicial review. Although the constitution does not make specific mention of the rule of law, it is clear that the relationship between law and government was to be predicated upon that basis. This is demonstrated by the fact that fundamental human rights are protected against

---

2. *Id.* Though said in the context of the reception of Western law, in general it remains true of the constitution in particular.

the arbitrary exercise of government power and by the use of judicial review, introduced in Article 81*.... However, there is what might seem to be something of an inconsistency between the concept of parliamentary supremacy based on popular sovereignty and the idea of judicial supremacy embodied in judicial review. This alleged inconsistency arises from Article 41* which designates the Diet as the 'highest organ of state power' and thereby seems to give the legislature some kind of superiority. Moreover, even if the superiority of the Diet is of 'symbolic rather than legal significance', it may be one explanation for the apparent reluctance of the Supreme Court to invalidate laws as unconstitutional.[3] Certainly in the 50 year history of the constitution, the Supreme Court has declared a law unconstitutional on only five occasions and invalidated the legislation in just four of the five cases. Given the volume of legislation during the period, this may be considered as something of a triumph for the process of legislative drafting in the Diet. On the other hand, there is considerable support for the view that the Supreme Court is self restraining and that "negativism in judicial review is one of the most characteristic features of the Japanese Supreme Court."[4]

With the move from the authoritarian Meiji era of rule by law, to the new postwar constitution based on the rule of law, the second 'revolution' was complete. How it has been sustained will be examined in the materials, but first a number of issues will be highlighted, in particular the role of the Supreme Court and the use of judicial review. Article 76* of the Constitution states that "the whole judicial power" is vested in the Supreme Court and Article 77* provides that it is "vested with the rule-making power under which it determines the rules of procedure and practice" for the courts, profession and administration of justice. In addition Article 81 states that the Supreme Court "is the court of last resort with power to determine the constitutionality of any law, order, regulation or official act." Thus, not only is it a court of last resort with powers of constitutional review, but it is also seized with responsibility for the administration and management of the profession ... However, in spite of its position as guardian of the constitution, the Supreme Court is not a constitutional court in the mould of continental European models, a fact that was made clear in a Supreme Court decision in 1952. In that case, whilst upholding the power of judicial review, the Supreme Court made the following statement clarifying the position:

> Under the system prevailing in our country, a judgment may be sought in the courts only when there exists a concrete legal dispute be-

---

3. Alfred C. Oppler, LEGAL REFORM IN OCCUPIED JAPAN: A PARTICIPANT LOOKS BACK 88 (1976).

4. Y. Okudaira, *Forty Years of the Constitution and Its Various Influences: Japanese, American and European* in JAPANESE CONSTITUTIONAL LAW 20 (Percy R. Luney and Kazuyuki Takahashi eds. 1976).

tween specific parties. The argument that courts have the power to determine in the abstract the constitutionality of laws, orders, and the
like, in the absence of a concrete case, has no foundation in the constitution itself, or any statute.[5]

....

Organization of the Court System

The postwar constitution established a unitary court system for civil, criminal and administrative cases, with the Supreme Court at its head. Article 76
states: "The whole judicial power is vested in the Supreme Court and in such
inferior courts as are established by law." The Court Organisation Law 1947*
provided for four types of inferior courts, Summary Courts, District and Family Courts and the High Courts ... Two appeals are allowed against an original
judgment thereby establishing a three-tiered court structure, but the only real
distinction drawn is that indicated in the Constitution as between the Supreme
Court and inferior courts....

The Supreme Court consists of 14 judges and the Chief Justice ... The
Supreme Court sits as a full court of 15, or in a division of five judges. These
divisions, or Petty Benches..., of which there are three, are the norm, but in
exceptional cases the judges must sit together as a Grand Bench..., with the
Chief Justice presiding. These exceptional cases fall into four categories: (1) an
appeal on a constitutional issue where there is no Supreme Court precedent;
(2) an appeal on a non-constitutional point of law, where a Petty Bench wishes
to overrule a Supreme Court precedent; (3) cases ereferred to the Grand Bench
by a Petty Bench on the grounds of their importance; and (4) cases where the
Petty Bench does not reach a majority view.

Sources of Law

... Modern Japanese law is drawn from a wide variety of legal sources, but
to present it merely as a system of law developed over the last 120 years and
consisting entirely of legal transplants, would be to ignore and misrepresent
the structure and operation of law in Japanese society. In spite of what might
be considered massive injections of Western legal and cultural influences, there
remain aspects of law and society which are fundamentally and uniquely
Japanese, the strength and resilience of which affect the operation of the law.
Thus, the place of custom *(kanshu)* and equitable principles of common reason *(jori)* need to be considered, as does 'administrative guidance' *(gyosei*

---

5. [Judgment Concerning the Question of Whether, in the Absence of a Concrete
Case, the Supreme Court Has Authority to Determine the Constitutionality of Any Law or
the like in the Abstract, Minshu Vol. 6, No. 9, at 783, Case Number: 1952 (Ma) No. 23
(Grand Bench, October 8, 1952).]

shido) which occupies a unique place in the Japanese legal system as what might be termed 'nonjusticiable law'. Issued by government departments it is an instrument of bureaucratic power which, whilst it is not 'law' in the strict sense, has a role and function beyond that of the mere bureaucratic circular....

... Japanese law is a complex mosaic ... where the apparent certainty of the written law can become less clear as a result of interpretation *(kaishaku)* or the meaning of the language itself.... First it is important to establish the hierarchy of sources of Japanese law. At its simplest, the distinction is between written and unwritten law, thus enacted law *(seiteiho)* is the prime source of law. Within this class of laws there is a sub-hierarchy consisting of the six codes *(roppa)* and statutes *(horitsu)....*

[I]n addition to the codes and statutes, written law also includes orders *(meirei)* issued by government agencies; foremost amongst these are Cabinet Orders *(seirei),* followed by Ministerial Orders *(furei* being an order issued by the Prime Minister and *sharei* issued by Ministers). Also under this heading are rules *(kisoku);* these fall into three categories, (1) Rules of the Ministries, issued to supplement general statutes with detail; (2) Rules of the House of Representatives or the House of Councillors, which govern procedural and administrative matters and are made pursuant to Article 58(2) of the constitution; (3) Rules of the Supreme Court which detail the administration of justice, rules of practice and procedure in relation to the courts and profession, pursuant to Article 77(1) of the constitution. Although not technically law in this context, there are also Local Ordinances *(jorei)* which are issued by prefectural or city authorities pursuant to Article 94* of the constitution. Last, but by no means least, there are treaties *(joyaku)* which whilst no doubt a source of law, are the subject of debate amongst Japanese academics as to their effect on domestic law.

C. The European Human Rights System

(Taken from the website of the European Court of Human Rights, http://www.echr.coe.int/ECHR/EN/Header/The+Court/The+Court/History+o f+the+Court/, visited December 27, 2006.)

1. The Council of Europe

The Council of Europe was established in 1949, with the objects of defending human rights, parliamentary democracy, and the rule of law. (It should be understood that the Council is an institution distinct from the 25-member European Union, although all members of the Union are also members of the Council.) Currently, the Council numbers 46 countries. It has promulgated a large number of treaties on a wide variety of subjects. Human rights is a subject to which the Council has paid particular attention. It is the parent organization of the European Court of Human Rights.

In addition to the Court, the organs of the Council are: the Committee of Ministers, composed of the 46 Foreign ministers or their Strasbourg-based deputies, which is the Council's decision-making body; the Parliamentary Assembly, grouping 630 members (315 representatives and 315 substitutes) from the 46 national parliaments; the Congress of Local and Regional Authorities, composed of a Chamber of Local Authorities and a Chamber of Regions; and the 1800-strong secretariat.

2. The European Court of Human Rights

Historical Background

The European Convention on Human Rights of 1950

1. The Convention for the Protection of Human Rights and Fundamental Freedoms was drawn up within the Council of Europe. It was opened for signature in Rome on 4 November 1950 and entered into force in September 1953. Taking as their starting point the 1948 Universal Declaration of Human Rights, the framers of the Convention sought to pursue the aims of the Council of Europe through the maintenance and further realisation of human rights and fundamental freedoms. The Convention was to represent the first steps for the collective enforcement of certain of the rights set out in the Universal Declaration.

2. In addition to laying down a catalogue of civil and political rights and freedoms, the Convention set up a mechanism for the enforcement of the obligations entered into by Contracting States. Three institutions were entrusted with this responsibility: the European Commission of Human Rights (set up in 1954), the European Court of Human Rights (set up in 1959) and the Committee of Ministers of the Council of Europe, the latter organ being composed of the Ministers of Foreign Affairs of the member States or their representatives.

3. Under the Convention in its original version, complaints could be brought against Contracting States either by other Contracting States or by individual applicants (individuals, groups of individuals or non-governmental organisations). Recognition of the right of individual application was, however, optional and it could therefore be exercised only against those States which had accepted it (Protocol No. 11 to the Convention was subsequently to make its acceptance compulsory, see paragraph 6 below).

The complaints were first the subject of a preliminary examination by the Commission, which determined their admissibility. Where an application was declared admissible, the Commission placed itself at the parties' disposal with a view to brokering a friendly settlement. If no settlement was forthcoming, it drew up a report establishing the facts and expressing an opinion on the merits of the case. The report was transmitted to the Committee of Ministers.

4. Where the respondent State had accepted the compulsory jurisdiction of the Court, the Commission and/or any Contracting State concerned had a period of three months following the transmission of the report to the Committee of Ministers within which to bring the case before the Court for a final, binding adjudication. Individuals were not entitled to bring their cases before the Court.

If a case was not referred to the Court, the Committee of Ministers decided whether there had been a violation of the Convention and, if appropriate, awarded "just satisfaction" to the victim. The Committee of Ministers also had responsibility for supervising the execution of the Court's judgments.

Subsequent Developments

5. Since the Convention's entry into force thirteen Protocols have been adopted. Protocols Nos. 1, 4, 6, 7, 12 [not yet in force] and 13 added further rights and liberties to those guaranteed by the Convention, while Protocol No. 2 conferred on the Court the power to give advisory opinions. Protocol No. 9 enabled individual applicants to bring their cases before the Court subject to ratification by the respondent State and acceptance by a screening panel. Protocol No. 11 restructured the enforcement machinery (see below). The remaining Protocols concerned the organisation of and procedure before the Convention institutions.

6. From 1980 onwards, the steady growth in the number of cases brought before the Convention institutions made it increasingly difficult to keep the length of proceedings within acceptable limits. The problem was aggravated by the accession of new Contracting States from 1990. The number of applications registered annually with the Commission increased from 404 in 1981 to 4,750 in 1997. By that year, the number of unregistered or provisional files opened each year in the Commission had risen to over 12,000. The Court's statistics reflected a similar story, with the number of cases referred annually rising from 7 in 1981 to 119 in 1997.

The increasing case-load prompted a lengthy debate on the necessity for a reform of the Convention supervisory machinery, resulting in the adoption of Protocol No. 11 to the Convention. The aim was to simplify the structure with a view to shortening the length of proceedings while strengthening the judicial character of the system by making it fully compulsory and abolishing the Committee of Ministers' adjudicative role.

Protocol No. 11, which came into force on 1 November 1998, replaced the existing, part-time Court and Commission by a single, full-time Court. For a transitional period of one year (until 31 October 1999) the Commission continued to deal with the cases which it had previously declared admissible.

7. During the three years which followed the entry into force of Protocol No. 11 the Court's case-load grew at an unprecedented rate. The number of applications registered rose from 5,979 in 1998 to 13,858 in 2001, an increase of approximately 130%. Concerns about the Court's capacity to deal with the growing volume of cases led to requests for additional resources and speculation about the need for further reform.

A Ministerial Conference on Human Rights, held in Rome on 3 and 4 November 2000 to mark the 50th anniversary of the opening of the Convention for signature, had initiated a process of reflection on reform of the system. In November 2002, as a follow-up to a Ministerial Declaration on "the Court of Human Rights for Europe", the Ministers' Deputies issued terms of reference to the Steering Committee for Human Rights (CDDH) to draw up a set of concrete and coherent proposals covering measures that could be implemented without delay and possible amendments to the Convention.

Organisation of the Court

8. The European Court of Human Rights ... is composed of a number of judges equal to that of the Contracting States (currently forty-five). There is no restriction on the number of judges of the same nationality. Judges are elected by the Parliamentary Assembly of the Council of Europe for a term of six years ... the terms of office of one half of the judges are renewed every three years.

Judges sit on the Court in their individual capacity and do not represent any State. They cannot engage in any activity which is incompatible with their independence or impartiality or with the demands of full-time office. Their terms of office expire when they reach the age of seventy.

The Plenary Court elects its President, two Vice-Presidents and two Presidents of Section for a period of three years.

9. [T]he Court is divided into four Sections, whose composition, fixed for three years, is geographically and gender balanced and takes account of the different legal systems of the Contracting States....

10. Committees of three judges are set up within each Section for twelve-month periods.

11. Chambers of seven members are constituted within each Section on the basis of rotation, with the Section President and the judge elected in respect of the State concerned sitting in each case. Where the latter is not a member of the Section, he or she sits as an *ex officio* member of the Chamber. The members of the Section who are not full members of the Chamber sit as substitute members.

12. The Grand Chamber of the Court is composed of seventeen judges, who include, as *ex officio* members, the President, Vice-Presidents and Section Presidents.

Procedure before the Court

General

13. Any Contracting State (State application) or individual claiming to be a victim of a violation of the Convention (individual application) may lodge directly with the Court … an application alleging a breach by a Contracting State of one of the Convention rights.

14. The procedure before the Court is adversarial and public. Hearings, which are held only in a minority of cases, are public, unless the Chamber/Grand Chamber decides otherwise on account of exceptional circumstances. Memorials and other documents filed with the Court's Registry by the parties are, in principle, accessible to the public.

15. Individual applicants may present their own cases, but legal representation is recommended, and indeed usually required once an application has been communicated to the respondent Government. The Council of Europe has set up a legal aid scheme for applicants who do not have sufficient means.

16. The official languages of the Court are English and French, but applications may be submitted in one of the official languages of the Contracting States. Once the application has been declared admissible, one of the Court's official languages must be used, unless the President of the Chamber/Grand Chamber authorizes the continued use of the language of the application.

Admissibility procedure

17. Each individual application is assigned to a Section, whose President designates a rapporteur. After a preliminary examination of the case, the rapporteur decides whether it should be dealt with by a three-member Committee or by a Chamber.

18. A Committee may decide, by unanimous vote, to declare inadmissible or strike out an application where it can do so without further examination.

19. Individual applications which are not declared inadmissible by Committees, or which are referred directly to a Chamber by the rapporteur, and State applications are examined by a Chamber. Chambers determine both admissibility and merits, in separate decisions or where appropriate together.

20. Chambers may at any time relinquish jurisdiction in favor of the Grand Chamber where a case raises a serious question of interpretation of the Convention or where there is a risk of departing from existing case-law, unless one of the parties objects to such relinquishment within one month of notification of the intention to relinquish. In the event of relinquishment the procedure followed is the same as that set out below for Chambers.

21. The first stage of the procedure is generally written, although the Chamber may decide to hold a public hearing, in which case issues arising in relation to the merits will normally also be addressed.

22. Decisions on admissibility, which are taken by majority vote, must contain reasons and be made public.

Procedure on the merits

23. Once the Chamber has decided to admit the application, it may invite the parties to submit further evidence and written observations, including any claims for just satisfaction by the applicant. If no hearing has taken place at the admissibility stage, it may decide to hold a hearing on the merits of the case.

24. The President of the Chamber may, in the interests of the proper administration of justice, invite or grant leave to any Contracting State which is not party to the proceedings, or any person concerned who is not the applicant, to submit written comments, and, in exceptional circumstances, to make representations at the hearing. A Contracting State whose national is an applicant in the case is entitled to intervene as of right.

25. During the procedure on the merits, negotiations aimed at securing a friendly settlement may be conducted through the Registrar. The negotiations are confidential.

Judgments

26. Chambers decide by a majority vote. Any judge who has taken part in the consideration of the case is entitled to append to the judgment a separate opinion, either concurring or dissenting, or a bare statement of dissent.

27. Within three months of delivery of the judgment of a Chamber, any party may request that the case be referred to the Grand Chamber if it raises a serious question of interpretation or application or a serious issue of general importance. Such requests are examined by a Grand Chamber panel of five judges composed of the President of the Court, the Section Presidents, with the exception of the Section President who presides over the Section to which the Chamber that gave judgment belongs, and another judge selected by rotation from judges who were not members of the original Chamber.

28. A Chambers judgment becomes final on expiry of the three-month period or earlier if the parties announce that they have no intention of requesting a referral or after a decision of the panel rejecting a request for referral.

29. If the panel accepts the request, the Grand Chamber renders its decision on the case in the form of a judgment. The Grand Chamber decides by a majority vote and its judgments are final.

30. All final judgments of the Court are binding on the respondent States concerned.

31. Responsibility for supervising the execution of judgments lies with the Committee of Ministers of the Council of Europe. The Committee of Ministers verifies whether States in respect of which a violation of the Convention is found have taken adequate remedial measures to comply with the specific or general obligations arising out of the Court's judgments.

Editor's Comment:
Compliance with the Court's Judgments

Generally speaking, states held by the European Court of Human Rights (ECHR) to have violated some provision of European human rights instruments have an excellent record of compliance with the Court's judgments. Not only do states generally implement the ECHR's judgments in particular cases, e.g., by paying a successful applicant a certain amount in damages, but they also generally alter domestic law when that law is held by the ECHR to be contrary to European human rights obligations.

However, though compliance with ECHR judgments is much greater than is compliance with the determinations of other international and regional human rights tribunals, it is not perfect. For example, according to a working paper prepared for a committee of the Parliamentary Assembly of the Council of Europe,[a] Italy has an abysmal record in this regard; as of June 9, 2005, Italy had failed to fully implement 2181 adverse judgments regarding the excessive length of its judicial proceedings and 140 cases in which judgments requiring evictions of tenants had not been enforced, as well as 30 other cases.[b] Poland has failed to implement 109 judgments, most of which relate to the excessive length of judicial proceedings,[c] and Turkey's compliance with 111 judgments is uncertain, for example, because of questions concerning the actual implementation by security forces of new legislative provisions directed at preventing torture.[d] There are also questions outstanding regarding compliance by 10 other states.[e] More recently, concerns have been expressed regarding Russian behavior in Chechnya.[f]

---

a. Council of Europe, *Implementation of judgments of the European Court of Human Rights: Court Judgments Pending Before the Committee of Ministers for Control of Execution for More than Five Years, or Otherwise Raising Important Issues*, AS/Jur (2005) 32, 9 June 2005, ajdoc32 2005.

b. Id. at 9–20.

c. Id. at 23–25.

d. Id. at 27–28.

e. Id. at 5–9, 19–23, 25–27, 38–43.

f. Council of Europe, *Implementation of judgments of the European Court of Human Rights: Supplementary Introductory Memorandum (Revised)*, AS/Jur (2005) 55, 20 December 2005, ajdoc55 2005rev at 12–13.

D. India

(Taken from "India" in Thomas H. Reynolds and Arturo A. Flores, Foreign Law Guide: Current Sources of Codes and Basic Legislation in Jurisdictions of the World, http://www.foreignlawguide.com/ip/, visited August 9, 2006.)

The Indian Legal System

The Indian legal system at the time of independence had been substantially molded in the British colonial image....

The contemporary Indian legal system continues to reflect the Common Law in all respects, although naturally there have been numerous, if not always successful, efforts at nationalizing major industries and socializing large sectors of the economy. Most of the laws and codes in force now date either from the colonial period or the immediate post-independence decade. This is to say that the structure and the nomenclature is British or British colonial, although, on analysis, one can see that a great many laws have been amended to meet modern needs, but almost always in accord with British models or even British legislation of the post-war years....

Personal law in British India had always been an exception to the Common Law approach. In the colonial period, the British discomfort with administering Hindu law was solved by a trend towards codifying Hindu (and also Muslim) law. The constitution directs that each state enact its own family code, thus ensuring a closer congruence between personal law and that of the various ethnic and linguistic communities; for the most part, the various laws follow the colonial tradition.

The Indian courts have held that colonial legislation is not applicable to India if it is "repugnant to the concept of a sovereign democratic republic." It has become the practice, however, that rather than leaving the decision to the courts, the legislature will make the necessary determination as to what British legislation is no long applicable. Occasionally a specific act is passed, repealing great numbers of colonial enactments in a sensible and comprehensive approach.

Precedent is strictly observed in Indian jurisprudence and is regarded as binding if made by a higher court. Thus, a decision of the Supreme Court would be binding on all Indian courts, while the decision of the High Court of a state would only have authority within that state's judicial system and not to that of another state. India is an enormous jurisdiction, the largest in the Commonwealth, and one with a vast body of case law that is regularly cited, published and digested....

The body of Indian law is so great, and so dependent on jurisprudence and the principles of the Common Law, that any researcher is strongly advised to approach the question through one of the numerous treatises or commentaries regularly published in almost annual editions on all aspects of law, both public and private, statutory and customary....

[India is currently organized into] 26 states and six territories. The federation's membership is not necessarily equal; the states were originally divided into four categories, but now there are only two, states and Union Territories, which latter are administered by a federally appointed governor. The states all have their own elected executives and legislatures while the legislatures of the territories may enact laws, but always subject to union or federal controls and guidelines. State legislation plays an important role at the local level....

The Indian judicial system is totally integrated, with a single system of law courts (federal and state), characterized by a high degree of uniformity. Each state has its own high court, some of the larger ones with "benches" in different locations. There are separate ranges of high courts for the Union Territories. The high courts have appellate jurisdiction from their district civil or session courts and the district criminal magistrate's courts. In addition the high courts are charged with the general administration of justice and also have a certain degree of original jurisdiction. The high courts are capable of administering the law of the entire nation, federal law, the law of the particular state and laws of all the other states. The Supreme Court has appellate jurisdiction over all courts and tribunals and, as well, has original jurisdictions in matters of basic civil and human rights and gives advisory opinions when requested. There is no separate judicial hierarchy for administrative courts; a great number of administrative tribunals function under certain specific statutes, but cases rarely move from these into the general court system. An exception is the range of labor tribunals that are subject to the appellate authority of the general court system.

[The Supreme Court includes the Chief Justice of India and 25 other justices. That court sits in "benches," varying from as few as two justices to as many as seven, depending upon the matter to be addressed. According to Article 145 of the Constitution, a panel considering a substantial question of law involving interpretation of the Constitution or providing an advisory opinion requested by the President of India must include no fewer than five justices.]

Chapter Two

Habeas Corpus

A. Japan

1. [Denial of an Application for a Writ of Habeas Corpus] 1955, IX Hanreishu No. 10 at 1453, (Grand Bench)[h]

References: Habeas Corpus Law, Article 2; Habeas Corpus Rules, Article 4.

FORMAL JUDGMENT

Appeal dismissed. Appellant to pay the court fees of the appeal.

REASONS: This Court has already decided ... that an application for relief under the Habeas Corpus Law may be made only where freedom of person is restrained other than in accordance with a lawful and proper procedure and such restraint, or the judgment or administrative decision relating to such restraint, is patently without authority or patently and seriously violates a form or procedure established by law.

The facts of the detention of the applicant found by the lower court are briefly as follows:

In October 27, 1953, the applicant [a Chinese citizen] was charged before the Hachioji branch of the Tokyo District Court with violating the Foreign Exchange Law and the Foreign Trade Control Law* and was remanded in custody. He was released on bail on March 26,1954. At about 6:30 P.M. on November 8, 1954, at Yokohama prison, he was served with a deportation order issued by an Immigration officer pursuant to ... the Immigration Control Order* ... and ... the supplementary regulations.... (The deportation order had originally been

---

h. EDITOR'S NOTE: This translation is from John M. Maki, *Court and Constitution in Japan: Selected Supreme Court Decisions, 1948–60* (University of Washington Press, 1964) and is reprinted with the permission of the University of Washington Press.

issued by an investigating officer of the Tokyo branch of the. Immigration Department on September 5, 1951, pursuant to ... the Aliens Registration Law, after it had been discovered that the applicant had entered Japan unlawfully, without the permission of the Supreme Commander for the Allied Powers. The execution of this deportation order had, however, been subsequently suspended.) At 4:10 P.M. on November 17, 1954, he was placed in confinement in the Yokohama Immigration Holding Center, of which the respondent is the superintendent. He has been confined there continuously ever since.[i] The appellant contends that the Immigration Control Order and the deportation order are contrary to the spirit of Articles 33 and 34 of the Constitution and that, moreover, the manner of his detention is contrary to ... the said cabinet order. It is, however, clear from the facts that the restraint is neither (in the words of our previous judgment) "patently without authority" nor "a patent and serious violation of a form or procedure established by law." Accordingly, the application should be dismissed without judging the issues that the appellant raises. The appeal should, therefore, be dismissed under ... the Habeas Corpus Rules as without grounds. Court fees in connection with the appeal shall, in accordance with ... the Habeas Corpus Rules and ... the Code of Civil Procedure be borne as decreed in the formal judgment (above).

[dissenting opinions omitted].

B. The European Human Rights System

1. Cases of De Wilde, Ooms and Versyp ("Vagrancy") v. Belgium, European Court of Human Rights, E.C.H.R. Series A., No. 12 (June 18, 1971)

....

[De Wilde, Ooms and Versyp were all Belgian nationals. All were determined to be vagrants by Belgian police magistrates in proceedings in which the magistrates were obliged to satisfy themselves as to "the identity, age, physical and mental state and manner of life" of the alleged vagrants, and to provide the alleged vagrant with an opportunity to reply. De Wilde and Versyp were found to fall under section 13* of Belgium's vagrancy statute and were, as the statute required, "placed ... at the disposal of the government to be detained in a va-

---

i. EDITOR's NOTE:: That is, through September 28, 1955.

grancy center for two years." Ooms was determined to fall under Section 16* of the statute and "was placed at the disposal of the Government to be detained in an assistance home." De Wilde was detained from April 19th, 1966 until November 16th, 1966, the period including a three month sentence on an unrelated criminal charge. Ooms was detained for exactly one year. Versyp was detained for one year, nine months and six days. Belgian law permitted no judicial review of the vagrancy determinations.]

D. Factors common to the three cases

33. According to ... the Belgian Criminal Code of 1867 "vagrants are persons who have no fixed abode, no means of subsistence and no regular trade or profession." These three conditions are cumulative: they must be fulfilled at the same time with regard to the same person.

34. Vagrancy was formerly a misdemeanour ... or a petty offence..., but no longer of itself constitutes a criminal offence since the entry into force of the 1891 Act: only "aggravated" vagrancy as defined in ... the present Criminal Code is a criminal offence and these articles were not applied in respect of any of the three applicants. "Simple" vagrancy is dealt with under the 1891 Act.

35. According to Section 8* of the said Act "every person picked up as a vagrant shall be arrested and brought before the police court"—composed of one judge, a magistrate. The public prosecutor or the court may nonetheless decide that he be provisionally released (Section 11)*.

"The person arrested shall be brought before the magistrate within twenty-four hours and in his ordinary court, or at a hearing applied for by the public prosecutor for the following day." If that person so requests "he (shall be) granted a three days' adjournment in order to prepare his defence," (Section 3 of the Act of 1st May 1849*); neither De Wilde, nor Ooms nor Versyp made use of this right.

36. Where, after having ascertained "the identity, age, physical and mental state and manner of life" of the person brought before him (Section 12*), the magistrate considers that such person is a vagrant, Section 13 or Section 16 of the 1891 Act becomes applicable.

Section 13 deals with "able-bodied persons who, instead of working for their livelihood, exploit charity as professional beggars," and with "persons who through idleness, drunkenness or immorality live in a state of vagrancy;" Section 16 with "persons found begging or picked up as vagrants when none of the circumstances specified in Section 13 ... apply."

In the first case the court shall place the vagrant "at the disposal of the Government to be detained in a vagrancy centre, for not less than two and not more than seven years;" in the second case, the court may "place (him) at the disposal of the Government to be detained in an assistance home" for an indeterminate period which in no case can exceed a year....

Section 13 was applied to Jacques De Wilde and Edgard Versyp and Section 16 to Franz Ooms.

The distinction between the "reformatory institutions" referred to as "vagrancy centres" and "assistance homes" or "welfare settlements" (Sections 1* and 2* of the Act) has become a purely theoretical one; it has been replaced by a system of individual treatment of the persons detained.

Detention in a vagrancy centre is entered on a person's criminal record; furthermore, vagrants "placed at the disposal of the Government" suffer certain electoral incapacities....

37. Magistrates form part of the judiciary and have the status of an officer vested with judicial power, with the guarantees of independence which this status implies.... The Court of Cassation, however, considers that the decisions given by them in accordance with Sections 13 and 16 of the 1891 Act are administrative acts and not judgments.... They are not therefore subject to challenge or to appeal nor—except when they are ultra vires ... to cassation proceedings. The decisions of the highest court in Belgium are uniform on this point....

40. "Persons detained in an assistance home"—as Franz Ooms—may not "in any case be kept against their will for more than one year" (Section 18*, first sentence, of the 1891 Act). They regain their freedom, as of right, before the expiry of this period "when their release savings (have reached) the amount ... fixed by the Minister of Justice," who shall, moreover, release them if he considers their detention "to be no longer necessary" (Sections 17 and 18, second sentence, of the 1891 Act).

As regards vagrants detained in a vagrancy centre—such as Jacques De Wilde and Edgard Versyp—they leave the centre either at the expiry of the period varying from two to seven years "fixed by the court" or at an earlier date if the Minister of Justice considers "that there is no reason to continue their detention" (Section 15* of the 1891 Act); the accumulation of the release savings and any other means which the detainee might have do not suffice for this purpose....

D. As to the alleged violation of paragraph (4) of article 5 (art. 5-4)

...

73. Although the Court has not found in the present cases any incompatibility with paragraph (1) of Article 5 (art. 5-1)..., this finding does not dispense it from now proceeding to examine whether there has been any violation of paragraph (4) (art. 5-4). The latter is, in effect, a separate provision, and its observance does not result eo ipso from the observance of the former: "everyone who is deprived of his liberty," lawfully or not, is entitled to a supervision of lawfulness by a court; a violation can therefore result either from a detention incom-

patible with paragraph (1) (art. 5-1) or from the absence of any proceedings satisfying paragraph (4) (art. 5-4), or even from both at the same time.

1. As to the decisions ordering detention

74. The Court began by investigating whether the conditions in which De Wilde, Ooms and Versyp appeared before the magistrates satisfied their right to take proceedings before a court to question the lawfulness of their detention.

75. The applicants were detained in execution of the magistrates' orders: their arrest by the police was merely a provisional act and no other authority intervened in the three cases....

A first question consequently arises. Does Article 5(4) ... require that two authorities should deal with the cases falling under it, that is, one which orders the detention and a second, having the attributes of a court, which examines the lawfulness of this measure on the application of the person concerned? Or, as against this, is it sufficient that the detention should be ordered by an authority which had the elements inherent in the concept of a "court" within the meaning of Article 5(4) ... ?

76. At first sight, the wording of Article 5(4) ... might make one think that it guarantees the right of the detainee always to have supervised by a court the lawfulness of a previous decision which has deprived him of his liberty. The two official texts do not however use the same terms, since the English text speaks of "proceedings" and not of "appeal," "recourse" or "remedy".... Besides, it is clear that the purpose of Article 5(4) ... is to assure to persons who are arrested and detained the right to a judicial supervision of the lawfulness of the measure to which they are thereby subjected; the word "court" ("tribunal") is there found in the singular and not in the plural. Where the decision depriving a person of his liberty is one taken by an administrative body, there is no doubt that Article 5(4) ... obliges the Contracting States to make available to the person detained a right of recourse to a court; but there is nothing to indicate that the same applies when the decision is made by a court at the close of judicial proceedings. In the latter case the supervision required by Article 5(4) ... is incorporated in the decision; this is so, for example, where a sentence of imprisonment is pronounced after "conviction by a competent court" (Article 5(1)(a) of the Convention).... It may therefore be concluded that Article 5(4) ... is observed if the arrest or detention of a vagrant, provided for in paragraph (1) (e) (art. 5-1-e), is ordered by a "court" within the meaning of paragraph (4) (art. 5-4).

It results, however, from the purpose and object of Article 5..., as well as from the very terms of paragraph (4) ... ("proceedings," "recours"), that in order to constitute such a "court" an authority must provide the fundamental guarantees of procedure applied in matters of deprivation of liberty. If the procedure of the competent authority does not provide them, the State could not be dispensed from making available to the person concerned a second authority

which does provide all the guarantees of In sum, the Court considers that the
intervention of one organ satisfies Article 5(4)..., but on condition that the
procedure followed has a judicial character and gives to the individual concerned guarantees appropriate to the kind of deprivation of liberty in question.

77. The Court has therefore enquired whether in the present cases the magistrate possessed the character of a "court" within the meaning of Article 5(4)...,
and especially whether the applicants enjoyed, when appearing before him, the
guarantees mentioned above.

There is no doubt that from an organisational point of view the magistrate is a
"court;" the Commission has, in fact, accepted this. The magistrate is independent both of the executive and of the parties to the case and he enjoys the benefit
of the guarantees afforded to the judges by ... the Constitution of Belgium.

The task the magistrate has to discharge in the matters under consideration consists in finding whether in law the statutory conditions required for the "placing
at the disposal of the Government" are fulfilled in respect of the person brought
before him. By this very finding, the police court necessarily decides "the lawfulness" of the detention which the prosecuting authority requests it to sanction.

The Commission has, however, emphasised that in vagrancy matters the magistrate exercises "an administrative function" and does not therefore carry out
the "judicial supervision" required by Article 5(4).... This opinion is grounded
on the case-law of the Court of Cassation and of the Conseil d'État (see paragraph 37 above). The Commission had concluded from this that the provision
of a judicial proceeding was essential.

78. It is true that the Convention uses the word "court" (French "tribunal") in
several of its Articles. It does so to mark out one of the constitutive elements of
the guarantee afforded to the individual by the provision in question.... In all
these different cases it denotes bodies which exhibit not only common fundamental features, of which the most important is independence of the executive
and of the parties to the case..., but also the guarantees of judicial procedure.
The forms of the procedure required by the Convention need not, however, necessarily be identical in each of the cases where the intervention of a court is required. In order to determine whether a proceeding provides adequate guarantees, regard must be had to the particular nature of the circumstances in which
such proceeding takes place. Thus, in [another] case, the Court considered that
the competent courts remained "courts" in spite of the lack of "equality of arms"
between the prosecution and an individual who requested provisional release....;
nevertheless, the same might not be true in a different context and, for example,
in another situation which is also governed by Article 5(4)....

79. It is therefore the duty of the Court to determine whether the proceedings
before the police courts of Charleroi, Namur and Brussels satisfied the requirements of Article 5(4) ... which follow from the interpretation adopted above.

The deprivation of liberty complained of by De Wilde, Ooms and Versyp resembles that imposed by a criminal court. Therefore, the procedure applicable should not have provided guarantees markedly inferior to those existing in criminal matters in the member States of the Council of Europe.

According to Belgian law, every individual found in a state of vagrancy is arrested and then brought—within twenty-four hours as a rule—before the police court.… Regarding the interrogation of this individual, the 1891 Act limits itself to specifying … that the magistrate ascertains the identity, age, physical and mental state and manner of life of the person brought before him. Regarding the right of defence, the only relevant provision is found in … the Act of 1st May 1849, which provides that the person concerned is granted a three-day adjournment if he so requests. According to information provided by the Government, the Code of Criminal Procedure does not apply to the detention of vagrants.

The procedure in question is affected by the administrative nature of the decision to be given. It does not ensure guarantees comparable to those which exist as regards detention in criminal cases, notwithstanding the fact that the detention of vagrants is very similar in many respects. It is hard to understand why persons arrested for simple vagrancy have to be content with such a summary procedure: individuals liable to sentences shorter than the terms provided for by Section 13, and even Section 16, of the 1891 Act—including those prosecuted for an offence under Articles 342* to 344* of the Criminal Code (aggravated vagrancy)—have the benefit of the extensive guarantees provided under the Code of Criminal Procedure. This procedure undoubtedly presents certain judicial features, such as the hearing taking place and the decision being given in public, but they are not sufficient to give the magistrate the character of a "court" within the meaning of Article 5(4) … when due account is taken of the seriousness of what is at stake, namely a long deprivation of liberty attended by various shameful consequences. Therefore it does not by itself satisfy the requirements of Article 5(4) … and the Commission was quite correct in considering that a remedy should have been open to the applicants. The Court, however, has already held that De Wilde, Ooms and Versyp had no access either to a superior court or, at least in practice, to the Conseil d'État (see paragraphs 37 and 62 above).

80. The Court therefore reaches the conclusion that on the point now under consideration there has been a violation of Article 5(4) … in that the three applicants did not enjoy the guarantees contained in that paragraph.…

FOR THESE REASONS, THE COURT,

II. AS TO THE MERITS

…

4. Holds by nine votes to seven that there has been a breach of Article 5 (4) … in that the applicants had no remedy open to them before a court against the decisions ordering their detention; …

13. Reserves for the applicants the right, should the occasion arise, to apply for just satisfaction on the issue referred to at point II-4 above.

[separate opinions omitted]

2. Case of Weeks v. the United Kingdom, E.C.H.R. Series A, No. 114 (March 2, 1987)

[Facts: The applicant was a British subject who, in 1966, was sentenced to life in prison for armed robbery. Under British law, a person in the position of the applicant could be released on "licence", i.e., on parole. In 1976, he was so released. In 1977, after his arrest for a number of petty crimes, his parole was revoked by the responsible government official, the Home Secretary. After his conviction for these crimes, the Parole Board, a body charged with advising the Home Secretary, recommended that the revocation of the applicant's parole be confirmed. He was subsequently released on licence in 1982; in 1984, it was learned that the applicant had violated the conditions of his licence by changing his residence to France and he was arrested upon his return to the United Kingdom in 1985. He was again released on licence later that year, and again moved to France. His licence was again revoked but, at the time the European Court heard his case, he was at large.]

III. ALLEGED BREACH OF ARTICLE 5 PARA. 4 (art. 5-4)

54. The applicant's second complaint was that he had not been able, either on his recall to prison in 1977 or at reasonable intervals throughout his detention, to take proceedings satisfying the requirements of paragraph 4 of Article 5 ...

A. Whether the requisite judicial control was incorporated in the original conviction

55. The Government shared the view of the minority of the Commission that, since Mr. Weeks was an offender sentenced to life imprisonment, the supervision of lawfulness required by Article 5 para. 4 ... was incorporated at the outset in the original trial and appeal. They referred in this connection to a passage from the De Wilde, Ooms and Versyp judgment [*supra*]..., para. 76):

> At first sight, the wording of Article 5 para. 4 ... might make one think that it guarantees the right of the detainee always to have supervised by a court the lawfulness of a previous decision which has deprived him of his liberty ... Where [this] decision ... is one taken by an administrative body, there is no doubt that Article 5 para. 4 ... obliges the Contracting States to make available to the person detained a right of recourse to a court; but there is nothing to indicate

that the same applies when the decision is made by a court at the close of judicial proceedings. In the latter case the supervision required by Article 5 para. 4 ... is incorporated in the decision; this is so, for example, where a sentence of imprisonment is pronounced after 'conviction by a competent court' (Article 5 para. 1(a) of the Convention)....

56. As has been pointed out in subsequent judgments, this passage speaks only of the initial decision depriving a person of his liberty; it does not purport to deal with an ensuing period of detention in which new issues affecting the lawfulness of the detention might arise....

The Court must therefore determine what new issues of lawfulness, if any, were capable of arising in relation to Mr. Weeks' recall to prison and continued detention subsequent to sentence and whether the proceedings available complied with paragraph 4 of Article 5....

57. Mr. Weeks did not dispute that in so far as he may have wished to challenge the lawfulness of his recall or detention in terms of English law he at all moments had available to him a remedy before the ordinary courts in the form of an application for judicial review....

However, for the purposes of Article 5 para. 4..., the "lawfulness" of an "arrest or detention" has to be determined in the light not only of domestic law but also of the text of the Convention, the general principles embodied therein and the aim of the restriction permitted by Article 5 para. 1....

58. The Court has already held in the context of paragraph 1(a) of Article 5 ... that the stated purpose of social protection and rehabilitation for which the "indeterminate" sentence was passed on Mr. Weeks, taken together with the particular circumstances of the offence for which he was convicted, places the sentence in a special category: unlike the case of a person sentenced to life imprisonment because of the gravity of the offence committed, the grounds relied on by the sentencing judges for deciding that the length of the deprivation of Mr. Weeks' liberty should be subject to the discretion of the executive for the rest of his life are by their nature susceptible of change with the passage of time. The Court inferred from this that if the decisions not to release or to redetain were based on grounds inconsistent with the objectives of the sentencing court, Mr. Weeks' detention would no longer be "lawful" for the purposes of sub-paragraph (a) of paragraph 1 of Article 5....

It follows that, by virtue of paragraph 4 of Article 5..., Mr. Weeks was entitled to apply to a "court" having jurisdiction to decide "speedily" whether or not his deprivation of liberty had become "unlawful" in this sense; this entitlement should have been exercisable by him at the moment of any return to custody after being at liberty and also at reasonable intervals during the course of his imprisonment.

59. Article 5 para. 4 ... does not guarantee a right to judicial control of such scope as to empower the "court," on all aspects of the case, including questions of expediency, to substitute its own discretion for that of the decision-making authority. The review should, however, be wide enough to bear on those conditions which, according to the Convention, are essential for the lawful detention of a person subject to the special kind of deprivation of liberty ordered against Mr. Weeks.

B. Whether the proceedings available subsequent to conviction satisfied the requirements of Article 5 para. 4 (art. 5-4)

60. The Government submitted in the alternative that the requirements of Article 5 para. 4 ... were sufficiently met by the Parole Board's jurisdiction, supplemented as it was by the availability of judicial review before the High Court. Both the applicant and the Commission disagreed with this analysis.

1. General principles

61. The "court" referred to in Article 5 para. 4 ... does not necessarily have to be a court of law of the classic kind integrated within the standard judicial machinery of the country.... The term "court" serves to denote "bodies which exhibit not only common fundamental features, of which the most important is independence of the executive and of the parties to the case..., but also the guarantees" — "appropriate to the kind of deprivation of liberty in question" — "of a judicial procedure," the forms of which may vary from one domain to another (see the above-mentioned De Wilde, Ooms and Versyp judgment, ... paras. 76 and 78). In addition, as the text of Article 5 para. 4 ... makes clear, the body in question must not have merely advisory functions but must have the competence to "decide" the "lawfulness" of the detention and to order release if the detention is unlawful. There is thus nothing to preclude a specialised body such as the Parole Board being considered as a "court" within the meaning of Article 5 para. 4..., provided it fulfils the foregoing conditions....

2. Parole Board

(a) Independence and impartiality

62.... The Parole Board sits in small panels, each of which in the case of life prisoners includes a High Court judge and a psychiatrist.... The manner of appointment of the Board's members does not, in the Court's opinion, establish a lack of independence on the part of the members.... Furthermore, the Court is satisfied that the judge member and the other members of the Board remain wholly independent of the executive and impartial in the performance of their duties.

There remains the question whether the Board presents an appearance of independence, notably to persons whose liberty it considers.... On this point, as the Government stated, the functions of the Board do not bring it into contact with officials of the prisons or of the Home Office in such a way as to identify it with the administration of the prison or of the Home Office.

The Court therefore sees no reason to conclude that the Parole Board and its members are not independent and impartial.

(b) Powers and procedural guarantees

....

(i) Powers

64. According to the wording of the 1967 Act, the duty of the Parole Board is to "advise" the Home Secretary on the exercise of his powers to release prisoners on licence and to revoke such licences, and its decisions take the form of "recommendations" to the Home Secretary....

The Board's functions are without doubt purely advisory, both in law and in substance, as regards the periodic review that it carries out in relation to the question of the possible release on licence of a detained person serving a sentence of life imprisonment.... The Home Secretary may not, it is true, release on licence a life prisoner unless recommended to do so by the Parole Board.... However, where the Board does recommend release of such prisoners, the Home Secretary must also consult the Lord Chief Justice, together with the trial judge if available ... ; and, as demonstrated by the facts of Mr. Weeks' own case..., the Home Secretary is free, in the light of all the material before him, not to accept the Board's recommendation. Quite apart from any consideration of procedural guarantees, the Board therefore lacks the power of decision required by Article 5 para. 4 ... when dealing with this category of case.

On the other hand, the Board's recommendation to release is binding on the Home Secretary when the Board has to consider, as it did in December 1977 in relation to Mr. Weeks, recall to prison after release on licence.... The procedure applicable in the event of recall must therefore be examined.

(ii) Procedural guarantees

65. The language of Article 5 para. 4 ... speaks of the detained individual being entitled to initiate proceedings. Under the British system of parole of life prisoners, although only the Home Secretary may refer a case to the Board, referral is obligatory in recall cases except where a person recalled after a recommendation to that effect by the Board has chosen not to make written representations.... In these circumstances, the recalled person can be considered as having sufficient access to the Parole Board for the purposes of Article 5 para. 4....

66. The Board deals with individual cases on consideration of the documents supplied to it by the Home Secretary and of any reports, information or interviews with the individual concerned it has itself called for.... The prisoner is entitled to make representations with respect to his recall, not only in writing to the Board but also orally to a member of the Local Review Committee....

The individual is free to take legal advice in preparing such representations. Furthermore, he must be sufficiently informed of the reasons for his recall in order to enable him to make sensible representations....

Whilst these safeguards are not negligible, there remains a certain procedural weakness in the case of a recalled prisoner. Thus, the Court of Appeal established ... that the duty on the Board to act fairly, as required under English law by the principles of natural justice, does not entail an entitlement to full disclosure of the adverse material which the Board has in its possession. The procedure followed does not therefore allow proper participation of the individual adversely affected by the contested decision, this being one of the principal guarantees of a judicial procedure for the purposes of the Convention, and cannot therefore be regarded as judicial in character.

67. In view of this finding, the Court does not consider it necessary to rule on the remaining points raised by the applicant and the Commission, that is: firstly, whether, in relation to the special category of deprivation of liberty ordered against Mr. Weeks, this requirement of a proper procedure calls for the holding of an oral hearing in addition to the existing possibility of making written submissions, and, secondly, whether the proceedings before the Board were "speedy."

(c) Conclusion

68. Consequently, neither in relation to consideration of Mr. Weeks' recall to prison in 1977 nor in relation to periodic examination of his detention with a view to release on licence can the Parole Board be regarded as satisfying the requirements of Article 5 para. 4....

3. Judicial review

69. The Court has in previous cases recognised the need to take a comprehensive view of the system in issue before it, as apparent shortcomings in one procedure may be remedied by safeguards available in other procedures. In this connection, an application for judicial review undoubtedly represents a useful supplement to the procedure before the Parole Board: it enables the individual concerned to obtain a control by the ordinary courts of both the Parole Board's decisions and the Home Secretary's decisions.

...

The grounds on which judicial review lies, as summarised by Lord Diplock in his speech in the Council of Civil Service Unions case, are "illegality," "irrationality" and "procedural impropriety." By "illegality" is meant incorrect application of the law governing the decision-making power and, in particular, breach of the relevant statutory requirements; "irrationality" covers a decision that is so outrageous in its defiance of logic or of accepted moral standards that no sensible person who had applied his mind to the question to be decided could have arrived at it; and "procedural impropriety" is a failure to observe expressly laid down procedural rules, a denial of natural justice or a lack of procedural fairness.

As the Commission pointed out, the scope of the control afforded is thus not wide enough to bear on the conditions essential for the "lawfulness," in the sense of Article 5 para. 4 ... of the Convention, of Mr. Weeks' detention, that is to say, whether it was consistent with and therefore justified by the objectives of the indeterminate sentence imposed on him (see paragraphs 58 and 59 above). In the Court's view, having regard to the nature of the control it allows, the remedy of judicial review can neither itself provide the proceedings required by Article 5 para. 4 ... nor serve to remedy the inadequacy, for the purposes of that provision, of the procedure before the Parole Board.

FOR THESE REASONS, THE COURT

...

2. Holds, by thirteen votes to four, that there has been a breach of Article 5 para. 4 (art. 5-4); ...

[separate opinions omitted]

C. India

1. General Observations

The courts of India have not described in detail the scope of the writ of habeas corpus as applied in that country, apparently because they have understood the application of the writ to be that which had been established by English practice prior to the independence of India, see, e.g., Kanu Sanyal v. District Magistrate, Darjeeijng and Others, 1973 A.I.R.(SC.). 2684, 2687–88, 2689–94; 1974 (1) S.C.R. 621. Thus, the writ has been held to be available not only when the government has taken the petitioner into custody without following the procedures required by law, Gunupati Keshavram Reddy v. Nafisul Hasan and The State of Uttar Pradesh, 1954 A.I.R.(S.C.) 636, but also when the seizure violated the petitioner's substantive rights, Ebrahim Vazir Mavat v. State of Bombay and Others (With Connected Appeals), 1954 A.I.R.(S.C.) 229, 1954 (1) S.C.R. 933.

However, Indian law differs from that of the United Kingdom (and the United States) in that Item 9 of List I and Item 3 of List III of the Seventh Schedule of the Constitution of India, read with Article 246 of that instrument, and subject to the limitations imposed by Article 22, permit both the Central and state governments of India to enact laws permitting preventive detention of persons, that is, their detention despite the non-existence of evidence that would permit their prosecution for violations of the criminal law. The decisions which follow explain the approach of India's courts to this element of the law of India.

2. A.K. Gopalan v. State of Madras;
Union of India, Intervener, 1950 (1)
S.C.R. 88, 1950 A.I.R. (S.C.) 27

KANIA C. J

This is a petition by the applicant under article 32(1) of the Constitution of India for a writ of habeas corpus against his detention in the Madras Jail. In the petition he has given various dates showing how he has been under detention since December, 1947. Under the ordinary Criminal Law he was sentenced to terms of imprisonment but those convictions were set aside. While he was thus under detention under one of the orders of the Madras State Government, on the 1st of March, 1950, he was served with an order made under section 3(1) of the Preventive Detention Act, IV of 1950. He challenges the legality of the order as it is contended that Act IV of 1950 contravenes the provisions of articles 13, 19 and 21 and the provisions of that Act are not in accordance with article 22 of the Constitution. He has also challenged the validity of the order on the ground that it is issued mala fide. The burden of proving that allegation is on the applicant. Because of the penal provisions ... of the impugned Act the applicant has not disclosed the grounds, supplied to him, for his detention and the question of mala fides of the order therefore cannot be gone into under this petition.

In order to appreciate the rival contentions it is useful first to bear in mind the general scheme of the Constitution.... Part III of the Constitution is an important innovation. It is headed "Fundamental Rights." In that Part the word "State" includes both the Government of the Union and the Government of the States. By article 13 it is expressly provided that all laws in force in the territory of India, immediately before the commencement of the Constitution, in so far as they are inconsistent with the provisions of this Part, to the extent of such inconsistency, are void. Therefore, all laws in operation in India on the day the Constitution came into force, unless otherwise saved, to the extent they are inconsistent with this Chapter on Fundamental Rights, become automatically void. Under article 13(2) provision is made for legislation after the Constitution comes into operation. It is there provided that the State shall not make any law which takes away or abridges the rights conferred by this Part and any law made in contravention of this clause shall to the extent of the contravention, be void. Therefore, as regards future legislation also the Fundamental Rights in Part III have to be respected and, unless otherwise saved by the provisions of the Constitution, they will be void to the extent they contravene the provisions of Part III.... [T]he legislative powers conferred under article 246 are also made "subject to the provisions of this Constitution," which of course includes Part III dealing with the Fundamental Rights.... In this case we are directly concerned only with the articles under the caption "Right to Freedom" ... and article 32 which gives a remedy to enforce the rights conferred by this Part. The rest of the articles may have to be referred to only to assist in the interpretation of the above-mentioned articles. It is obvious that by the insertion of this Part the powers of the Legislature and the Executive, both of the Union and the States, are further curtailed and the right to enforce the Fundamental Rights found in Part III by a direct application to the Supreme Court is removed from the legislative control. The wording of article 32 shows that the Supreme Court can be moved to grant a suitable relief, mentioned in article 32(2), only in respect of the Fundamental Rights mentioned in Part III of the Constitution.

The petitioner is detained under a preventive detention order, made under Act IV of 1950, which has been passed by the Parliament of India. In the Seventh Schedule of the Constitution, List I contains entries specifying items in respect of which the Parliament has exclusive legislative powers. Entry 9 is in these terms: "preventive detention for reasons connected with Defence, Foreign Affairs or the Security of India; persons subjected to such detention." List III of that Schedule enumerates topics on which both the Union and the States have concurrent legislative powers. Entry 3 of that List is in these terms: "Preventive detention for reasons connected with the security of a State, the maintenance of public order or the maintenance of supplies and services essential to the community; persons subjected to such detention." It is not disputed that Act IV of 1950 is covered by these two Entries in List I and List III of the Seventh Schedule. The contention of the petitioner is that the impugned legislation ... is ... not in accordance with the permissive legislation on preventive detention allowed under articles 22(4) and (7) and in particular is an infringement of the provisions of article 22(5). It is therefore necessary to consider in detail each of these articles and the arguments advanced in respect thereof.

A detailed discussion of the true limits of article 21 [which provides "No person shall be deprived of his life or personal liberty except according to procedure established by law," and is interpreted in an omitted portion of this opinion as *not* requiring that such procedures conform to concepts of natural justice] will not be necessary if article 22 is considered a code to the extent there are provisions therein for preventive detention. In this connection it may be noticed that the articles in Part III deal with different and separate rights. Under the caption "Right to Freedom" articles 19–22 are grouped but each with a separate marginal note. It is obvious that article 22(1) and (2) prescribe limitations on the right given by article 21. If the procedure mentioned in those articles is followed the arrest and detention contemplated by article 22(1) and (2), although they infringe the personal liberty of the individual, will be legal, because that becomes the established legal procedure in respect of arrest and detention....

The learned Attorney-General contended that the subject of preventive detention does not fall under article 21 at all and is covered wholly by article 22. According to him, article 22 is a complete code. I am unable to accept that contention. It is obvious that in respect of arrest and detention article 22(1) and
(2) provide safeguards. These safeguards are excluded in the case of preventive
detention by article 22(3), but safeguards in connection with such detention
are provided by clauses (4) to (7) of the same article. It is therefore clear that
article 21 has to be read as supplemented by article 22. Reading in that way the
proper mode of construction will be that to the extent the procedure is prescribed by article 22 the same is to be observed; otherwise article 21 will apply.
But if certain procedural safeguards are expressly stated as not required, or
specific rules on certain points of procedure are prescribed, it seems improper
to interpret these points as not covered by article 22 and left open for consideration under article 21. To the extent the points are dealt with, and included or
excluded, article 22 is a complete code. On the points of procedure which expressly or by necessary implication are not dealt with by article 22, the operation of article 21 will remain unaffected. It is thus necessary first to look at article 22(4) to (7) and next at the provisions of the impugned Act to determine
if the Act or any of its provisions are ultra vires.... Preventive detention in normal times, i.e., without the existence of an emergency like war, is recognised as
a normal topic of legislation in List I, Entry 9, and List III, Entry 3, of the Seventh Schedule. Even in the Chapter on Fundamental Rights article 22 envisages
legislation in respect of preventive detention in normal times. The provisions
of article 22(4) to (7) by their very wording leave unaffected the large powers
of legislation on this point and emphasize particularly by article 22(7) the
power of the Parliament to deprive a person of a right to have his case considered by an advisory board. Part III and. article 22 in particular are the only restrictions on that power and but for those provisions the power to legislate on
this subject would have been quite unrestricted. Parliament could have made a
law without any safeguard or any procedure for preventive detention. Such an
autocratic supremacy of the legislature is certainly cut down by article 21.
Therefore, if the legislature prescribes a procedure by a validly enacted law and
such procedure in the case of preventive detention does not come in conflict
with the express provisions of Part III or article 22(4) to (7), the Preventive
Detention Act must be held valid notwithstanding that the Court may not fully
approve of the procedure prescribed under such Act. Article 22(4) opens with
a double negative. Put in a positive form it will mean that a law which provides
for preventive detention for a period longer than three months shall contain a
provision establishing an advisory board, (consisting of persons with the qualifications mentioned in sub-clause (a)), and which has to report before the expiration of three months if in its opinion there was sufficient cause for such detention. This clause, if it stood by itself and without the remaining provisions
of article 22, will apply both to the Parliament and the State Legislatures. The

proviso to this clause further enjoins that even though the advisory board may be of the opinion that there was sufficient cause for such detention, i.e., detention beyond the period of three months, still the detention is not to be permitted beyond the maximum period, if any, prescribed by Parliament under article 22(7)(b). Again the whole of this sub-clause is made inoperative by article 22(4)(b) in respect of an Act of preventive detention passed by Parliament under clauses (7)(a) and (b). Inasmuch as the impugned Act is an Act of the Parliament purported to be so made, clause 22(4) has no operation and may for the present discussion be kept aside. Article 22 prescribes that when any person under a preventive detention law is detained, the authority making the order shall, as soon as may be, communicate to such person the grounds on which the order has been made and shall afford him the earliest opportunity of making a representation against the order. This clause is of general operation in respect of every detention order made under any law permitting detention. Article 22(6) permits the authority making the order to withhold disclosure of facts which such authority considers against the public interest to disclose. It may be noticed that this clause only permits the non-disclosure of facts, and reading clauses (5) and (6) together a distinction is drawn between facts and grounds of detention. Article 22(4) and (7) deal not with the period of detention only but with other requirements in the case of preventive detention also. They provide for the establishment of an advisory board, and the necessity of furnishing grounds to the detenue and also to give him a right to make a representation. Reading article 22 clauses (4) and (7) together it appears to be implied that preventive detention for less than three months, without an advisory board, is permitted under the Chapter on Fundamental Rights, provided such legislation is within the legislative competence of the Parliament or the State Legislature, as the case may be. Article 22(5) permits the detained person to make a representation. The Constitution is silent as to the person to whom it has to be made, or how it has to be dealt with. But that is the procedure laid down by the Constitution. It does not therefore mean that if a law made by the Parliament in respect of preventive detention does not make provision on those two points it is invalid. Silence on these points does not make the impugned Act in contravention of the Constitution because the first question is what are the rights given by the Constitution in the case of preventive detention. The contention that the representation should be to an outside body has no support in law.... After such representation was made, another advisory board had to consider it, but it was not necessary to make the representation itself to a third party. Article 22(4) and (7) permit the non-establishment of an advisory board expressly in a parliamentary legislation providing for preventive detention beyond three months. If so, how can it be urged that the non-establishment of an advisory board is a fundamental right violated by the procedure prescribed in the Act passed by the Parliament?

The important clause to be considered is article 22(7). Sub-clause (a) is important for this case. In the case of an Act of preventive detention passed by the Parliament this clause contained in the Chapter on Fundamental Rights, thus permits detention beyond a period of three months and excludes the necessity of consulting an advisory board, if the opening words of the sub-clause are complied with. Sub-clause (b) is permissive. It is not obligatory on the Parliament to prescribe any maximum period. It was argued that this gives the Parliament a right to allow a person to be detained indefinitely. If that construction is correct, it springs out of the words of sub-clause (7) itself and the Court cannot help in the matter. Subclause (c) permits the Parliament to lay down the procedure to be followed by the advisory board in an inquiry under sub-clause (a) of clause (4). I am unable to accept the contention that article 22(4)(a) is the rule and article 22(7) the exception. I read them as two alternatives provided by the Constitution for making laws on preventive detention. Bearing in mind the provisions of article 22 read with article 246 and Schedule VII, List I, Entry 9, and List III, Entry 3, it is thus clear that the Parliament is empowered to enact a law of preventive detention (a) for reasons connected with defence, (b) for reasons connected with foreign affairs, (c) for reasons connected with the security of India; and (under List III), (d) for reasons connected with the security of a State, (e) for reasons connected with the maintenance of public order, or (f) for reasons connected with the maintenance of supplies and services essential to the community. Counsel for the petitioner has challenged the validity of several provisions of the Act.

… There is considerable authority for the statement that the Courts are not at liberty to declare an Act void because in their opinion it is opposed to a spirit supposed to pervade the Constitution but not expressed in words. Where the fundamental law has not limited, either in terms or by necessary implication, the general powers conferred upon the Legislature we cannot declare a limitation under the notion of having discovered something in the spirit of the Constitution which is not even mentioned in the instrument. It is difficult upon any general principles to limit the omnipotence of the sovereign legislative power by judicial interposition, except so far as the express words of a written Constitution give that authority. It is also stated, if the words be positive and without ambiguity, there is no authority for a Court to vacate or repeal a Statute on that ground alone. But it is only in express constitutional provisions limiting legislative power and controlling the temporary will of a majority by a permanent and paramount law settled by the deliberate wisdom of the nation that one can find a safe and solid ground for the authority of Courts of justice to declare void, any legislative enactment. Any assumption of authority beyond this would be to place in the hands of the judiciary powers too great and too indefinite either for its own security or the protection of private rights. It was first argued that by section 3 the Parliament had delegated its legislative power to the executive officer in detaining a person on his being satisfied of its necessity. It was urged that the satisfaction must be of the legislative body. This contention of delegation of the legislative power in such cases has been considered and rejected in numerous cases by our Federal Court and by the English Courts.... Section 3 of the impugned Act is no delegation of legislative power to make laws. It only confers discretion on the officer to enforce the law made by the legislature. Section 3 is also impugned on the ground that it does not provide an objective standard which the Court can utilize for determining whether the requirements of law have been complied with. It is clear that no such objective standard of conduct can be prescribed, except as laying down conduct tending to achieve or to avoid a particular object. For preventive detention action must be taken on good suspicion.... The contention is urged in respect of preventive detention and not punitive detention. Before a person can be held liable for an offence it is obvious that he should be in a position to know what he may do or not do, and an omission to do or not to do will result in the State considering him guilty according to the penal enactment. When it comes however to preventive detention, the very purpose is to prevent the individual not merely from acting in a particular way but, as the sub-heads summarized above show, from achieving a particular object. It will not be humanly possible to tabulate exhaustively all actions which may lead to a particular object. It has therefore been considered that a preventive detention Act which sufficiently prescribes the objects which the legislature considers have not to be worked up to is a sufficient standard to prevent the legislation being vague. In my opinion, therefore, the argument of the petitioner against section 3 of the impugned Act fails. It was also contended that section 3 prescribes no limit of time for detention and therefore the legislation is ultra vires. The answer is found in article 22(7)(b). A perusal of the provisions of the impugned Act moreover shows that in section 12 provision is made for detention for a period longer than three months but not exceeding one year in respect of clauses (a) and (b) of that section. It appears therefore that in respect of the rest of the clauses mentioned in section 3(1)(a) the detention is not contemplated to be for a period longer than three months, and in such cases a reference to the advisory board under section 9 is contemplated. Section 7 of the Act which is next challenged, runs on the same lines as article 22(5) and (6) and in my opinion infringes no provision of the Constitution. It was argued that this gave only the right of making a representation without being heard orally or without affording an opportunity to lead evidence and therefore was not an orderly course of procedure, as required by the rules of natural justice. The Parliament by the Act has expressly given a right to the person detained under a preventive detention order to receive the grounds for detention and also has given him a right to make a representation. The Act has thus complied with the requirements of article 22(5). That clause, which prescribes what procedure has to be followed as a matter of fundamental right, is silent about the person detained having a right to be heard orally or by a lawyer. The Constituent Assembly had before them the provisions of clause (1) of the same article. The Assembly having dealt with the requirements of receiving grounds and giving an opportunity to make a representation has deliberately refrained from providing a right to be heard orally. If so, I do not read the clause as guaranteeing such right under article 22(5). An "orderly course of procedure" is not limited to procedure which has been sanctioned by settled usage. New forms of procedure are as much ... due process of law as old forms, provided they give a person a fair opportunity to present his case. It was contended that the right to make a representation in article 22(5) must carry with it a right to be heard by an independent tribunal; otherwise the making of a representation has no substance because it is not an effective remedy. I am unable to read clause (5) of article 22 as giving a fundamental right to be heard by an independent tribunal. The Constitution deliberately stops at giving the right of representation. This is natural because under article 22(7), in terms, the Constitution permits the making of a law by Parliament in which a reference to an advisory board may be omitted. To consider the right to make a representation as necessarily including a right to be heard by an independent judicial, administrative or advisory tribunal will thus be directly in conflict with the express words of article 22(7)....

Again, I am not prepared to accept the contention that a right to be heard orally is an essential right of procedure even according to the rules of natural justice. The right to make a defence may be admitted, but there is nothing to support the contention that an oral interview is compulsory.... A right to lead evidence against facts suspected to exist is also not essential in the case of preventive detention. Article 22(6) permits the non-disclosure of facts. That is one of the clauses of the Constitution dealing with fundamental rights. If even the non-disclosure of facts is permitted, I fail to see how there can exist a right to contest facts by evidence and the noninclusion of such procedural right could make this Act invalid.

Section 10(3) was challenged on the ground that it excludes the right to appear in person or by any lawyer before the advisory board and it was argued that this was an infringement of a fundamental right. It must be noticed that article 22(1) which gives a detained person a right to consult or be defended by his own legal practitioner is specifically excluded by article 22(3) in the case of legislation dealing with preventive detention. Moreover, the Parliament is expressly given power under article 22(7)(c) to lay down the procedure in an inquiry by an advisory board. This is also a part of article 22 itself. If so, how can the omission to give a right to audience be considered against the constitutional rights? It was pointed out that section 10(3) prevents even the disclosure of a portion of the report and opinion of the advisory board. It was argued that if so how can the detained person put forth his case before a Court and challenge the conclusions? ... In my opinion, the answer is in the provision found in article 22(7)(c) of the Constitution of India.

It was argued that section 11 of the impugned Act was invalid as it permitted the continuance of the detention for such period as the Central Government or the State Government thought fit. This may mean an indefinite period. In my opinion this argument has no substance because the Act has to be read as a whole. The whole life of the Act is for a year and therefore the argument that the detention may be for an indefinite period is unsound. Again, by virtue of article 22(7)(b), the Parliament is not obliged to fix the maximum term of such detention. It has not so fixed it, except under section 12, and therefore it cannot be stated that section 11 is in contravention of article 22(7). Section 12 of the impugned Act is challenged on the ground that it does not conform to the provisions of article 22(7). It is argued that article 22(7) permits preventive detention beyond three months, when the Parliament prescribes "the circumstances in which, and the class or classes of cases in which," a person may be detained. It was argued that both these conditions must be fulfilled. In my opinion, this argument is unsound, because the words used in article 22(7) themselves are against such interpretation. The use of the word "which" twice in the first part of the sub-clause, read with the comma put after each, shows that the legislature wanted these to be read as disjunctive and not conjunctive. Such argument might have been possible (though not necessarily accepted) if the article in the Constitution was "the circumstances and the class or classes of cases in which ..." I have no doubt that by the clause, as worded, the legislature intended that the power of preventive detention beyond three months may be exercised either if the circumstances in which, or the class or classes of cases in which, a person is suspected or apprehended to be doing the objectionable things mentioned in the section. This contention therefore fails.

It was next contended that by section 12 the Parliament had provided that a person might be detained for a period longer than three months but not exceeding one year from the date of his detention, without obtaining the opinion of an advisory board, with a view to prevent him from acting in any manner prejudicial to (a) the defence of India, relations of India with foreign powers or the security of India; or (b) the security of a State or the maintenance of public order. It must be noticed that the contingency provided in section 3(1)(a)(iii), viz., the maintenance of supplies and services essential to the community is omitted in section 12. Relying on the wording of these two sub-sections in section 12, it was argued that in the impugned Act the wording of Schedule VII List I, Entry 9, and List III, Entry 3, except the last part, are only copied. This did not comply with the requirement to specify either the circumstances or the class or classes of cases as is necessary to be done under article 22(7) of the Constitution. Circumstances ordinarily mean events or situation extraneous to the actions of the individual concerned, while a class of cases mean determinable groups based on the actions of the individuals with a common aim or idea. Determinable may be according to the nature of the object also. It is obvious that the classification can be by grouping the activities of people or by specifying the objectives to be attained or avoided. The argument advanced on behalf of the petitioner on this point does not appeal to me because it assumes that the words of Schedule VII List I, Entry 9, and List III, Entry 3 are never capable of being considered as circumstances or classes of cases. In my opinion, that assumption is not justified, particularly when we have to take into consideration cases of preventive detention and not of conviction and punitive detention. Each of the expressions used in those entries is capable of complying with the requirement of mentioning circumstances or classes of cases. The classification of cases, having regard to an object, may itself amount to a description of the circumstances. It is not disputed that each of the entries in the Legislative Lists in the Seventh Schedule has a specific connotation well understood and ascertainable in law. If so, there appears no reason why the same expression when used in section 12(1)(a) and (b) of the impugned Act should not be held to have such specific meaning and thus comply with the requirement of prescribing circumstances or classes of cases. This argument therefore must be rejected.

Section 13(2) was attacked on the ground that even if a detention order was revoked, another detention order under section 3 might be made against the same person on the same grounds. This clause appears to be inserted to prevent a man being released if a detention order was held invalid on some technical ground. There is nothing in the Chapter on Fundamental Rights and in article 21 or 22 to prevent the inclusion of such a clause in a parliamentary legislation permitting preventive detention. Article 20(2) may be read as a contrast on this point.

... [I]t is thus clear that in respect of preventive detention no question of an objective standard of human conduct can be laid down. It is conceded that no notice before detention can be claimed by the very nature of such detention. The argument that after detention intimation of the grounds should be given has been recognised in article 22(5) and incorporated in the impugned Act. As regards an impartial tribunal, article 22(4) and (7) read together give the Parliament ample discretion. When in specified circumstances and classes of cases the preventive detention exceeds three months, the absence of an advisory board is expressly permitted by article 22(7). Under article 22(4) it appears implied that a provision for such tribunal is not necessary if the detention is for less than three months. As regards an opportunity to be heard, there is no absolute natural right recognised in respect of oral representation. It has been held to depend on the nature of the tribunal. The right to make a representation is affirmed by the Constitution in article 22(5) and finds a place in the impugned Act. The right to an orderly course of procedure to the extent it is guaranteed by article 22(4) read with article 22(7)(c), and by article 22(7)(a) and (b), has also been thus provided in the Act. It seems to me therefore that the petitioner's contentions even on these points fail.

Section 14 was strongly attacked on the ground that it violated all principles of natural justice and even infringed the right given by article 22(5) of the Constitution. It runs as follows:

> 14. (1) No Court shall, except for the purposes of a prosecution for an offence punishable under subsection (2), allow any statement to be made, or any evidence to be given, before it of the substance of any communication made under section 7 of the grounds on which a detention order has been made against any person or of any representation made by him against such order; and, notwithstanding anything contained in any other law, no Court shall be entitled to require any public officer to produce before it, or to disclose the substance of, any such communication or representation made, or the proceedings of an Advisory Board or that part of the report of an Advisory Board which is confidential.
>
> (2) It shall be an offence punishable with imprisonment for a term which may extend to one year, or with fine, or with both, for any person to disclose or publish without the previous authorisation of the Central Government or the State Government, as the case may be, any contents or matter purporting to be contents of any such communication or representation as is referred to in sub-section (1):
>
> Provided that nothing in this sub-section shall apply to a disclosure made to his legal adviser by a person who is the subject of a detention order.

By that section the Court is prevented (except for the purpose of punishment for such disclosure) from being informed, either by a statement or by leading evidence, of the substance of the grounds conveyed to the detained person under section 7 on which the order was made, or of any representation made by him against such order. It also prevents the Court from calling upon any public officer to disclose the substance of those grounds or from the production of the proceedings or report of the advisory board which may be declared confidential. It is clear that if this provision is permitted to stand the Court can have no material before it to determine whether the detention is proper or not. I do not mean whether the grounds are sufficient or not. It even prevents the Court from ascertaining whether the alleged grounds of detention have anything to do with the circumstances or class or classes of cases mentioned in section 12(1)(a) or (b). In Machindar Shivaji Mahar v. The King, 1949 F.C.R. 827, the Federal Court. held that the Court can examine the grounds given by the Government to see if they are relevant to the object which the legislation has in view. The provisions of article 22(5) do not exclude that right of the

Court. Section 14 of the impugned Act appears to be a drastic provision. which requires considerable support to sustain it in a preventive detention Act. The learned Attorney-General urged that the whole object of the section was to prevent ventilation in public of the grounds and the representations, and that it was a rule of evidence only which the Parliament could prescribe. I do not agree. This argument is clearly not sustainable on the words of article 22 clauses(5) and (6). The Government has the right under article 22(6) not to disclose facts which it considers undesirable to disclose in the public interest. It does not permit the Government to refrain from disclosing grounds which fall under clause (5). Therefore, it cannot successfully be contended that the disclosure of grounds may be withheld from the Court in public interest, as a rule of evidence. Moreover, the position is made clear by the words of article 22(5). It provides that the detaining authority shall communicate to such detained person the grounds on which the order has been made. It is therefore, essential that the grounds must be connected with the order of preventive detention. If they are not so connected the requirements of article 22(5) are not complied with and the detention order will be invalid. Therefore, it is open to a detained person to contend before a Court that the grounds on which the order has been made have no connection at all with the order, or have no connection with the circumstances or class or classes of cases under which a preventive detention order could be supported under section 12. To urge this argument the aggrieved party must have a right to intimate to the Court the grounds given for the alleged detention and the representation made by him. For instance, a person is served with a paper on which there are written three stanzas of a poem or three alphabets written in three different ways. For the validity of the detention order it is necessary that the grounds should be those on which the order has been made. If the detained person is not in a position to put before the Court this paper, the Court will be prevented from considering whether the requirements of article 22(5) are complied with and that is a right which is guaranteed to every person. It seems to me therefore that the provisions .of section 14 abridge the right given under article 22(5) and are therefore ultra vires. It next remains to be considered how far the invalidity of this section affects the rest of the impugned Act. The impugned Act minus this section can remain unaffected. The omission of this section will not change the nature or the structure or the object of the legislation. Therefore the decision that section 14 is ultra vires does not affect the validity of the rest of the Act. In my opinion therefore Act IV of 1950, except section 14, is not ultra vires. It does not infringe any provisions of Part III of the Constitution and the contention of the applicant against the validity of that Act except to the extent of section 14, fails. The petition therefore fails and is dismissed.

Notes

1. The Indian courts have been quite demanding in their interpretation of Article 22. Regarding paragraph 5 of that Article, they have held that they have the authority to examine the grounds for detention communicated to the detained person in order to determine whether they fall among the bases for detention prescribed in the relevant preventive detention law, Vijay Narain Singh v. Bihar, 1984 A.I.R.(S.C.) 1334, 1984 (3) S.C.R. 435. They have further held that "the communication made to the detained person to enable him to make the representation should, consistently with the privilege not to disclose facts which are not desirable to be disclosed in public interest, be as full and adequate as the circumstances permit and should be made as soon as it can be done," State of Bombay v. Atma Ram Sridhar Vaidya, 1951 A.I.R.(S.C.) 157, 165; 1951 (2) S.C.R. 167. If the communication was too vague to meet this standard, the person was entitled to release. If more than one ground for detention is cited, the vagueness or irrelevancy of any of the grounds renders the detention unconstitutional, Dr. Ram Krishan Bhardwaj v. State of Delhi and Others, 1953 A.I.R.(S.C.) 318, 1953 (4) S.C.R. 708. Jayanarayan Sukul v. State of West Bengal, 1970 A.I.R.(S.C.) 675, 1970 (3) S.C.R. 225, held that a government detaining a person under a preventive detention law was obliged to consider any representation made by that person as soon as possible; failure to consider the representation as soon as possible entitled the person to release. Furthermore, although Article 22(3) would appear to eliminate the right to counsel guaranteed by Article 22(2), the Court has held that a detained person is entitled to be represented by counsel before any advisory board convened pursuant to Article 22(4) if the government is represented either by a legal practicioner or by officers of the government departments involved in the matter; further, the Court held that the detainee is, in any event, entitled to be assisted by a friend who is not a legal practicioner, A. K. Roy, Etc v. Union of India and Another, 1982 A.I.R.(S.C.) 710, 747–48, 1982 (2) S.C.R. 272.

2. The Court has also addressed conditions of detention. In A. K. Roy, Etc v. Union of India and Another, 1982 A.I.R.(S.C.) 710, 1982 (2) S.C.R. 272, the Court held that, since "whatever smacks of punishment must be scrupulously avoided in matters of preventive detention," 1982 A.I.R. (S.C.) at 740, only exceptional circumstances could justify detaining someone under a preventive detention statute in any place other than the locality where he usually resides. For similar reasons, the Court held that detainees had the rights "to wear their own clothes, eat their own food, have interview with the members of their families at least once a week and, last but not the least, have reading and writing material according to their reasonable requirement," id. at 752, and could not be housed with convicts, id.

3. Article 21 of the Constitution forbids deprivations of life or personal liberty "except according to procedure established by law." As stated at page 31,

in an omitted portion of this opinion the Court held that Article 21 should *not* be interpreted as requiring that such procedures conform to concepts of natural justice. This reading of Article 21 was rejected in Maneka Gandhi v. Union of India, 1978 AIR (SC) 597, which held in paragraph 56 that Article 21 required that a procedure established by law be " 'right and just and fair' and not arbitrary, fanciful, or oppressive; otherwise, it should be no procedure at all...."

D. The United States

1. Immigration and Naturalization Service v. Enrico St. Cyr, 533 U.S. 289, 121 S. Ct. 2271 (2001)

JUSTICE STEVENS delivered the opinion of the Court.

Both the Antiterrorism and Effective Death Penalty Act of 1996 (AEDPA) ... and the Illegal Immigration Reform and Immigrant Responsibility Act of 1996 (IIRIRA) ... contain comprehensive amendments to the Immigration and Nationality Act (INA), 8 U.S.C. § 1101* et seq. This case raises two important questions about the impact of those amendments. The first question is a procedural one, concerning the effect of those amendments on the availability of habeas corpus jurisdiction under 28 U.S.C. § 2241. The second question is a substantive one....

Respondent, Enrico St. Cyr, is a citizen of Haiti who was admitted to the United States as a lawful permanent resident in 1986. Ten years later, on March 8, 1996, he pled guilty in a state court to a charge of selling a controlled substance in violation of Connecticut law. That conviction made him deportable. Under pre-AEDPA law applicable at the time of his conviction, St. Cyr would have been eligible for a waiver of deportation at the discretion of the Attorney General. However, removal proceedings against him were not commenced until April 10, 1997, after both AEDPA and IIRIRA became effective, and, as the Attorney General interprets those statutes, he no longer has discretion to grant such a waiver.

In his habeas corpus petition, respondent has alleged that the restrictions on discretionary relief from deportation contained in the 1996 statutes do not apply to removal proceedings brought against an alien who pled guilty to a deportable crime before their enactment. The District Court accepted jurisdiction of his application and agreed with his submission. In accord with the decisions of four other Circuits, the Court of Appeals for the Second Circuit affirmed. The importance of both questions warranted our grant of certiorari.

I

The character of the pre-AEDPA and pre-IIRIRA law that gave the Attorney General discretion to waive deportation in certain cases is relevant to our appraisal of both the substantive and the procedural questions raised by the petition of the Immigration and Naturalization Service (INS). We shall therefore preface our discussion of those questions with an overview of the sources, history, and scope of that law.

Subject to certain exceptions, § 3* of the Immigration Act of 1917 excluded from admission to the United States several classes of aliens, including, for example, those who had committed crimes "involving moral turpitude." The seventh exception provided "that aliens returning after a temporary absence to an unrelinquished United States domicile of seven consecutive years may be admitted in the discretion of the Secretary of Labor, and under such conditions as he may prescribe." Although that provision applied literally only to exclusion proceedings, and although the deportation provisions of the statute did not contain a similar provision, the Immigration and Naturalization Service (INS) relied on § 3 to grant relief in deportation proceedings involving aliens who had departed and returned to this country after the ground for deportation arose ...

Section 212* of the Immigration and Nationality Act of 1952, which replaced and roughly paralleled § 3 of the 1917 Act, excluded from the United States several classes of aliens, including those convicted of offenses involving moral turpitude or the illicit traffic in narcotics. As with the prior law, this section was subject to a proviso granting the Attorney General broad discretion to admit excludable aliens ... That proviso, codified at 8 U.S.C. § 1182(c)**, stated:

> Aliens lawfully admitted for permanent residence who temporarily proceeded abroad voluntarily and not under an order of deportation, and who are returning to a lawful unrelinquished domicile of seven consecutive years, may be admitted in the discretion of the Attorney General....

Like § 3 of the 1917 Act, § 212(c) was literally applicable only to exclusion proceedings, but it too has been interpreted by the Board of Immigration Appeals (BIA) to authorize any permanent resident alien with "a lawful unrelinquished domicile of seven consecutive years" to apply for a discretionary waiver from deportation ... If relief is granted, the deportation proceeding is terminated and the alien remains a permanent resident.

The extension of § 212(c) relief to the deportation context has had great practical importance, because deportable offenses have historically been defined broadly.... [T]he class of aliens whose continued residence in this country has depended on their eligibility for § 212(c) relief is extremely large, and not surprisingly, a substantial percentage of their applications for §212(c) relief have been granted.

Three statutes enacted in recent years have reduced the size of the class of aliens eligible for such discretionary relief. In 1990, Congress amended §212(c) to preclude from discretionary relief anyone convicted of an aggravated felony who had served a term of imprisonment of at least five years.... In 1996, in §440(d)* of AEDPA, Congress identified a broad set of offenses for which convictions would preclude such relief. See 110 Stat. 1277 (amending 8 U.S.C. §1182(c)*). And finally, that same year, Congress passed IIRIRA. That statute, inter alia, repealed §212(c), see §304(b)*, ... and replaced it with a new section that gives the Attorney General the authority to cancel removal for a narrow class of inadmissible or deportable aliens, see id. at 3009–594 (creating 8 U.S.C. §1229b*). So narrowed, that class does not include anyone previously "convicted of any aggravated felony."

In the Attorney General's opinion, these amendments have entirely withdrawn his §212(c) authority to waive deportation for aliens previously convicted of aggravated felonies. Moreover, as a result of other amendments adopted in AEDPA and IIRIRA, the Attorney General also maintains that there is no judicial forum available to decide whether these statutes did, in fact, deprive him of the power to grant such relief. As we shall explain below, we disagree on both points. In our view, a federal court does have jurisdiction to decide the merits of the legal question, and the District Court and the Court of Appeals decided that question correctly in this case.

II

The first question we must consider is whether the District Court retains jurisdiction under the general habeas corpus statute, 28 U.S.C. §2241, to entertain St. Cyr's challenge. His application for a writ raises a pure question of law. He does not dispute any of the facts that establish his deportability or the conclusion that he is deportable. Nor does he contend that he would have any right to have an unfavorable exercise of the Attorney General's discretion reviewed in a judicial forum. Rather, he contests the Attorney General's conclusion that, as a matter of statutory interpretation, he is not eligible for discretionary relief.

The District Court held, and the Court of Appeals agreed, that it had jurisdiction to answer that question in a habeas corpus proceeding. The INS argues, however, that four sections of the 1996 statutes—specifically, §401(e)* of AEDPA and three sections of IIRIRA (8 U.S.C. §§1252(a)(1)*, 1252(a)(2)(C)*, and 1252(b)(9)*—stripped the courts of jurisdiction to decide the question of law presented by respondent's habeas corpus application.

For the INS to prevail it must overcome both the strong presumption in favor of judicial review of administrative action and the longstanding rule requiring a clear statement of congressional intent to repeal habeas jurisdiction....

In this case, the plain statement rule draws additional reinforcement from other canons of statutory construction. First, as a general matter, when a particular interpretation of a statute invokes the outer limits of Congress' power, we expect a clear indication that Congress intended that result ... Second, if an otherwise acceptable construction of a statute would raise serious constitutional problems, and where an alternative interpretation of the statute is "fairly possible," ... we are obligated to construe the statute to avoid such problems....

A construction of the amendments at issue that would entirely preclude review of a pure question of law by any court would give rise to substantial constitutional questions. Article I, §9, cl. 2, of the Constitution provides: "The Privilege of the Writ of Habeas Corpus shall not be suspended, unless when in Cases of Rebellion or Invasion the public Safety may require it." Because of that Clause, some "judicial intervention in deportation cases" is unquestionably "required by the Constitution." Heikkila v. Barber, 345 U.S. 229, 235, 97 L. Ed. 972 (1953).

Unlike the provisions of AEDPA that we construed in Felker v. Turpin, 518 U.S. 651, 135 L. Ed. 2d 827 (1996), this case involves an alien subject to a federal removal order rather than a person confined pursuant to a state-court conviction. Accordingly, regardless of whether the protection of the Suspension Clause encompasses all cases covered by the 1867 Amendment extending the protection of the writ to state prisoners, cf. id. at 663–664, or by subsequent legal developments ... at the absolute minimum, the Suspension Clause protects the writ "as it existed in 1789." Felker, 518 U.S. at 663–664.

At its historical core, the writ of habeas corpus has served as a means of reviewing the legality of executive detention, and it is in that context that its protections have been strongest.... In England prior to 1789, in the Colonies, and in this Nation during the formative years of our Government, the writ of habeas corpus was available to nonenemy aliens as well as to citizens. It enabled them to challenge executive and private detention in civil cases as well as criminal. Moreover, the issuance of the writ was not limited to challenges to the jurisdiction of the custodian, but encompassed detentions based on errors of law, including the erroneous application or interpretation of statutes. It was used to command the discharge of seamen who had a statutory exemption from impressment into the British Navy, to emancipate slaves, and to obtain the freedom of apprentices and asylum inmates. Most important, for our purposes, those early cases contain no suggestion that habeas relief in cases involving executive detention was only available for constitutional error.

Notwithstanding the historical use of habeas corpus to remedy unlawful executive action, the INS argues that this case falls outside the traditional scope of the writ at common law. It acknowledges that the writ protected an individual who was held without legal authority, but argues that the writ would not issue where "an official had statutory authorization to detain the individual but ... the official was not properly exercising his discretionary power to determine whether the individual should be released." ... In this case, the INS points out, there is no dispute that the INS had authority in law to hold St. Cyr, as he is eligible for removal. St. Cyr counters that there is historical evidence of the writ issuing to redress the improper exercise of official discretion....

St. Cyr's constitutional position also finds some support in our prior immigration cases. In Heikkila v. Barber, the Court observed that the then-existing statutory immigration scheme "had the effect of precluding judicial intervention in deportation cases *except insofar as it was required by the Constitution*," 345 U.S. at 234–235 (emphasis added)—and that scheme, as discussed below, did allow for review on habeas of questions of law concerning an alien's eligibility for discretionary relief. Therefore, while the INS' historical arguments are not insubstantial, the ambiguities in the scope of the exercise of the writ at common law identified by St. Cyr, and the suggestions in this Court's prior decisions as to the extent to which habeas review could be limited consistent with the Constitution, convince us that the Suspension Clause questions that would be presented by the INS' reading of the immigration statutes before us are difficult and significant.

In sum, even assuming that the Suspension Clause protects only the writ as it existed in 1789, there is substantial evidence to support the proposition that pure questions of law like the one raised by the respondent in this case could have been answered in 1789 by a common law judge with power to issue the writ of habeas corpus. It necessarily follows that a serious Suspension Clause issue would be presented if we were to accept the INS's submission that the 1996 statutes have withdrawn that power from federal judges and provided no adequate substitute for its exercise.... The necessity of resolving such a serious and difficult constitutional issue—and the desirability of avoiding that necessity—simply reinforce the reasons for requiring a clear and unambiguous statement of constitutional intent.

Moreover, to conclude that the writ is no longer available in this context would represent a departure from historical practice in immigration law. The writ of habeas corpus has always been available to review the legality of executive detention.... Federal courts have been authorized to issue writs of habeas corpus since the enactment of the Judiciary Act of 1789, and § 2241 of the Judicial Code provides that federal judges may grant the writ of habeas corpus on the application of a prisoner held "in custody in violation of the Constitution or laws or treaties of the United States ..." Before and after the enactment in 1875 of the first statute regulating immigration ... that jurisdiction was regularly invoked on behalf of noncitizens, particularly in the immigration context.

Until the enactment of the 1952 Immigration and Nationality Act, the sole means by which an alien could test the legality of his or her deportation order was by bringing a habeas corpus action in district court.... In such cases, other than the question whether there was some evidence to support the order, the courts generally did not review factual determinations made by the Executive.... However, they did review the Executive's legal determinations.... In case after case, courts answered questions of law in habeas corpus proceedings brought by aliens challenging Executive interpretations of the immigration laws.

Habeas courts also regularly answered questions of law that arose in the context of discretionary relief.... Traditionally, courts recognized a distinction between eligibility for discretionary relief, on the one hand, and the favorable exercise of discretion, on the other hand.... Eligibility that was "governed by specific statutory standards" provided "a right to a ruling on an applicant's eligibility," even though the actual granting of relief was "not a matter of right under any circumstances, but rather is in all cases a matter of grace." Jay v. Boyd, 351 U.S. 345, 353–354, 100 L. Ed. 1242 (1956). Thus, even though the actual suspension of deportation authorized by § 19(c) of the Immigration Act of 1917 was a matter of grace, in United States ex rel. Accardi v. Shaughnessy, 347 U.S. 260, 98 L. Ed. 681 (1954), we held that a deportable alien had a right to challenge the Executive's failure to exercise the discretion authorized by the law. The exercise of the District Court's habeas corpus jurisdiction to answer a pure question of law in this case is entirely consistent with the exercise of such jurisdiction in *Accardi*....

Thus, under the pre-1996 statutory scheme—and consistent with its common-law antecedents—it is clear that St. Cyr could have brought his challenge to the Board of Immigration Appeals' legal determination in a habeas corpus petition under 28 U.S.C. § 2241. The INS argues, however, that AEDPA and IIRIRA contain four provisions that express a clear and unambiguous statement of Congress' intent to bar petitions brought under § 2241, despite the fact that none of them mention that section. The first of those provisions is AEDPA's § 401(e).

While the title of § 401(e)—"ELIMINATION OF CUSTODY REVIEW BY HABEAS CORPUS"—would seem to support the INS' submission, the actual text of that provision does not. As we have previously noted, a title alone is not controlling.... The actual text of § 401(e), unlike its title, merely repeals a subsection of the 1961 statute amending the judicial review provisions of the 1952 Immigration and Nationality Act.... Neither the title nor the text makes any mention of 28 U.S.C. § 2241.

. . . .

In any case, whether [the subsection] served as an independent grant of habeas jurisdiction or simply as an acknowledgement of continued jurisdiction pursuant to § 2241, its repeal cannot be sufficient to eliminate what it did not originally grant—namely, habeas jurisdiction pursuant to 28 U.S.C. § 2241.

...

The INS also relies on three provisions of IIRIRA, now codified at 8 U.S.C. §§ 1252(a)(1), 1252(a)(2)(C), and 1252(b)(9). As amended by § 306* of IIRIRA, 8 U.S.C. § 1252(a)(1) now provides that, with certain exceptions, including those set out in subsection (b) of the same statutory provision, "judicial review of a final order of removal ... is governed only by" the Hobbs Act's procedures for review of agency orders in the courts of appeals. Similarly, § 1252(b)(9), which addresses the "consolidation of questions for judicial review," provides that "judicial review of all questions of law and fact, including interpretation and application of constitutional and statutory provisions, arising from any action taken or proceeding brought to remove an alien from the United States under this subchapter shall be available only in judicial review of a final order under this section." Finally, § 1252(a)(2)(C), which concerns "matters not subject to judicial review," states: "Notwithstanding any other provision of law, no court shall have jurisdiction to review any final order of removal against an alien who is removable by reason of having committed" certain enumerated criminal offenses.

The term "judicial review" or "jurisdiction to review" is the focus of each of these three provisions. In the immigration context, "judicial review" and "habeas corpus" have historically distinct meanings.... In Heikkila, the Court concluded that the finality provisions at issue "precluded judicial review" to the maximum extent possible under the Constitution, and thus concluded that the APA was inapplicable. Id. at 235. Nevertheless, the Court reaffirmed the right to habeas corpus. Ibid. Noting that the limited role played by the courts in habeas corpus proceedings was far narrower than the judicial review authorized by the APA, the Court concluded that "it is the scope of inquiry on habeas corpus that differentiates" habeas review from "judicial review." Id. at 236; ... Both §§ 1252(a)(1) and (a)(2)(C) speak of "judicial review"—that is, full, nonhabeas review. Neither explicitly mentions habeas, or 28 U.S.C. § 2241. Accordingly, neither provision speaks with sufficient clarity to bar jurisdiction pursuant to the general habeas statute.

The INS also makes a separate argument based on 8 U.S.C. § 1252(b)(9). We have previously described § 1252(b)(9) as a "zipper clause...." Its purpose is to consolidate "judicial review" of immigration proceedings into one action in the court of appeals, but it applies only "with respect to review of an order of removal under subsection (a)(1)." 8 U.S.C. § 1252(b). Accordingly, this provision, by its own terms, does not bar habeas jurisdiction over removal orders not subject to judicial review under § 1252(a)(1)—including orders against aliens who are removable by reason of having committed one or more criminal offenses. Subsection (b)(9) simply provides for the consolidation of issues to be brought in petitions for "judicial review," which, as we note above, is a term historically distinct from habeas.... It follows that §1252(b)(9) does not clearly apply to actions brought pursuant to the general habeas statute, and thus cannot repeal that statute either in part or in whole.

If it were clear that the question of law could be answered in another judicial forum, it might be permissible to accept the INS' reading of §1252*. But the absence of such a forum, coupled with the lack of a clear, unambiguous, and express statement of congressional intent to preclude judicial consideration on habeas of such an important question of law, strongly counsels against adopting a construction that would raise serious constitutional questions. Cf. Felker, 518 U.S. at 660–661. Accordingly, we conclude that habeas jurisdiction under §2241 was not repealed by AEDPA and IIRIRA.

III

[In Part III of its opinion, the Court concluded that the Attorney General had misread the IIPIRA, reading that statute as not affecting the eligibility for discretionary waivers of deportation of persons eligible for such waivers as of the effective date of the statute. Since habeas corpus was available to require an executive branch official to use his discretion when the official's failure to do so resulted from the official's mistaken conclusion that he had no discretion to use, the Court affirmed the lower courts.]

(dissenting opinions omitted)

Notes

1. It is impossible to describe briefly the complexities of federal habeas corpus law; discussion of the variations in the remedy under the law of different states would require a volume. The observations that follow should therefore be understood as addressing only certain very basic questions.

2. As St. Cyr makes clear, the federal courts have the authority to grant habeas corpus relief against confinement by federal officials in connection with immigration matters. More recently, the Supreme Court has held that an American citizen, alleged to have been captured on the battlefield in Afghanistan serving as part of a military force fighting against the United States, denying that he was in fact an "enemy combatant", and seeking a writ of habeas corpus, "must receive notice of the factual basis for his classification, and a fair opportunity to rebut the Government's factual assertions before a neutral decisionmaker," Hamdi v. Rumsfeld, 542 U.S. 507, 533, 124 S. Ct. 2633, 159 L. Ed. 2d 578 (2004). In addition, Rasul v. Bush, 542 U.S. 466, 124 S. Ct. 2686, 159 L. Ed. 2d 548 (2004), held that the federal courts had jurisdiction to hear applications for the writ of habeas corpus brought by aliens held in

military custody at the United States base at Guantanamo Bay, Cuba, who asserted that their detentions were illegal. On October 17, 2006, the Military Commissions Act of 2006, P.L. 109-336 (MCA) became effective; section 7* of that Act, by amending 28 U.S.C. §2241, purports to deny jurisdiction to hear an alien's petition for a writ of habeas corpus to any federal court, justice or judge, if the petitioner is an alien either determined by the United States to be an unlawful enemy combatant or awaiting such determination. Defining an "unlawful enemy combatant", in turn, requires consideration of section 948a* of chapter 47a of Title 10 of the United States Code, added to Title 10 by section 3* of the MCA. Section 948a defines that term as meaning "a person who ... has been determined to be an unlawful enemy combatant by a Combatant Status Review Tribunal or another competent tribunal established under the authority of the President or the Secretary of Defense," 10 U.S.C. §948a (1)(ii). Section 1005 (e)(2) of Detainee Treatment Act of 2005, title X of P.L. 109-148 (December 30, 2005), as amended by section 10 of the MCA and codified as a note to 10 U.S.C.§801, provides for the review of determinations of Combatant Status Review Tribunals by the U.S. Court of Appeals for the District of Columbia Circuit; it provides no relief, however, for any detainee as to whom such a tribunal has made no determination.

3. Section 2254* of title 28 of the U.S. Code permits federal courts, in some circumstances, to grant writs of habeas corpus to persons held in custody by state authorities. The complexity of identifying the circumstances in which such relief is available preclude any discussion of this subject here; those interested should consult cases and texts regarding criminal procedure in the United States.

Chapter Three

Criminal Procedure

A. Japan

1. Right to Counsel

a. *Judgment on the Right of the Suspect in Criminal Procedure to Communicate with the Defence Counsel, Case Number: (o) No. 1189 of 1993, (Grand Bench, March 24, 1999)*

The Main Text of the Judgment

The second point of the grounds for the ... appeal is unfounded.

References: Articles 34, 37 and 38 of the Constitution; Article 39 of the Code of Criminal Procedure

Reasons

1. The main text of Article 39, paragraph 3 of the Code of Criminal Procedure and the first part of Article 34 of the Constitution

The gist of the appellant's argument is that the main text of Article 39, paragraph 3 of the Code of Criminal Procedure which allows imposition of ex-parte restrictions by the public prosecutor, the clerk of the Public Prosecutors' Office, or a police officer (hereinafter investigating agencies) on the interview between a suspect in custody and the defence counsel, or a person who is to be a defence counsel upon request of a person who is empowered to appoint a counsel for the suspect (hereafter defence counsel), is against the first part of Article 34 of the Constitution.

1) The first part of Article 34 of the Constitution provides that no one shall be detained or confined without immediately being given the reason and immediately given the right to retain a defence counsel. This right to defence is designed to enable a suspect in custody to seek assistance from the defence coun-

sel in order to defend his freedom and rights for purposes such as exonerating him/herself from the charge which serves as a basis of his detention, and to be released. Therefore, this provision does not merely prohibit the obstruction by officials of the appointment of the defence counsel by the suspect, but also in substance, guarantees that the suspect, upon appointment of the defence counsel, is granted opportunities to consult the defence counsel, seek advice from the counsel and thus be assisted by the counsel.

The aim of Article 39, paragraph 1 of the Code of Criminal Procedure, which provides that "a suspect or defendant in custody is entitled to meet the defence counsel, or a person who is to be a defence counsel upon request of a person who is empowered to appoint a counsel (if this person is not a qualified attorney, this is limited to cases where the permission as provided by Article 31, paragraph 2 has been granted) without the presence of any person, or receive documents and other things" and thus grants the right to have contacts with the defence counsel is, in accordance with the meaning of Article 34 of the Constitution, to ensure that suspects in custody are given opportunities of consulting the defence counsel and to receive advice and thus be assisted by the counsel; in this sense, this provision of the Code of Criminal Procedure emanates from constitutional guarantee....

2) However, since the Constitution presupposes the exercise of the power to penalise people or the enforcement of investigative power for the exercise of such power to be a function of the state as a matter of course, it cannot be concluded from the fact that the right of the suspect to consult and communicate with the defence counsel originates from constitutional guarantee, that this right has by its nature, absolute priority to the right to penalise people and the right to investigation. In order to exercise investigative power, there may be instances where it is necessary to hold the suspect in custody and interrogate the suspect. The Constitution does not deny such interrogations, and therefore, a reasonable balance must be struck between the exercise of the right to consult and communicate with the defense counsel and the exercise of investigative power. It should be acknowledged that Article 34 of the Constitution does not deny the possibility of enacting a provision which strikes such a balance by law, provided that the goal of the Constitution to guarantee opportunities for suspects in custody to be assisted by the defence counsel is not harmed in a substantial way.

3) While Article 39, paragraph 1 of the Code of Criminal Procedure provides for the right to consult and communicate with the defence counsel as mentioned above, in the main part of paragraph 3, it provides that "public prosecutors, clerks of the Public Prosecutors' Office, or police officers (i.e. police officers and sergeants) may, when it is needed for investigation, and provided that it is before indictment, designate the place and time of the consultation and the reception of documents" and acknowledges the possibility of investiga-

tion agencies to impose restrictions on the exercise of the right to consult and communicate with the defence counsel. This provision was introduced in order to balance the necessity of investigation such as interrogating the suspect and the exercise of the right to consult and communicate with the defence counsel by taking into consideration that by the Code of Criminal Procedure, it is allowed to interrogate a suspect who is held in custody (Art.198, para.1), and that in restricting the right of the suspect in preparing the defence, there is a strict limit on the length of custody, i.e. maximum 23 days (for internal strife, 28 days).... Furthermore, the final part of Article 39, paragraph 3 provides that "however, this designation shall not be of a nature that unreasonably restricts the right of the suspect in preparing the defence," and makes it clear that the designation of the place and time etc., is a necessary and indispensable, but exceptional measure, and that it is not allowed to restrict the right of the suspect in preparing the defence in an unreasonable way.

In the light of such legislative purpose and the content of Article 39, as a rule, the investigating agency is under obligations to provide opportunities for interviews etc., when so requested by the defence counsel. 'Necessity for investigation,' as provided in the main text of Article 39, paragraph 3 should be limited to instances where, if an interview is allowed, an obvious obstruction to investigation emerges, such as an obstruction by interruption of interrogation. If these conditions are met and the place and time etc. of the interview etc. are to be designated, the investigating agency should designate the time which is as early as possible upon consultation with the defence counsel and take measures to ensure that the suspect is able to prepare the defence with the defence counsel and others. If, at the time of the request by the defence counsel for an interview, the investigation agency is actually interrogating the suspect, the suspect is attending an on site investigation, or where there is a fixed schedule to interrogate the suspect shortly and if an interview is allowed in accordance with the request of the defence counsel, the scheduled interrogation would not be able to start as planned, as a rule, these should be understood as instances as cited above, where, 'if an interview is allowed, an obvious obstruction emerges, such as obstruction by interruption of interrogation'....

The appellant argues that since Article 38, paragraph 1 of the Constitution provides for the right against self-incrimination, suspects who are arrested or detained are under no obligation to endure interrogation, and therefore, the qualifying proviso of Article 198, paragraph 1 of the Code of Criminal Procedure is unconstitutional, if it provides for the duty of the suspect to endure interrogation; if the suspect chooses to do so, the interrogation has to be suspended any time, and therefore, interrogation of the suspect cannot serve as a ground for restricting the right to consult and communicate with the defence counsel. However, the interpretation that the suspect in custody has a duty to be present for interrogation and to stay for interrogation does not necessarily mean that the suspect is deprived of the right against self-incrimination. This is obvious, and thus, the appellant's argument in this respect is without premise and cannot be accepted.

4) As mentioned above, the Code of Criminal Procedure allows the interrogation of suspects who are held in custody, but sets the limit of the time in custody to a maximum of 23 days (or 28 days). It is necessary to balance the need for the investigation such as interrogation, and the exercise of the right to consult and communicate with the defence counsel. The following points should be taken into consideration; (1) restrictions on the interview etc. as provided by the main text of Article 39, paragraph 3 of the Code of Criminal Procedure do not allow the total rejection of the request of the defence counsel for an interview etc., but only allow the designation of a time which is different from the time proposed by the defence counsel, or shortening the interview, and therefore, the level of restriction should be regarded to be low. Also, as mentioned above, (2) designation by the investigating agency is possible only when, by allowing an interview, there would be an obvious obstruction to the investigation, such as in cases where, at the time an interview was requested by the defence counsel, the investigation agency was actually interrogating the suspect. Furthermore, (3) if these conditions are met and the place and time etc. of the interview etc. are to be designated, the investigating agency should designate the time which is as early as possible upon consultation with the defence counsel and take measures to ensure that the suspect is able to prepare the defence with the defence counsel. In view of these considerations, the main text of Article 39, paragraph 3 of the Code of Criminal Procedure is, in substance, not against the guarantee of the right to defence as provided by the first part of Article 34 of the Constitution.

In addition, the fact that the main text of Article 39, paragraph 3 of the Code of Criminal Procedure grants the power of designation to investigating agencies, which are on the opposite side to the suspect, is not against the first part of Article 34, since Article 430*, paragraphs 1 and 2 of the Code of Criminal Procedure provides that those who do not agree with the designation based upon Article 39, paragraph 3 have recourse to the court in order to have the decision revoked or altered and thus provides a simple and expedient means of judicial review against restrictions imposed on interviews.

5) Based upon the above, the main part of Article 39, paragraph 3 of the Code of Criminal Procedure is not against the first part of Article 34 of the Constitution. The argument of the appellant cannot be accepted....

3. The main part of Article 39, paragraph 3 of the Code of Criminal Procedure and Article 38, paragraph 1 of the Constitution

The appellant argues that Article 38, paragraph 1 of the Constitution also guarantees the right of the suspect held in custody to consult and communicate with the defence counsel in order to ensure the prohibition against forcing a statement of self-incrimination in an effective way, and based on this view, claims that the main part of Article 39, paragraph 3 of the Code of Criminal Procedure is against Article 38, paragraph 1 of the Constitution.

However, by what means the prohibition against forcing a statement of self-incrimination should be effectively guaranteed is basically left to the legislative policy, based upon the actual practice of investigation and other matters. Guarantee of the right of the suspect held in custody to consult and communicate with the defence counsel cannot be automatically derived from the prohibition against forcing a statement of self-incrimination by Article 38, paragraph 1 of the Constitution. The appellant's argument claims unconstitutionality based upon a unique view and cannot be accepted.

Conclusion

… The appealed judgment is not against the law as claimed by the appellant, and the arguments in point 2 of the reasons for appeal are all without grounds.

* Translated by Sir Ernest Satow, Chair of Japanese Law, University College, University of London

Note

Regarding the right to confront witnesses under Japanese law, the Court in the Decision Concerning the Admissibility as Evidence of the On-the-Spot Inspection Report Recording the Scenes of Victimization and Perpetration Reproduced by the Victim or the Suspect as Instructed by the Investigating Officers, in Cases Where It May Be Understood That the Existence of the Criminal Fact So Reproduced Is Essentially the Fact Required to Be Established in Order to Prove the Charge, Keishu Vol. 59, No. 7; Case number: 2005 (A) No. 684 (Second Petty Bench, September 27, 2005), held that photographs of the reinactment of a crime, with the victim portraying herself and a police officer playing the alleged perpetrator, and accompanied by captions containing the victims statements during the reinactment, were inadmissable at trial. However, the ground of inadmissability was apparently the failure of the photographs to satisfy certain technical requirements imposed by statute, the decision making no reference to any fairness concerns.

2. Limitations on Interrogation Methods

a. Decision Concerning the Case in which the Interrogation over Long Hours of the Suspect Was Ruled Not to Have Transgressed Permissible Limits of Non-Compulsory Investigation; Keishu Vol. 43, No.7, at 581; Case Number: 1985 (A) No. 826 (Third Petty Bench, July 4, 1989)

References: Articles 197 and 198 of the Code of Criminal Procedure

Main text of the decision:

The ... appeal in this case shall be dismissed.

The 500 days detention pending trial for this case shall be included as time served for the principal punishment.

Reasons:

...

2. Judgment by virtue of the court authority

a. According to the findings and records of the judgment of the second instance court, the circumstances and conditions of the investigation in this case in relation to the criminal defendant are as follows.

(1) The investigation in this case was initiated at 8:48pm on February 1, 1983, when the younger sister of the victim contacted the police stating that the then apartment residence of the victim had remained locked for approximately 10 days and that the victim's whereabouts were unknown. Police officers proceeded to the victim's apartment, whereupon the discovery was made that the victim had been killed. The aforementioned younger sister informed police officers that, until approximately one month earlier, the victim had been living with and been engaged in an intimate relationship with the criminal defendant. In respect of the severity and urgency of the case, police officers immediately proceeded to the criminal defendant's residence and requested voluntary attendance by the criminal defendant for questioning concerning the victim's lifestyle and social relationships prior to her death, to which the criminal defendant consented and was consequently accompanied to the Hiratsuka Police Station at 11:00pm on the same day.

(2) Following initial inquiries regarding personal circumstances such as how the criminal defendant first came into contact with the victim, interrogation commenced in earnest after 11:30pm on the same day, conducted mainly by one officer in the presence of one or two other officers. From the outset, a request was put to the criminal defendant for cooperation regarding investiga-

tions into this case, the criminal defendant responded stating, "We lived together and I will tell you everything I know. I too ask that the perpetrator is apprehended as soon as possible" and promised his cooperation. The interrogation continued throughout the night, during which time the criminal defendant consented to and underwent a polygraph test. The activities of the defendant following the last day the criminal defendant alleged to have met the victim were initially corroborated, but on the morning of the following day, February 2, after 9:30am, the criminal defendant began to confess to the killing of the victim at the victim's residence and the taking off the victim's money and valuables.

(3) Accordingly, police officers continued interrogation for approximately one hour, and after 11:00am, asked the criminal defendant to write a report outlining the crime, whereupon the criminal defendant complied, completing a six and a half page report by 2:00pm, during which time a twenty to thirty minute break for lunch was taken, detailing the circumstances under which the criminal defendant first met the victim up until the death of the victim, the motives for the crime, how the crime was committed, activities of the criminal defendant after the crime, etc.

(4) However, as details in the aforementioned report and statements made by the criminal defendant during this time regarding the timing of reimbursement for postal savings in the name of the victim and the method used to kill the victim differed from the objective facts hitherto ascertained by the police, and statements concerning the criminal defendant's intentions to rob the victim's money and valuables at the time of killing were extremely vague, police officers deemed that the aforementioned statements, etc, contained falsehoods, and began to suspect the criminal defendant of Robbery resulting in Death instead of Homicide and Theft as stated by the criminal defendant. The interrogation continued and at the point when the criminal defendant admitted to having killed the victim because he had been enraged by the victim's attitude immediately prior to the crime and wanted the victim's postal savings, corroborating the aforementioned intention to rob, a further report was requested. The criminal defendant complied, and in approximately one hour from 4:00pm, wrote a further report of about one page in length entitled "My true feelings as to why I killed Midori," specifically detailing the aforementioned intentions.

(5) Consequently, police officers began preparations to apply for an arrest warrant, attaching the two aforementioned reports as prima facie evidence, and at 7:50pm, applied for an arrest warrant to be issued for the charges of robbery resulting in death and theft in response to the content of the criminal defendant's confession. Upon obtaining the arrest warrant, the criminal defendant was arrested at 9:25pm and interrogation of the criminal defendant for that day concluded shortly afterwards. At 2:30pm on the third day of the same month, procedures were instigated to send the criminal defendant to the

public prosecutor, an application for detention was made on the same day, and a warrant for detention was served at 11:23am on the fourth day of the same month.

(6) The criminal defendant, other than pleading that there was no intention of robbery during detention for questioning, consistently issued statements confirming the intent to rob in subsequent interrogations, while during interrogation on the seventh day of the same month, having continuously given false statements concerning the timing of reimbursement for the above mentioned postal savings in the name of the victim and the method used to kill the victim, these points were amended during the interrogation of this day, and the criminal defendant subsequently maintained a confession consistent with the facts of the public indictment. On the twenty-second day of the same month the criminal defendant was prosecuted for the charges of Robbery resulting in Death, etc, in relation to this case during his detention.

b. Based on the above mentioned facts, the interrogation of the criminal defendant from the time of voluntary attendance at the Hiratsuka Police Station after 11:00pm on February 1, 1983 until his arrest at 9:25pm of February 2 is accepted as having been conducted as non-compulsory investigation in accordance with Article 198 of the Code of Criminal Procedure, taking into account the various factors such as the nature of the case, the degree of suspicion that the suspect was under, the attitude of the suspect, etc, the interrogation of the suspect as part of those non-compulsory investigations are permissible within the accepted methods, modes and limits of social convention.

In consideration of the appropriateness of the voluntary interrogation in this case from the above perspective, the voluntary interrogation conducted throughout the night without allowing the criminal defendant to sleep, moreover, continued for the best part of half a day even after the criminal defendant had provided an initial confession, cannot be readily approved without the presence of exceptional circumstances, as in general, this type of interrogation of a suspect over long hours, even in cases of voluntary investigation, inflicts substantial mental and physical pain and fatigue on the suspect. Particularly in this case, as other methods could have been employed, such as the prompt undertaking of corroborative investigation, the instigation of arrest procedures followed by the discontinuation of interrogation after the criminal defendant had provided a confession to the killing of the victim, prudence must be exercised when approving the legitimacy of such actions. Furthermore, should the interrogation in this case cast any doubt on the voluntary nature of the criminal defendant's statement, then the interrogation must be deemed illegitimate, and any confession obtained during that time must be denied as inadmissible.

c. Consequently, in further consideration of the voluntary interrogation in this case, the presence of the following exceptional circumstances must be acknowledged.

Namely, that as previously stated, the police officers began the interrogation to the criminal defendant in this case under the context of questioning an unsworn witness with intimate knowledge of the victim's lifestyle prior to her death, and from the outset had obtained the approval of the criminal defendant who asserted his willingness to undergo interrogation.

In addition, the criminal defendant began his confession regarding the killing of the victim after 9:30am the following morning, and it is acknowledged that the interrogation continued for long hours after this not because the police officers insisted on a confession of criminal intent concerning robbery with the intention of obtaining the materials required for an arrest, or as a result of officers continuing the interrogation under the pretense of voluntary interrogation with the intention of avoiding time restrictions at the time of an arrest, but because, although hitherto investigations had already provided enough materials for an arrest, aspects of the criminal defendant's confession pertaining to the homicide and theft did not correspond to the objective conditions and were judged to contain falsehoods, causing officers to suspect that the truth lay in robbery resulting in death and continue the interrogation.

Furthermore, the lack of evidence suggesting that at any time during the voluntary interrogation in this case, the criminal defendant refused interrogation and attempted to leave or asked for a break, and the criminal defendant's attitude during the voluntary interrogation and in subsequent interrogations, in continuing to make false statements and excuses concerning important points such as the timing of reimbursement for the aforementioned postal savings when officers repeatedly pressed the point, make it difficult to accept the argument that the criminal defendant was at the time, not thinking clearly due to a cold and drowsiness.

d. In addition to the above circumstances, considering the overall nature and severity of this case, the interrogation in this case cannot be judged to have transgressed permissible limits of social convention pertaining to non-compulsory investigation, and the suggestion that the interrogation was such as to cast doubt on the voluntary nature of the criminal defendant's confession is unacceptable.

e. Therefore, the voluntary nature of reports written by the criminal defendant during the voluntary investigation in this case, reports written by the criminal defendant during the course of ensuing interrogations, and written statements submitted to judicial police officials and public prosecutors is affirmed, and the judgment in the second instance court upholding the judgment of the first instance court which approves their admissibility of evidence cannot be deemed illegitimate.

3. Conclusions

Therefore, the decision is rendered in the form of the Main Text.

(dissenting opinion omitted)

b. Decision upon the Case Concerning: (1) Limits on the Use of Physical Force in Voluntary Investigations; (2) Use of Physical Force in Voluntary Investigations Deemed to Be Permissible, Keishu, Vol. 30, No. 2 at 187; Case Number: 1975 (A) No. 146 (Third Petty Bench, March 16, 1976)

References: Article 197 and Article 198 of the Code of Criminal Procedure

Main Text of the Decision:

[A]ppeal is dismissed.

Reasons:

Concerning the grounds for ... Appeal ...:

In light of the arguments presented, this Court makes the ex officio determination to uphold the judgment of the Court of Appeals of guilt in obstructing a police officer in executing his duties for the following reasons.

1. The facts in the judgment of the Court of Appeals of obstructing a police officer from performing his duties are the same as those in the arraignment, as follows: "At approximately 6:00 a.m. on August 31, 1973, Defendant A was being questioned on suspicion of violation of the Road Traffic Law in the communications command room of the Gifu-Naka Police Station ... Police Officers B ... and C ... conducted the questioning. When asked to submit to a breath analysis test to determine whether he was driving under the influence of alcohol, the Defendant obstructed Officer B from performing his official duties as follows. Defendant grabbed and pulled the left shoulder and uniform collar of Officer B with his right hand while Officer B was carrying out his official duties. Next, the Defendant ripped off Officer B's left epaulette and committed battery by hitting Officer B once in the face with his right fist."

2. The judgment of the Court of Appeals found the following facts: (1) At approximately 4:10 a.m. on August 31, 1973, the Defendant, while driving under the influence of alcohol, crashed his vehicle into a concrete garbage disposal container located at the side of the road ... thereby causing a property-damage traffic accident. Shortly thereafter, Police Officers B and C arrived on the scene of the accident by patrol car and instructed the Defendant to show his driver's license and to blow into a balloon to test for breath alcohol content. Defendant refused to comply with either request.

Thereupon, the police officers placed the Defendant in their patrol car and took him to the Gifu-Naka Police Station for questioning under voluntary investigation on suspicion of violation of the Road Traffic Law. They arrived at the police station at approximately 4:30 a.m.

(2) Between the hours of 1:00 a.m. and 4:00 a.m. on that day, the Defendant had consumed [considerable alcohol]. Thereafter while driving home ... he caused the accident. At the time of the accident, his face was red, he smelled strongly of alcohol, was physically unsteady, and used rough language. From his appearance, it could be surmised that he was drunk.

(3) Defendant was questioned by the two police officers in the communications command room located in the police station and immediately complied with instructions to show his driver's license. Although he was informed that the breath analysis test complied with the Road Traffic Law, the Defendant repeatedly refused to take it. At approximately 5:30 a.m., the Defendant's father arrived at the police station at the request of the police officers. He attempted to persuade the Defendant to take the test but gave up as the Defendant became increasingly defiant. When the Defendant indicated that he would take the test if his mother came to the police station, the father returned home to call in the Defendant's mother.

(4) The two police officers continued to try to persuade the Defendant while awaiting the arrival of his mother. At approximately 6:00 a.m., the Defendant asked for matches and was refused. Thereupon the Defendant said, "I am going to get some matches," and suddenly got up from his chair and moved quickly towards the exit. Believing that the Defendant might attempt to flee, Officer B approached the Defendant to the Defendant's left and said, "You can leave after you blow the balloon," and used both hands to hold the Defendant's left wrist. The Defendant immediately pushed away the officer's hands, grabbed the officer's left shoulder and uniform collar with his right hand, ripped off the officer's left epaulette and hit him in the face once with his right fist. In the meantime, Officer B had extended both hands in an effort to stop the Defendant. However, since the Defendant continued to engage in violent behavior, Officers B and C acted together to restrain him and seat him again in his chair. Immediately thereafter, the officers arrested the Defendant for flagrantly obstructing a police officer from performing his law duties.

(5) The series of acts the Defendant took after pushing away the officer's hands do not constitute a legitimate counterattack in self-defense to Police Officer B's holding of his wrist; rather, the Defendant initiated a new attack.

(6) Defendant persisted in refusing to submit to a breath analysis test because, drawing on experience with questioning in two similar prior incidents, he was attempting to lower his alcohol content by delaying the administration of the test.

3. The court of the first instance held as follows: the restraining actions of Officer B described above exceeded reasonable limits in the context of a voluntary investigation and constituted coercive measures aimed at achieving what was

virtually the arrest of the Defendant. Since these acts were unlawful, they do not constitute official duties as prescribed under the crime of obstruction of official duties. Moreover, because those acts constituted an immediate and wrongful infringement upon the Defendant's rights, the Defendant's violent response constituted legitimate acts of self-defense necessary for obtaining the Defendant's freedom of action. Thus, the Defendant's actions do not constitute battery.

The Court of Appeals found this judgment to be in error. It held that the actions of Police Officer B, who approached the Defendant to the Defendant's left and used both hands to hold the Defendant's left wrist, constituted an objectively reasonable use of force since excessive force was not applied, and considering the necessity and urgency of the investigation, the police officer's action constituted an appropriate means to persuade the Defendant to change his mind and to submit to the breath analysis test. Moreover, Police Officer B's actions immediately after this incident were taken with the intent to restrain the violent behavior of the Defendant and do not represent coercion intended to have the same results as the arrest of the Defendant. Further, the acts of violence perpetrated by the Defendant upon Police Officer B after pushing away the officer's hands did not constitute a legitimate counterattack but a new attack, and this Court judges that none of the Defendant's acts of violence could be justified as legitimate acts of self-defense.

4. The legal issue before the Court of Appeals in the determination of facts focuses on the question of whether the actions taken by Police Officer B, who approached the Defendant to the left of the Defendant to block his access to the door and used both hands to hold the Defendant's left wrist, are permissible in the course of a voluntary investigation.

The use of coercive measures in the course of an investigation is permitted only where explicitly provided for under the law. However, coercive measures in this context do not denote measures accompanied by the use of physical force. Rather, they refer to measures that are not permitted in the absence of special rules and provisions justifying such action, such as suppressing or subjecting the individual to unreasonable duress and placing restrictions on his person, residence, or property for the purpose of carrying out the coercive investigation. Any exercise of physical force that does not involve coercive measures may be considered permissible, depending on the circumstances of each case. However, even the use of physical force that does not employ coercive measures may infringe upon or threaten to infringe upon certain benefits of the law. It is therefore inappropriate to give carte blanche to the use of physical force. Rather, the permissible use of physical force is contingent upon a determination of the urgency and necessity for employing such force, and of the allowable limit under the specific circumstances of each case.

In applying this principle to the case on hand, the actions of Police Officer B cannot be judged to constitute a virtual arrest or other forms of coercive measures, insofar as the officer's actions were intended to persuade the Defendant to undergo to a breath analysis test and were not excessively forceful. Prior to this incident, the Defendant had been voluntarily brought to the police station under strong suspicion of driving under the influence of alcohol. Defendant's father was thereafter called to the police station to persuade him to take the breath analysis test. At that time, the Defendant indicated that he would submit to the test if his mother were present at the police station. Thereupon the father was requested to convey this matter to the Defendant's mother. While awaiting the arrival of the mother, the Defendant suddenly attempted to exit the room. The actions of Police Officer B constituted actions to restrain and further persuade the Defendant and were not excessively forceful. Hence, the police officer's actions cannot be judged inappropriate and outside the permissible limits of investigative activities, and cannot be charged with unlawful exercise of official duties. Therefore, this Court affirms the Court of Appeals in its finding that Police Officer B acted legitimately in performing his official duties including the above actions, and in finding the Defendant guilty of the obstruction of the execution of official duties.

Therefore, … this Court unanimously finds as stated in the Main Text of the Decision above.

(This translation is provisional and subject to revision.)

Note

The result in the principal case should be compared to that in the Decision of August 1, 1951, Hanreishu V, No. 9 at 1684 (Grand Bench), in which the Supreme Court squarely held that confessions extracted by torture are inadmissible under the Constitution of Japan. It is also interesting to compare the result in the main case with that in the Judgment Upon the Case Concerning the Relationship Between Evidential Capacity of a Confession Provoked by a Fraudulent Means and Article 38(2) of the Constitution of Japan; Keishu Vol. 24, No. 12, at 1670, Case number: 1967(A) No.1546 (Grand Bench, November 25, 1970). In that case, the defendant and his wife were suspected of engaging in a conspiracy. A public prosecutor had induced the defendant to confess by stating, falsely, that the wife had all ready confessed, and by suggesting that the wife would not be prosecuted if the defendant took responsibility for the crime. The defendant's conviction was based on the confession. The Supreme Court held that the use of fraudulent means to induce a defendant to confess amounted to the employment of unfair mental pressure and rendered the confession involuntary. His conviction was therefore thrown out, as violating article 38(2) of the Japanese Constitution.

B. The European Human Rights System

1. Drawing Inferences from Defendant's Silence; Questioning Defendant without Access to an Attorney

a. In the Case of John Murray v. the United Kingdom, 1996-I E.C.H.R. 30

....

AS TO THE FACTS

I. Particular circumstances of the case

A. The applicant's arrest and detention

11. The applicant was arrested by police officers at 5.40 p.m. on 7 January 1990 under section 14* of the Prevention of Terrorism (Temporary Provisions) Act 1989. Pursuant to Article 3* of the Criminal Evidence (Northern Ireland) Order 1988 ("the Order")..., he was cautioned by the police in the following terms:

> You do not have to say anything unless you wish to do so but I must warn you that if you fail to mention any fact which you rely on in your defence in court, your failure to take this opportunity to mention it may be treated in court as supporting any relevant evidence against you. If you do wish to say anything, what you say may be given in evidence.

In response to the police caution the applicant stated that he had nothing to say.

12. On arrival at Castlereagh Police Office at about 7 p.m., he refused to give his personal details to the officer in charge of the custody record ... At 7.06 p.m. he indicated that he wished to consult with a solicitor. At 7.30 p.m. his access to a solicitor was delayed on the authority of a detective superintendent pursuant to section 15(1)* of the Northern Ireland (Emergency Provisions) Act 1987 ("the 1987 Act"). The delay was authorised for a period of 48 hours from the time of detention (i.e. from 5.40 p.m. on 7 January) on the basis that the detective superintendent had reasonable grounds to believe that the exercise of the right of access would, inter alia, interfere with the gathering of information about the commission of acts of terrorism or make it more difficult to prevent an act of terrorism....

13. At 9.27 p.m. on 7 January a police constable cautioned the applicant pursuant to Article 6* of the Order, inter alia, requesting him to account for his presence at the house where he was arrested. He was warned that if he failed or

refused to do so, a court, judge or jury might draw such inference from his failure or refusal as appears proper. He was also served with a written copy of Article 6 of the Order....

In reply to this caution the applicant stated: "Nothing to say."

14. At 10.40 p.m. he was reminded of his right to have a friend or relative notified of his detention and stated that he did not want anyone notified. He was also informed that his right of access to a solicitor had been delayed. He then requested consultation with a different firm of solicitors. A police inspector reviewed the reasons for the delay and concluded that the reasons remained valid.

15. The applicant was interviewed by police detectives at Castlereagh Police Office on twelve occasions during 8 and 9 January. In total he was interviewed for 21 hours and 39 minutes. At the commencement of these interviews he was either cautioned pursuant to Article 3 of the Order or reminded of the terms of the caution.

16. During the first ten interviews on 8 and 9 January 1990 the applicant made no reply to any questions put to him. He was able to see his solicitor for the first time at 6.33 p.m. on 9 January. At 7.10 p.m. he was interviewed again and reminded of the Article 3 caution. He replied: "I have been advised by my solicitor not to answer any of your questions." A final interview, during which the applicant said nothing, took place between 9.40 p.m. and 11.45 p.m. on 9 January.

His solicitor was not permitted to be present at any of these interviews.

B. The trial proceedings

17. In May 1991 the applicant was tried by a single judge, the Lord Chief Justice of Northern Ireland, sitting without a jury, for the offences of conspiracy to murder, the unlawful imprisonment, with seven other people, of a certain Mr L. and of belonging to a proscribed organisation, the Provisional Irish Republican Army (IRA).

18. According to the Crown, Mr L. had been a member of the IRA who had been providing information about their activities to the Royal Ulster Constabulary. On discovering that Mr L. was an informer, the IRA tricked him into visiting a house in Belfast on 5 January 1990. He was falsely imprisoned in one of the rear bedrooms of the house and interrogated by the IRA until the arrival of the police and the army at the house on 7 January 1990. It was also alleged by the Crown that there was a conspiracy to murder Mr L. as punishment for being a police informer.

19. In the course of the trial, evidence was given that when the police entered the house on 7 January, the applicant was seen by a police constable coming down a flight of stairs wearing a raincoat over his clothes and was arrested in the hall of the house. Mr L. testified that he was forced under threat of being

killed to make a taped confession to his captors that he was an informer. He further said that on the evening of 7 January he had heard scurrying and had been told to take off his blindfold, that he had done so and had opened the spare bedroom door. He had then seen the applicant standing at the stairs. The applicant had told him that the police were at the door and to go downstairs and watch television. While he was talking to him the applicant was pulling tape out of a cassette. On a search of the house by the police items of clothing of Mr L. were subsequently found in the spare bedroom, whilst a tangled tape was discovered in the upstairs bathroom. The salvaged portions of the tape revealed a confession by Mr L. that he had agreed to work for the police and had been paid for so doing. At no time, either on his arrest or during the trial proceedings, did the applicant give any explanation for his presence in the house.

20. At the close of the prosecution case the trial judge, acting in accordance with Article 4* of the Order, called upon each of the eight accused to give evidence in their own defence. The trial judge informed them inter alia:

> I am also required by law to tell you that if you refuse to come into the witness box to be sworn or if, after having been sworn, you refuse, without good reason, to answer any question, then the court in deciding whether you are guilty or not guilty may take into account against you to the extent that it considers proper your refusal to give evidence or to answer any questions.

21. Acting on the advice of his solicitor and counsel, the applicant chose not to give any evidence. No witnesses were called on his behalf. Counsel, with support from the evidence of a co-accused, D.M., submitted, inter alia, that the applicant's presence in the house just before the police arrived was recent and innocent.

22. On 8 May 1991 the applicant was found guilty of the offence of aiding and abetting the unlawful imprisonment of Mr L. and sentenced to eight years' imprisonment. He was acquitted on the remaining charges.

23. The trial judge rejected D.M.'s evidence (see paragraph 21 above) as untruthful. He considered that

> the surrounding facts, including the finding of the tangled tape in the bathroom with the broken cassette case, and the fact that, on entering the house some appreciable time after they arrived outside it and some appreciable time after they first knocked on the door, the police found Murray coming down the stairs at the time when all the other occupants of the house were in the living room, strongly confirm L's evidence that after the police knocked on the door Murray was upstairs pulling the tape out of the cassette.

24. In rejecting a submission by the applicant that ... the Order did not operate to permit the court to draw an adverse inference against him, where, at the

end of the Crown case, there was a reasonably plausible explanation for the accused's conduct consistent with his innocence, the trial judge stated as follows:

> There can be debate as to the extent to which, before the making of the Criminal Evidence (Northern Ireland) Order 1988, a tribunal of fact in this jurisdiction was entitled to draw an adverse inference against an accused because he failed to give evidence on his own behalf, or to account for his presence at a particular place or to mention particular facts when questioned by the police. But I consider that the purpose of … the 1988 Order was to make it clear that, whatever was the effect of the previous legal rules, a judge trying a criminal case without a jury, or a jury in a criminal case, was entitled to apply common sense in drawing inferences against the accused in the circumstances specified in [the Order].

> I think it is clear that the purpose of Article 4 is to permit the tribunal of fact to draw such inferences against the accused from his failure to give evidence in his own defence as common sense requires. The inference which it is proper to draw against an accused will vary from case to case depending on the particular circumstances of the case and, of course, the failure of the accused to give evidence on his own behalf does not in itself indicate guilt. Nor does the failure to mention particular facts when questioned or the failure to account for presence in a particular place in itself indicate guilt. But I consider that the intendment of [the Order] is to enable the tribunal of fact to exercise ordinary common sense in drawing inferences against an accused …

> Therefore when I come to consider the case against the accused … I propose to draw such inferences against [him] … as ordinary common sense dictates.

25. In concluding that the applicant was guilty of the offence of aiding and abetting false imprisonment, the trial judge drew adverse inferences against the applicant under both Articles 4 and 6 of the Order. The judge stated that in the particular circumstances of the case he did not propose to draw inferences against the applicant under Article 3 of the Order. He stated furthermore:

> I accept the submissions of counsel for the accused that as demonstrated by his replies in cross-examination, L. is a man who is fully prepared to lie on oath to advance his own interests and is a man of no moral worth whatever. I, therefore, accept the further submissions of counsel for the accused that, unless his evidence were confirmed by other evidence, a court should not act on his evidence, particularly against accused persons in a criminal trial …

> I now turn to consider the fifth count charging the false imprisonment of L. against the accused [the applicant]. For the reasons which I have

already stated, I am satisfied that, as L. described in his evidence, [the applicant] was at the top of the stairs pulling the tape out of the cassette after the police arrived outside the house.

I am also satisfied, for the reasons which I have already stated, that [the applicant] was in the house for longer than the short period described by his co-accused, [D.M.]. I am further satisfied that it is an irresistible inference that while he was in the house [the applicant] was in contact with the men holding L. captive and that he knew that L. was being held a captive. I also draw very strong inferences against [the applicant] ... by reason of his failure to give an account of his presence in the house when cautioned by the police on the evening of 7 January 1990..., and I also draw very strong inferences against [the applicant] ... by reason of his refusal to give evidence in his own defence when called upon by the Court to do so.

Therefore I find [the applicant] guilty of aiding and abetting the false imprisonment of L. because, knowing he was being held captive in the house, he was present in the house concurring in L. being falsely imprisoned. As Vaughan J. stated in R. v. Young ... [the applicant] was "near enough to give [his] aid and to give [his] countenance and assistance."

C. The appeal proceedings

26. The applicant appealed against conviction and sentence to the Court of Appeal in Northern Ireland. In a judgment of 7 July 1992, the court dismissed the applicant's appeal holding, inter alia:

... to suggest, with respect, that [the applicant] went into the house just as the police were arriving outside, immediately went upstairs, attempted to destroy a tape and then walked downstairs, and that this was the sum of his time and activity in the house defies common sense ...

We are satisfied that it can reasonably be inferred that [the applicant] knew before he came to the house that [L.] was being held captive there. With this knowledge he assisted in the false imprisonment by directing the captive from the bedroom where he had been held and by giving him the directions and admonition [L.] said. Accordingly [the applicant] aided and abetted the crime. We do not accept that [L.] would have been free to leave the house, if the police and army had been taken in by the pretence of the television watching and had departed without making any arrests. We have no doubt that [L.] remained under restraint in the living room when the police were there and if they had left, he would have remained a prisoner to await the fate that his captors would determine.

We consider that there was a formidable case against [the applicant]. He was the only one of the accused whom [L.] observed and identified as playing a positive part in the activities touching his captivity. [L.]'s evidence therefore called for an answer. No answer was forthcoming of any kind to the police or throughout the length of his trial. It was inevitable that the judge would draw 'very strong inferences' against him.

The Crown case deeply implicated [the applicant] in the false imprisonment of [L.].... .

AS TO THE LAW

I. ALLEGED VIOLATION OF ARTICLE 6 ... OF THE CONVENTION

40. The applicant alleged that there had been a violation of the right to silence and the right not to incriminate oneself contrary to Article 6 paras. 1 and 2 ... of the Convention....

A. Article 6 paras. 1 and 2 ...: right to silence

41. In the submission of the applicant, the drawing of incriminating inferences against him under the Criminal Evidence (Northern Ireland) Order 1988 ("the Order") violated Article 6 paras. 1 and 2 ... of the Convention. It amounted to an infringement of the right to silence, the right not to incriminate oneself and the principle that the prosecution bear the burden of proving the case without assistance from the accused.

He contended that a first, and most obvious element of the right to silence is the right to remain silent in the face of police questioning and not to have to testify against oneself at trial. In his submission, these have always been essential and fundamental elements of the British criminal justice system. Moreover the Commission ... and the Court ... have accepted that they are an inherent part of the right to a fair hearing under Article 6.... In his view these are absolute rights which an accused is entitled to enjoy without restriction.

A second, equally essential element of the right to silence was that the exercise of the right by an accused would not be used as evidence against him in his trial. However, the trial judge drew very strong inferences ... from his decision to remain silent under police questioning and during the trial. Indeed, it was clear from the trial judge's remarks and from the judgment of the Court of Appeal in his case that the inferences were an integral part of his decision to find him guilty.

Accordingly, he was severely and doubly penalised for choosing to remain silent: once for his silence under police interrogation and once for his failure to testify during the trial. To use against him silence under police questioning and his refusal to testify during trial amounted to subverting the presumption of innocence and the onus of proof resulting from that presumption: it is for the prosecution to prove the accused's guilt without any assistance from the latter being required.

42. Amnesty International submitted that permitting adverse inferences to be drawn from the silence of the accused was an effective means of compulsion which shifted the burden of proof from the prosecution to the accused and was inconsistent with the right not to be compelled to testify against oneself or to confess guilt because the accused is left with no reasonable choice between silence—which will be taken as testimony against oneself—and testifying. It pointed out that Article 14(3)(g)* of the United Nations International Covenant on Civil and Political Rights explicitly provides that an accused shall "not be compelled to testify against himself or to confess guilt." Reference was also made to Rule 42(A)* of the Rules of Procedure and Evidence of the International Criminal Tribunal for the Former Yugoslavia which expressly provides that a suspect has the right to remain silent and to the Draft Statute for an International Criminal Court, submitted to the United Nations General Assembly by the International Law Commission, which in Draft Article 26(6)(a)(i)* qualifies the right to silence with the words "without such silence being a consideration in the determination of guilt or innocence."

...

The Northern Ireland Standing Advisory Commission on Human Rights, for its part, considered that the right to silence was not an absolute right, but rather a safeguard which might, in certain circumstances, be removed provided other appropriate safeguards for accused persons were introduced to compensate for the potential risk of unjust convictions.

43. The Government contended that what is at issue is not whether the Order as such is compatible with the right to silence but rather whether, on the facts of the case, the drawing of inferences under ... the Order rendered the criminal proceedings against the applicant unfair contrary to Article 6 ... of the Convention.

They maintained, however, that the first question should be answered in the negative. They emphasised that the Order did not detract from the right to remain silent in the face of police questioning and explicitly confirmed the right not to have to testify at trial. They further noted that the Order in no way changed either the burden or the standard of proof: it remained for the prosecution to prove an accused's guilt beyond reasonable doubt. What the Order did was to confer a discretionary power to draw inferences from the silence of an accused in carefully defined circumstances. They maintained that this did not, of itself, violate the right to silence.

In this respect, they emphasised the safeguards governing the drawing of inferences under the Order which had been highlighted in national judicial decisions. In particular, it had been consistently stressed by the courts that the Order merely allows the trier of fact to draw such inferences as common sense dictates. The question in each case is whether the evidence adduced by the prosecution is sufficiently strong to call for an answer.

With regard to the international standards to which reference had been made by Amnesty International, it was contended that they did not demonstrate any internationally-accepted prohibition on the drawing of common-sense inferences from the silence of an accused whether at trial or pre-trial. In particular, the Draft Statute for an International Criminal Court is far from final and cannot be said to have been adopted by the international community.

As to the question whether, on the facts of the case, the drawing of inferences ... the Order rendered the criminal proceedings against the applicant unfair, the Government comprehensively analysed the trial court's assessment of the evidence against the applicant. On the basis of this analysis they submitted that on the evidence adduced against the applicant by the Crown, the Court of Appeal was right to conclude that a formidable case had been made out against him which deeply implicated him in the false imprisonment of Mr L. and that this case "called for an answer." The drawing of inferences therefore had been quite natural and in accordance with common sense.

44. The Court must, confining its attention to the facts of the case, consider whether the drawing of inferences against the applicant under ... Order rendered the criminal proceedings against him—and especially his conviction— unfair within the meaning of Article 6 ... of the Convention. It is recalled in this context that no inference was drawn under Article 3 of the Order. It is not the Court's role to examine whether, in general, the drawing of inferences under the scheme contained in the Order is compatible with the notion of a fair hearing under Article 6....

45. Although not specifically mentioned in Article 6 ... of the Convention, there can be no doubt that the right to remain silent under police questioning and the privilege against self-incrimination are generally recognised international standards which lie at the heart of the notion of a fair procedure under Article 6.... By providing the accused with protection against improper compulsion by the authorities these immunities contribute to avoiding miscarriages of justice and to securing the aims of Article 6....

46. The Court does not consider that it is called upon to give an abstract analysis of the scope of these immunities and, in particular, of what constitutes in this context "improper compulsion." What is at stake in the present case is whether these immunities are absolute in the sense that the exercise by an accused of the right to silence cannot under any circumstances be used against him at trial or, alternatively, whether informing him in advance that, under certain conditions, his silence may be so used, is always to be regarded as "improper compulsion."

47. On the one hand, it is self-evident that it is incompatible with the immunities under consideration to base a conviction solely or mainly on the accused's silence or on a refusal to answer questions or to give evidence himself. On the

other hand, the Court deems it equally obvious that these immunities cannot and should not prevent that the accused's silence, in situations which clearly call for an explanation from him, be taken into account in assessing the persuasiveness of the evidence adduced by the prosecution.

Wherever the line between these two extremes is to be drawn, it follows from this understanding of "the right to silence" that the question whether the right is absolute must be answered in the negative.

It cannot be said therefore that an accused's decision to remain silent throughout criminal proceedings should necessarily have no implications when the trial court seeks to evaluate the evidence against him. In particular, as the Government have pointed out, established international standards in this area, while providing for the right to silence and the privilege against self-incrimination, are silent on this point.

Whether the drawing of adverse inferences from an accused's silence infringes Article 6 ... is a matter to be determined in the light of all the circumstances of the case, having particular regard to the situations where inferences may be drawn, the weight attached to them by the national courts in their assessment of the evidence and the degree of compulsion inherent in the situation.

48. As regards the degree of compulsion involved in the present case, it is recalled that the applicant was in fact able to remain silent. Notwithstanding the repeated warnings as to the possibility that inferences might be drawn from his silence, he did not make any statements to the police and did not give evidence during his trial. Moreover ... he remained a non-compellable witness. Thus his insistence in maintaining silence throughout the proceedings did not amount to a criminal offence or contempt of court. Furthermore, as has been stressed in national court decisions, silence, in itself, cannot be regarded as an indication of guilt.

49. The facts of the present case accordingly fall to be distinguished from those in [a case] where criminal proceedings were brought against the applicant by the customs authorities in an attempt to compel him to provide evidence of offences he had allegedly committed. Such a degree of compulsion in that case was found by the Court to be incompatible with Article 6 ... since, in effect, it destroyed the very essence of the privilege against self-incrimination.

50. Admittedly a system which warns the accused—who is possibly without legal assistance (as in the applicant's case)—that adverse inferences may be drawn from a refusal to provide an explanation to the police for his presence at the scene of a crime or to testify during his trial, when taken in conjunction with the weight of the case against him, involves a certain level of indirect compulsion. However, since the applicant could not be compelled to speak or to testify, as indicated above, this factor on its own cannot be decisive. The Court must rather concentrate its attention on the role played by the inferences in the proceedings against the applicant and especially in his conviction.

51. In this context, it is recalled that these were proceedings without a jury, the trier of fact being an experienced judge. Furthermore, the drawing of inferences under the Order is subject to an important series of safeguards designed to respect the rights of the defence and to limit the extent to which reliance can be placed on inferences.

In the first place, before inferences can be drawn under ... the Order appropriate warnings must have been given to the accused as to the legal effects of maintaining silence. Moreover, as indicated by [a] judgment of the House of Lords ... the prosecutor must first establish a prima facie case against the accused, i.e. a case consisting of direct evidence which, if believed and combined with legitimate inferences based upon it, could lead a properly directed jury to be satisfied beyond reasonable doubt that each of the essential elements of the offence is proved.

The question in each particular case is whether the evidence adduced by the prosecution is sufficiently strong to require an answer. The national court cannot conclude that the accused is guilty merely because he chooses to remain silent. It is only if the evidence against the accused "calls" for an explanation which the accused ought to be in a position to give that a failure to give any explanation "may as a matter of common sense allow the drawing of an inference that there is no explanation and that the accused is guilty." Conversely if the case presented by the prosecution had so little evidential value that it called for no answer, a failure to provide one could not justify an inference of guilt.... In sum, it is only common-sense inferences which the judge considers proper, in the light of the evidence against the accused, that can be drawn under the Order.

In addition, the trial judge has a discretion whether, on the facts of the particular case, an inference should be drawn. As indicated by the Court of Appeal in the present case, if a judge accepted that an accused did not understand the warning given or if he had doubts about it, "we are confident that he would not [draw inferences] against him." Furthermore in Northern Ireland, where trial judges sit without a jury, the judge must explain the reasons for the decision to draw inferences and the weight attached to them. The exercise of discretion in this regard is subject to review by the appellate courts.

52. In the present case, the evidence presented against the applicant by the prosecution was considered by the Court of Appeal to constitute a "formidable" case against him (see paragraph 26 above)....

53. The trial judge drew strong inferences against the applicant under ... the Order by reason of his failure to give an account of his presence in the house when arrested and interrogated by the police. He also drew strong inferences under ... the Order by reason of the applicant's refusal to give evidence in his own defence when asked by the court to do so (see paragraph 25 above).

54. In the Court's view, having regard to the weight of the evidence against the applicant, as outlined above, the drawing of inferences from his refusal, at ar-

rest, during police questioning and at trial, to provide an explanation for his presence in the house was a matter of common sense and cannot be regarded as unfair or unreasonable in the circumstances. As pointed out by the Delegate of the Commission, the courts in a considerable number of countries where evidence is freely assessed may have regard to all relevant circumstances, including the manner in which the accused has behaved or has conducted his defence, when evaluating the evidence in the case. It considers that, what distinguishes the drawing of inferences under the Order is that, in addition to the existence of the specific safeguards mentioned above, it constitutes, as described by the Commission, "a formalised system which aims at allowing common-sense implications to play an open role in the assessment of evidence."

Nor can it be said, against this background, that the drawing of reasonable inferences from the applicant's behaviour had the effect of shifting the burden of proof from the prosecution to the defence so as to infringe the principle of the presumption of innocence.

55. The applicant submitted that it was unfair to draw inferences under ... the Order from his silence at a time when he had not had the benefit of legal advice. In his view the question of access to a solicitor was inextricably entwined with that of the drawing of adverse inferences from pre-trial silence under police questioning. In this context he emphasised that under the Order once an accused has remained silent a trap is set from which he cannot escape: if an accused chooses to give evidence or to call witnesses he is, by reason of his prior silence, exposed to the risk of an Article 3 inference sufficient to bring about a conviction; on the other hand, if he maintains his silence inferences may be drawn against him under other provisions of the Order.

56. The Court recalls that it must confine its attention to the facts of the present case.... The reality of this case is that the applicant maintained silence right from the first questioning by the police to the end of his trial. It is not for the Court therefore to speculate on the question whether inferences would have been drawn under the Order had the applicant, at any moment after his first interrogation, chosen to speak to the police or to give evidence at his trial or call witnesses. Nor should it speculate on the question whether it was the possibility of such inferences being drawn that explains why the applicant was advised by his solicitor to remain silent. Immediately after arrest the applicant was warned in accordance with the provisions of the Order but chose to remain silent. The Court, like the Commission, observes that there is no indication that the applicant failed to understand the significance of the warning given to him by the police prior to seeing his solicitor. Under these circumstances the fact that during the first 48 hours of his detention the applicant had been refused access to a lawyer does not detract from the above conclusion that the drawing of inferences was not unfair or unreasonable (see paragraph 54 above)....

57. Against the above background, and taking into account the role played by inferences under the Order during the trial and their impact on the rights of the defence, the Court does not consider that the criminal proceedings were unfair or that there had been an infringement of the presumption of innocence.

58. Accordingly, there has been no violation of Article 6 paras. 1 and 2 ... of the Convention.

....

FOR THESE REASONS, THE COURT

1. Holds by fourteen votes to five that there has been no violation of Article 6 paras. 1 and 2 ... of the Convention arising out of the drawing of adverse inferences on account of the applicant's silence;....

(dissenting opinions omitted)

2. Right to Confront Witnesses

a. Van Mechelen and Others v. the Netherlands, 1997-III E.C.H.R. 691

...

AS TO THE FACTS

I. Particular circumstances of the case

A. Background to the case

9. The police received information to the effect that the applicants were the perpetrators of several robberies, and that they operated from two residential caravan sites. It was decided to detail a police observation team ("OT") to keep these caravan sites under observation as from 25 January 1989.

10. On 26 January 1989 at around 5.15 p.m. three motor cars, a Mercedes estate car, a BMW and a Lancia, were seen to leave one of the two caravan sites shortly after each other. Their registration numbers were noted.

11. On 26 January 1989 at around 6 p.m. the post office of the town of Oirschot was robbed. The window of the post office was broken down by backing a Mercedes estate car equipped with a steel girder into it. One of the robbers, wearing a black balaclava helmet and armed with a pistol, forced the staff to surrender some 70,000 Netherlands guilders. The robbers then set the Mercedes car alight and made off in a BMW.

Police cars alerted by radio followed the BMW. Police officers saw the BMW drive onto a sand track leading into a nearby forest. Later they saw a column of smoke coming out of the forest. The BMW was subsequently found there, burnt out.

Four police officers in a police car saw a red car (later found to be a Lancia) leave the forest via the same sand track used by the BMW and gave chase. In the course of the chase the boot of the car was opened from the inside and men squatting in the back opened fire at the pursuing police car with a pistol and a sub-machine gun. A car containing civilians was hit by a stray bullet but its occupants were not hurt.

The Lancia made off at high speed and entered a side road. When the police car caught up with it the Lancia was stationary. A man standing in the road fired at the police car with a sub-machine gun. The police car was hit and its occupants injured, after which the gunman and the persons in the Lancia made their escape.

12. All three cars—the Mercedes, the BMW and the Lancia—were later identified as the cars which had been seen leaving the caravan site (see paragraph 10 above).

B. The criminal proceedings

1. Proceedings in the 's-Hertogenbosch Regional Court

13. The applicants and one other man, called Amandus Pruijmboom (not to be confused with the applicant Antonius Amandus Pruijmboom), were charged with attempted murder—or, in the alternative, attempted manslaughter—and robbery with the threat of violence and summoned to appear for trial before the 's-Hertogenbosch Regional Court on 19 May 1989.

Evidence proffered by the prosecution included statements made to a named police officer by police officers identified only by a number.

14....

Counsel for Mr Willem Venerius argued, inter alia, that the police officers identified only by a number were anonymous witnesses, so that their statements did not constitute sufficient proof, in the absence of corroborating evidence, to support a conviction. The Regional Court rejected this argument, holding that since the police officers in question had investigative competence, the evidential value of their statements was not affected by their anonymity.

The Regional Court convicted the accused of attempted manslaughter and robbery with the threat of violence. The evidence identifying the applicants as perpetrators of these crimes was constituted by the statements made before the trial by the anonymous police officers, none of whom gave evidence before either the Regional Court or the investigating judge.

All five accused were sentenced to ten years' imprisonment.

2. Proceedings in the 's-Hertogenbosch Court of Appeal

15. The five convicted men appealed to the 's-Hertogenbosch Court of Appeal.

At the hearing before that court on 2 May 1990 the applicants' lawyers made requests for several named and anonymous witnesses to be heard. The Court of Appeal thereupon referred the case to the investigating judge, firstly because it considered it necessary to find out what objections the police officers themselves had against the lifting of their anonymity and secondly because the number of persons to be heard was such that it could not conveniently be done in open court. The persons to be heard were four named police officers, eleven anonymous police officers (identified to the defence and the court only by a number) and two civilians.

16. The named and anonymous witnesses were questioned on 24 and 27 September and on 5–8 and 13 November 1990.

All of the anonymous witnesses were—or had at the relevant time been—police officers invested with investigative competence.

The procedure followed for questioning them was that the investigating judge, the witness and a registrar were together in one room, and the defendants, their lawyers and the advocate-general in another. The defendants, the lawyers and the advocate-general could hear all the questions asked to the witnesses and their replies through a sound link. The statements of the witnesses were repeated by the investigating judge to the registrar, who took them down.

[The opinion then recounts the testimony before the investigating magistrate of the eleven anonymous witnesses, which testimony strongly supported the allegations against the applicants. These witnesses further explained their requests for anonymity as motivated by a desire to avoid reducing their effectiveness as police officers by exposing their identities and also because of fears for themselves and their families, based on the fact that these officers had either themselves been threatened in the past or knew of other officers who had been. There was no testimony by any of the anonymous witnesses that they or anyone else had been threatened in connection with this case. The investigating judge made a detailed report of this testimony, stressing that counsel for both sides were given unlimited time to examine the witnesses, that their testimony in fact took considerable time, that the investigating judge was thoroughly convinced of the witnesses' credibility, and that he believed the reasons the witnesses put forward for seeking anonymity were such as to justify permitting them to testify anonymously. He explained this last conclusion only by reference to the very violent character of the crime of which the applicants were accused.]

....

25. The hearing before the Court of Appeal was resumed on 16, 17 and 18 January 1991.

On 16 January a named witness, Mr Engelen, was heard in open court. He had stated to the police in March 1989, and to the investigating judge in September 1990, that he recognised the applicant Van Mechelen as the man who had fired a sub-machine gun at a police car in the village of Leende. Before the Court of Appeal he stated that on the latter occasion he had been allowed to re-read his earlier statement, but that he was no longer sure whether he could still recognise either the weapon or the man who had fired it. He also said that he had not been threatened in connection with the case.

On 18 January the lawyer acting for the applicant Van Mechelen brought forward two persons chosen for their excellent eyesight (both having participated in the Olympic games as members of the Netherlands rifle-shooting team), and who had participated in a reconstruction of the shooting in light and weather conditions similar to those obtaining at the time of the crime. These witnesses both stated that they had been unable to distinguish the features of the persons acting the parts of the perpetrators at the distances at which it had been alleged that the accused had been seen by Mr Engelen. A video recording had been made of the reconstruction, in the presence of a notary who had kept the original videotape under seal.

The hearing was again resumed on 21 January 1991, and the video of the reconstruction was shown.

26. The Court of Appeal convicted all four applicants in four separate but similar judgments on 4 February 1991.

All four applicants were found guilty of attempted murder and robbery with the threat of violence and sentenced to fourteen years' imprisonment. The fifth suspect, Mr Amandus Pruijmboom, was acquitted.

The Court of Appeal's judgment in the case of the applicant Van Mechelen contained the following:

> Considering with regard to the statements, used in evidence, of the persons who remained anonymous, that these statements were taken down by a judge, more particularly the investigating judge responsible for criminal cases within the jurisdiction of the 's-Hertogenbosch Regional Court, who himself knows the identity of the witnesses, who has heard these witnesses on oath, who in his official record of his findings ... has given his reasoned opinion of the reliability of the witnesses and their reasons for wishing to remain anonymous, and who, moreover, has offered the accused and the defence the opportunity to question these witnesses, of which opportunity, as appears from the official records of the interrogations, extensive use has been made.

> The objections of the witnesses heard by the investigating judge and identified only by a number to remain anonymous (sic) are sufficient reason for the Court of Appeal to continue this anonymity. The Court of Appeal refuses the request made by counsel at the hearing to have these witnesses heard in open court, even if this request should be understood to imply that the witnesses might be disguised, since the

possibility that the witnesses may be recognised in open court cannot be excluded.

Of the arguments for continuing the anonymity of the witnesses, the Court of Appeal considers particularly persuasive the personal safety of these witnesses and their families, and it makes no difference that these witnesses have not yet been threatened. As already noted in the Court of Appeal's interlocutory decision of 3 October 1990, the present case concerns extremely serious crimes, the [attempted murder] having been committed so as to evade recognition and arrest by the police, the perpetrators having been prepared to sacrifice a number of human lives. In these circumstances, the risk run by the witnesses identified only by a number and their families if their anonymity is lifted or insufficiently guaranteed is decisive. In so far as anonymous witnesses have refused to answer questions this was done in order not to disclose methods of investigation or to maintain the anonymity of other investigating officers involved in the case.

The Court of Appeal considered the statements of the anonymous police officers to be corroborated by each other and by the evidence available from non-anonymous sources. This other evidence included a transcript of a telephone conversation between the wife of Mr Johan Venerius and her mother intercepted two days after the date of the crime, from which it appeared that Mr Johan Venerius had not returned home in the meanwhile and his whereabouts were unknown, as well as forensic reports relating to the cars and the weapons used for the crime and the above-mentioned statements of the named civilians and police officers. However, the Court of Appeal did not rely on the statements of Mr Engelen.

3. Proceedings in the Supreme Court

27. The applicants filed appeals on points of law to the Supreme Court.

In accordance with the advisory opinion of the advocate-general, the Supreme Court dismissed the appeals in a series of judgments of 9 June 1992. It held that in the circumstances the evidence given by the unnamed police officers was admissible, since on the one hand their evidence was sufficiently corroborated by the evidence obtained from named sources and on the other the procedure followed provided sufficient compensation for the handicaps under which the defence had laboured....

28. It has not been alleged that any named or anonymous witnesses were at any time threatened by or on behalf of the applicants.

AS TO THE LAW

I. Alleged Violation of Article 6 Paras. 1 and 3(d) of the Convention ...

46. The applicants complained that their conviction had been based essentially on the evidence of police officers whose identity was not disclosed to them and

who were not heard either in public or in their presence. They alleged a violation of Article 6 paras. 1 and 3(d)....,

Neither the Government nor the Commission shared this view.

....

B. The Court's assessment

1. Applicable principles

49. As the requirements of Article 6 para. 3 ... are to be seen as particular aspects of the right to a fair trial guaranteed by Article 6 para. 1..., the Court will examine the complaints under Article 6 paras. 1 and 3(d) taken together....

50. The Court reiterates that the admissibility of evidence is primarily a matter for regulation by national law and as a general rule it is for the national courts to assess the evidence before them. The Court's task under the Convention is not to give a ruling as to whether statements of witnesses were properly admitted as evidence, but rather to ascertain whether the proceedings as a whole, including the way in which evidence was taken, were fair ...

51. In addition, all the evidence must normally be produced at a public hearing, in the presence of the accused, with a view to adversarial argument. There are exceptions to this principle, but they must not infringe the rights of the defence; as a general rule, paragraphs 1 and 3 (d) of Article 6 ... require that the defendant be given an adequate and proper opportunity to challenge and question a witness against him, either when he makes his statements or at a later stage.

52. As the Court had occasion to state [in an earlier judgment], the use of statements made by anonymous witnesses to found a conviction is not under all circumstances incompatible with the Convention.

53. In that same judgment the Court noted the following:

> It is true that Article 6 ... does not explicitly require the interests of witnesses in general, and those of victims called upon to testify in particular, to be taken into consideration. However, their life, liberty or security of person may be at stake, as may interests coming generally within the ambit of Article 8 of the Convention.... Such interests of witnesses and victims are in principle protected by other, substantive provisions of the Convention, which imply that Contracting States should organise their criminal proceedings in such a way that those interests are not unjustifiably imperilled. Against this background, principles of fair trial also require that in appropriate cases the interests of the defence are balanced against those of witnesses or victims called upon to testify....

54. However, if the anonymity of prosecution witnesses is maintained, the defence will be faced with difficulties which criminal proceedings should not nor-

mally involve. Accordingly, the Court has recognised that in such cases Article 6 para. 1 taken together with Article 6 para. 3 (d) of the Convention ... requires that the handicaps under which the defence labours be sufficiently counterbalanced by the procedures followed by the judicial authorities....

55. Finally, it should be recalled that a conviction should not be based either solely or to a decisive extent on anonymous statements....

2. Application of the above principles

56. In the Court's opinion, the balancing of the interests of the defence against arguments in favour of maintaining the anonymity of witnesses raises special problems if the witnesses in question are members of the police force of the State. Although their interests—and indeed those of their families—also deserve protection under the Convention, it must be recognised that their position is to some extent different from that of a disinterested witness or a victim. They owe a general duty of obedience to the State's executive authorities and usually have links with the prosecution; for these reasons alone their use as anonymous witnesses should be resorted to only in exceptional circumstances. In addition, it is in the nature of things that their duties, particularly in the case of arresting officers, may involve giving evidence in open court.

57. On the other hand, the Court has recognised in principle that, provided that the rights of the defence are respected, it may be legitimate for the police authorities to wish to preserve the anonymity of an agent deployed in undercover activities, for his own or his family's protection and so as not to impair his usefulness for future operations.

58. Having regard to the place that the right to a fair administration of justice holds in a democratic society, any measures restricting the rights of the defence should be strictly necessary. If a less restrictive measure can suffice then that measure should be applied.

59. In the present case, the police officers in question were in a separate room with the investigating judge, from which the accused and even their counsel were excluded. All communication was via a sound link. The defence was thus not only unaware of the identity of the police witnesses but were also prevented from observing their demeanour under direct questioning, and thus from testing their reliability.

60. It has not been explained to the Court's satisfaction why it was necessary to resort to such extreme limitations on the right of the accused to have the evidence against them given in their presence, or why less far-reaching measures were not considered.

In the absence of any further information, the Court cannot find that the operational needs of the police provide sufficient justification. It should be noted that the explanatory memorandum of the bill which became the Act of 11 November 1993 [changing the evidence law of the Netherlands regarding the use of anonymous witnesses] refers in this connection to the possibilities of using make-up or disguise and the prevention of eye contact.

61. Nor is the Court persuaded that the Court of Appeal made sufficient effort to assess the threat of reprisals against the police officers or their families. It does not appear from that court's judgment that it sought to address the question whether the applicants would have been in a position to carry out any such threats or to incite others to do so on their behalf. Its decision was based exclusively on the seriousness of the crimes committed.

In this connection, it is to be noted that Mr Engelen, a civilian witness who in the early stages of the proceedings had made statements identifying one of the applicants as one of the perpetrators, did not enjoy the protection of anonymity and it has not been claimed that he was at any time threatened.

62. It is true—as noted by the Government and the Commission—that the anonymous police officers were interrogated before an investigating judge, who had himself ascertained their identity and had, in a very detailed official report of his findings, stated his opinion on their reliability and credibility as well as their reasons for remaining anonymous.

However these measures cannot be considered a proper substitute for the possibility of the defence to question the witnesses in their presence and make their own judgment as to their demeanour and reliability. It thus cannot be said that the handicaps under which the defence laboured were counterbalanced by the above procedures.

63. Moreover, the only evidence relied on by the Court of Appeal which provided positive identification of the applicants as the perpetrators of the crimes were the statements of the anonymous police officers. That being so the conviction of the applicants was based "to a decisive extent" on these anonymous statements.

64. In the Court's view, the present case falls to be distinguished from [another]; in the latter case it was decided on the basis of information contained in the case file itself that the witnesses Y.15 and Y.16—who were both civilians, and who knew the accused personally—had sufficient reason to believe that he might resort to violence, and they were heard in the presence of counsel....

In addition, in the latter case other evidence providing positive identification of the accused as the perpetrator of the crimes charged was available from sources unrelated to the anonymous witnesses ...

65. Against this background the Court cannot find that the proceedings taken as a whole were fair.

C. *Conclusion*

66. There has been a violation of Article 6 para. 1 taken together with Article 6 para. 3 (d)....

FOR THESE REASONS, THE COURT

1. Holds by six votes to three that there has been a violation of Article 6 para. 1 of the Convention taken together with Article 6 para. 3 (d)....

(dissenting opinions omitted)

C. India

1. Interrogation: Right to Confront Witnesses; Right to Silence

a. *Kartar Singh v. State of Punjab, 1994 (2) S.C.R. 375, 1995 A.I.R.(S.C.W.) 2698*

The Judgments of the Court were delivered by S. RATNAVEL PANDIAN, J. (on behalf of himself, Punchhi, J., K. Ramaswamy, J., Agrawal, J. and Sahai, J.). The above batch of matters consisting of a number of writ petitions, criminal appeals and SLPs [Special Leave Petitions] are filed challenging the vires of the Terrorist Affected Areas (Special Courts) Act (No. 61 of 1984)*, the Terrorists and Disruptive Activities (Prevention) Act (No. 31 of 1985)* and the Terrorists and Disruptive Activities (Prevention) Act, 1987 (No. 28 of 1987) commonly known as TADA Acts (hereinafter referred to as the Act of 1984, Act of 1985 and Act of 1987 respectively)....

2. [W]e are now rendering a common judgment pertaining to the vires of these three Acts.... At the same time, we make it clear that the merits of the individual cases will have to be decided separately after the validity of these three Acts is decided.

....

20. Before we make an in-depth examination of the challenges canvassed which are manifestly and pristinely legal, with regard to the impugned Acts and some of their provisions with a comprehensive and exclusive survey, it has become inevitable for us to give a brief sketch of the historical background and the circumstances which forced the legislature to enact these laws, as gathered from the parliamentary debates, Statement of Objects and Reasons and prefatory notes of the impugned Acts, etc., etc.

21. From the recent past, in many parts of the world, terrorism and disruption are spearheading for one reason or another and resultantly great leaders have been assassinated by suicide bombers and many dastardly murders have been committed. Deplorably, determined youths lured by hardcore criminals and

underground extremists and attracted by the ideology of terrorism are indulging in committing serious crimes against the humanity. In spite of the drastic actions taken and intense vigilance activated, the terrorists and militants do not desist from triggering lawlessness if it suits their purpose. In short, they are waging a domestic war against the sovereignty of their respective nations or against a race or community in order to create an embryonic imbalance and nervous disorder in the society either on being stimulated or instigated by the national, transnational or international hard-core criminals or secessionists etc. Resultantly, the security and integrity of the countries concerned are at peril and the law and order in many countries is disrupted. To say differently, the logic of the cult of the bullet is hovering the globe completely robbing off the reasons and rhymes. Therefore, every country has now felt the need to strengthen vigilance against the spurt in the illegal and criminal activities of the militants and terrorists so that the danger to its sovereignty is averted and the community is protected.

22. Thus, terrorism and disruptive activities are a worldwide phenomenon and India is not an exception. Unfortunately in the recent past this country has fallen in the firm grip of spiraling terrorists' violence and is caught between the deadly pangs of disruptive activities. As seen from the Objects and Reasons of the Act ... of 1985, "Terrorists had been indulging in wanton killings, arson, looting of properties and other heinous crimes mostly in Punjab and Chandigarh," and then slowly they expanded their activities to other parts of the country i.e. Delhi, Haryana, U.P. and Rajasthan. At present they have outstretched their activities by spreading their wings far and wide almost bringing the major part of the country under the extreme violence and terrorism by letting loose unprecedented and unprovoked repression and disruption unmindful of the security of the nation, personal liberty and right, inclusive of the right to live with human dignity of the innocent citizens of this country and destroying the image of many glitzy cities like Chandigarh, Srinagar, Delhi and Bombay by strangulating the normal life of the citizens. Apart from many skirmishes in various parts of the country, there were countless serious and horrendous events engulfing many cities with blood-bath, firing, looting, mad killing even without sparing women and children and reducing those areas into a graveyard, which brutal atrocities have rocked and shocked the whole nation.

....

28. We feel that it is not necessary to swell this judgment by reproducing the entire speeches made by the then Home Minister, the Minister of State for Home Affairs and some Members of Parliament on the atrocities committed by terrorists and disruptionists and on the necessity of bringing the Acts (TADA) to effectively prevent the consequent violence. But suffice to give the compelling reasons as shown in the Statements of Objects and Reasons for enacting

the Acts of 1985 and 1987 which are to the effect that the terrorists and disruptionists by their expanded activities have created dreadful fear and panic in the minds of the citizens and disrupted communal peace and harmony; that their activities are on an escalation in many parts of the country; that it has been felt that in order to combat and cope with such activities effectively, it had become necessary to take appropriate legal steps effectively and expeditiously so that the alarming increase of these activities which are a matter of serious concern, could be prevented and severely dealt with.

29. The totality of the speeches made by the Ministers, Members of the Parliament during the debates in the Parliament, the Statement of Objects and Reasons, the submissions made by the learned Additional Solicitors General converge to the following conclusions:

(1) From mid-eighties, the prevailing conditions have been surcharged with the terrorism and disruption posing a serious threat to the sovereignty and integrity of India as well as creating panic and sense of insecurity in the minds of the people. Added to that the brutality of terrorism let loose, by the secessionists and anti-nationals in the highly vulnerable area of Indian territory, (prejudicial to the defence of India), is causing grave concern even about the chances of survival of the democratic polity and process;

(2) there were also continuous commission of heinous offenses such as gruesome mass killings of defenseless innocent people including women, children and bystanders, disturbing the peace, tranquility and security;

(3) the existing ordinary criminal laws are found to be inadequate to sternly deal with such activities perpetrated on humanity.

30. It was only in the above prevailing circumstances, the Legislature has been compelled to bring forth these Acts (TADA) to prevent and deal with the peril of the erupting terrorism and the consequent potential disorder among others disrupting the law and order and to sternly deal with many groups lurking beneath the murky surface, aiding, abetting, nourishing and fomenting terrorism besides giving financial support and supplying sophisticated automatic lethal arms and ammunitions both from inside and outside of India. It may not be out of place to mention that the facts of the cases appealed against and set out in the writ petitions and SLP, if accepted in their entirety, reveal the multiple acts of violence let loose; and the acts of savage revenge perpetrated against individuals, group of persons or any particular community or religious sects show that the violent threat which has manifested itself is not evidently going to vanish with such inexplicable suddenness as would seem to have been visually presumed.

....

33. The Parliament, evidently, taking note of the gravity of terrorism committed by terrorists either with an intention to overawe the Government as by law

established or to strike terror in the people or any section of the people or to alienate any section of the people or to adversely affect the harmony amongst different sections of the people and the consequent widespread apparent danger to the nation, has felt the need of not only continuing but also further strengthening the provisions of TADA Act (Act ... of 1985) in order to cope with the menace of terrorism, enacted Act ... of 1987 bringing drastic changes with regard to the admissibility of confessions made to police officials prescribing special procedures and providing condign punishments etc., leave apart the question with regard to the validity of these provisions to be tested on the touchstone of the Constitution.

34. Keeping in view the above historical background, we shall unbiasedly and without any preconceived notion, examine the various legal problems presented inclusive of the constitutional validity of the three Acts (TADA) in general and of the various provisions in particular of those Acts on the touchstone of the Constitution of India.

....

42. Harking back to the Acts with which we are concerned, Act ... of 1985 and Act ... of 1987 have been enacted by Parliament as a piece of emergency legislation for a certain length of time which period has been extended periodically by the Parliament on revision and they have been extended to the whole of India and made applicable to citizens of India even outside India, to persons in the service of the Government, wherever they may be; and to persons on ships and aircraft registered in India, wherever they may be.

43. With the above brief introduction, we shall now proceed to deal with the submissions made by the learned counsel for the parties with reference to ... whether the Acts or any of the provisions thereof contravene any fundamental right specified in Part III of the Constitution, as well as other cognate questions.

....

Section 15 of 1987 Act

192. A blistering attack was made on the validity of the hotly debated Section 15 as per which the confession made by a person before a police officer not lower in rank than a Superintendent of Police and recorded by such police officer either in writing or on any mechanical device like cassettes, tapes or sound tracks, shall be admissible in the trial of such person or co-accused, abettor or conspirator for an offence under this Act or rules made thereunder. [It may be mentioned that the words "or co-accused, abettor or conspirator" are inserted after the words "trial of such person" by the TADA (Amendment) Act, 1993 (No. 43 of 1993) [effective May 22, 1993], with a proviso, reading, "Provided that co-accused, abettor or conspirator is charged and tried in the same case together with the accused."] But before recording the confession under sub-

section (1), the person making the confession should be given a statutory warning as contemplated under subsection (2) of Section 15.

193. Mr Ram Jethmalani made a scathing attack on this provision contending that this provision is atrocious and totally subversive of any civilized trial system and overrides Sections 25 and 26 of the Evidence Act and Sections 162 and 164 of the Code of Criminal Procedure.

According to him when the existing Codes of Law which have a life history of more than a century proceed on the footing that police confessions are untrustworthy, a fortiori, the confessions recorded on mechanical devices are certainly inferior to confessions recorded by Magistrates in open courts with all the precautions prescribed by the statute, High Court rules and judicial decisions. There will be many infirmities in such recording of confessions such as selective recordings, tampering, tailoring and editing and the confessions so recorded on mechanical devices are not as reliable as written confessions and signed by the makers of those confessions. Therefore, he contends that this provision should be held to be unjust and unreasonable and bad in law under both Articles 14 and 21 of the Constitution. In this connection, he made reference to Section 21(1)(c)[j] as per which a confession made by a co-accused that the accused has committed the offence, if proved, a presumption shall be drawn by the Designated Court that the accused has committed such offence unless the contrary is proved. This provision, according to him, totally subverts Section 30 of the Evidence Act and that the confession by the co-accused is not evidence as defined in the Evidence Act. Two decisions were cited by him to strengthen his submission, firstly, Bhuboni Sahu v. King, wherein the Privy Council after having approved the observation ... that where there is evidence against the co-accused sufficient, if believed, to support his conviction, then the kind of confession described in Section 30 may be thrown into the scale as an additional reason for believing that evidence has held that

> ... a confession of a co-accused is obviously evidence of a very weak type. It does not indeed come within the definition of 'evidence' contained in Section 3* of the Evidence Act. It is not required to be given on oath, nor in the presence of the accused, and it cannot be tested by cross-examination.

and secondly Hari Charan Kurmi and Jogia Hajam v. State of Bihar in which Gajendragadkar, C.J. speaking for the Constitution Bench stated that:

> Though a confession mentioned in Section 30 of the Indian Evidence Act is not evidence as defined by Section 3 of the Act, it is an element which may be taken into consideration by the criminal courts and in that sense, it may be described as evidence in a non-technical way. But

---

j. EDITOR'S NOTE: That is, Section 21 of the 1987 Act.

in dealing with a case against an accused person, the court cannot start with the confession of a co-accused person, it must begin with other evidence adduced by the prosecution and after it has formed its opinion with regard to the quality and effect of the said evidence, then it is permissible to turn to the confession in order to lend assurance to the conclusion of guilt which the judicial mind is about to reach on the said other evidence.

194. In continuation of his argument, the learned senior counsel has stressed that a police officer can easily find his own favourite informer, record his confession implicating whomsoever he wants and all those persons, forfeit their life and liberty unless they prove the contrary, namely, their innocence, which is an impossible burden to discharge and in that sense Section 21(1)(c) is subversive of all civilized notions of justice and renders a criminal trial a total farce.

195. Mr Harjinder Singh, the learned counsel supplementing the arguments of the other counsel cited the decision, namely, Olga Tellis v. Bombay Municipal Corpn. wherein it has been observed that,

[i]f a law is found to direct the doing of an act which is forbidden by the Constitution or to compel, in the performance of an act, the adoption of a procedure which is impermissible under the Constitution, it would have to be struck down,

and also made reference to [other decisions].

196. On the dictum laid down in the above decisions, he concluded by saying that unreasonableness vitiates not only law but also the procedure alike and, therefore, it is essential that the procedure prescribed by law for depriving a person of his fundamental right must conform to the norms of justice and fair play.

197. All the counsel who challenged the validity of the provisions of this Act made similar submissions as that of Mr Jethmalani and stated in chorus that Section 15 of the Act gives a death-knell to the very basic principle hitherto recognised and followed that a confession made before a police officer under any circumstance as well as a confession to a Magistrate or a third party while in police custody is totally inadmissible and that such a confession cannot be proved as against a person accused of any offence.

198. The learned Additional Solicitor General strains his every nerve to overthrow the above argument articulating that the constitutional validity of Section 15 is to be determined on the basis of the competence of the Parliament to vary the procedure which is just and fair in the facts and circumstances of the situation with which the statute tends to grapple and not on the touchstone of the Evidence Act. This section, according to him, contains a significant safeguard by vesting the power of recording confession in superior police officer in order to prevent any misuse or abuse which safeguard has been approved by

this Court in Gurbachan Singh v. State of Bombay wherein it has been held that a law which contains an extraordinary procedure can be made to meet the exceptional circumstances otherwise the purpose and object of the Act would be defeated.

199. Coming to the intrinsic value to be attached to the evidence, it has been said by Additional Solicitor General that this section does not lay down the probative value of the confession nor does it indicate that conviction can be based on confession alone made before a police officer. He continues to state that the probative value of the confessions is left to the court to be determined in each case on its own facts and circumstances. Then he drew our attention to certain provisions in various statutes empowering the officers specified therein to secure or arrest the offenders and to record statements from them which statements are held to be admissible in evidence in criminal proceeding as against them by judicial pronouncements of the various High Courts and this Court.

200. Now let us analyse Section 15 as amended by Act 43* of 1993 and examine the merit of the contentions of the respective parties with reference to certain relevant provisions of the Constitution, general procedural law and Evidence Act.

...

202. In recording a confession by a police officer, the said police officer under Rule 15** of the Rules made under the Act has to observe some legal formalities and comply with certain conditions. If the confession is reduced into writing, then under sub-rule (3) of Rule 15, the said confession should be signed by the person making the confession and the police officer who records the confession should append a certificate as required by the rule. As Rule 15 has to be read with Section 15 of the TADA Act, we feel that it would be necessary to reproduce the rule so that the legal formality to be observed may be properly understood.

203. Rule 15 of the Terrorist and Disruptive Activities (Prevention) Rules, 1987 is as follows:

15. Recording of confession made to police officers.—

(1)A confession made by a person before a police officer and recorded by such police officer under Section 15 of the Act shall invariably be recorded in the language in which such confession is made and if that is not practicable, in the language used by such police officer for official purposes or in the language of the Designated Court and it shall form part of the record.

(2) The confession so recorded shall be shown, read or played back to the person concerned and if he does not understand the language in which it is recorded, it shall be interpreted to him in a language which he understands and he shall be at liberty to explain or add to his confession.

(3) The confession shall, if it is in writing, be (a) signed by the person who makes the confession; and (b) by the police officer who shall also certify under his own hand that such confession was taken in his presence and recorded by him and that the record contains a full and true account of the confession made by the person and such police officer shall make a memorandum at the end of the confession to the following effect: "I have explained to (name) that he is not bound to make a confession and that, if he does so, any confession he may make may be used as evidence against him and I believe that this confession was voluntarily made. It was taken in my presence and hearing and recorded by me and was read over to the person making it and admitted by him to be correct, and it contains a full and true account of the statement made by him. Sd/-Police Officer."

(4) Where the confession is recorded on any mechanical device, the memorandum referred to in sub-rule (3) insofar as it is applicable and a declaration made by the person making the confession that the said confession recorded on the mechanical device has been correctly recorded in his presence shall also be recorded in the mechanical device at the end of the confession.

(5) Every confession recorded under the said Section 15 shall be sent forthwith to the Chief Metropolitan Magistrate or the Chief Judicial Magistrate having jurisdiction over the area in which such confession has been recorded and such Magistrate shall forward the recorded confession so received to the Designated Court which may take cognizance of the offence.

204. Before proceeding further, we may point out that Section 21(1)(c) in respect of which some argument has been advanced is omitted along with Section 21(1)(d) by the Amendment Act 43 of 1993.

205. In our Constitution as well as procedural law and law of Evidence, there are certain guarantees protecting the right and liberty of a person in a criminal proceeding and safeguards in making use of any statement made by him. Article 20(3) of the Constitution declares that, "No person accused of any offence shall be compelled to be a witness against himself."

206. Article 20(3) of our Constitution embodies the principle of protection against compulsion of self-incrimination which is one of the fundamental canons of the British System of Criminal Jurisprudence and which has been adopted by the American System and incorporated in the Federal Acts. The Fifth Amendment of the Constitution of the United States of America provides,

> No person shall be held to answer for a capital, or otherwise infamous crime, unless on a presentment or indictment of a Grand Jury, ... nor shall be compelled in any criminal case to be a witness against himself ...

207. The above principle is recognised to a substantial extent in the criminal administration of justice in our country by incorporating various statutory provisions. One of the components of the guarantee contained in Article 20(3) of the Constitution is that it is a protection against compulsion resulting in the accused of any offence giving evidence against himself. There are a number of outstanding decisions of this Court in explaining the intendment of Article 20(3).... Article 22(1) and (2) confer certain rights upon a person who has been arrested. Coming to the provisions of Code of Criminal Procedure, Section 161* empowers a police officer making an investigation to examine orally any person supposed to be acquainted with the facts and circumstances of the case and to reduce into writing any statement made to him in the course of such examination. Section 162 which speaks of the use of the statement so recorded, states that no statement recorded by a police officer, if reduced into writing, be signed by the person making it and that the statement shall not be used for any purpose save as provided in the Code and the provisions of the Evidence Act. The ban imposed by Section 162 applies to all the statements whether confessional or otherwise, made to a police officer by any person whether accused or not during the course of the investigation under Chapter XII of the Code. But the statement given by an accused can be used in the manner provided by Section 145* of the Evidence Act in case the accused examines himself as a witness for the defence by availing Section 315(1)* of the Code corresponding to Section 342-A* of the old Code and to give evidence on oath in disproof of the charges made against him or any person charged together with him at the same trial.

209. There is a clear embargo in making use of this statement of an accused given to a police officer under Section 25 of the Evidence Act, according to which, no confession made to a police officer shall be proved as against a person accused of any offence and under Section 26 according to which no confession made by any person whilst he is in custody of a police officer, unless it is made in the immediate presence of a Magistrate, shall be proved as against such person. The only exception is given under Section 27 which serves as a proviso to Section 26. Section 27 contemplates that only so much of information whether amounts to confession or not, as relates distinctly to the fact thereby discovered, in consequence of that information received from a person accused of any offence while in custody of the police can be proved as against the accused.

210. In the context of the matter under discussion, two more provisions also may be referred to namely Sections 24* and 30 of the Evidence Act and Section 164 of the Code.

211. Section 24 of the Evidence Act makes a confession, caused to be made before any authority by an accused by any inducement, threat or promise, irrelevant in a criminal proceeding. Section 30 of the Evidence Act is to the effect that if a confession made by one or more persons, affecting himself and some others jointly tried for the same offence is proved, the court may take into con-

sideration such confession as against such other persons as well as the maker of the confession. The explanation to the section reads that "offence" as used in this section includes the abetment of, or attempt to commit, the offence.

212. Section 164 of the Code speaks of recording of confessions and statements by Magistrates specified in that section by complying with the legal formalities and observing the statutory conditions including the appendage of a Certificate by the Magistrate recording the confession as contemplated under sub-sections (2) to (6) thereof.

213. Though in the old Code, there was a specific embargo on a police officer recording any statement or confession made to him in the course of an investigation embodied in the main sub-section (1) of Section 164 itself, in the present Code the legal bar is now brought by a separate proviso to subsection (1) of Section 164 which reads:

> Provided that no confession shall be recorded by a police officer on whom any power of a Magistrate has been conferred under any law for the time being in force.

This is a new provision but conveys the same meaning as embodied in the main sub-section (1) of Section 164 of the old Code.

214. Thus, an accused or a person accused of any offence is protected by the constitutional provisions as well as the statutory provisions to the extent that no self-incriminating statement made by an accused to the police officer while he is in custody, could be used against such maker. The submission of the Additional Solicitor General that while a confession by an accused before a specified officer either under the Railway Protection Force Act or Railway Property (Unlawful Possession) Act or Customs Act or Foreign Exchange Regulation Act is made admissible, the special procedure prescribed under this Act making a confession of a person indicted under the TADA Act given to a police officer admissible cannot be questioned, is misnomer because all the officials empowered to record statements under those special Acts are not police officers as per the judicial pronouncements of this Court as well the High Courts which principle holds the field till date.

215. The above constitutional and statutory procedural guarantees and safeguards are in consonance with the expression, "according to procedure established by law" enshrined in Article 21 of the Constitution within which fold the principle of just and fair trial is read into.

216. The procedure contemplated by Article 21 is that the procedure must be "right, just and fair" and not arbitrary, fanciful or oppressive. In order that the procedure is right, just and fair, it should conform to the principle of natural justice, that is, "fair play in action." ... If the procedural law is oppressive and violates the principle of just and fair trial offending Article 21 of the Constitution and is discriminatory violating the equal protection of laws offending Ar-

ticle 14 of the Constitution, then Section 15 of TADA Act is to be struck down. Therefore, it has become inevitably essential to examine the classification of 'offenders' and 'offenses' so as to enable us in deciding whether Section 15 is violative of Articles 14 and 21 of the Constitution.

....

245. The next question is whether the procedure in recording the confession is just and fair.

246. The counsel were severely critical of the mode and method of obtaining a confession from an accused person. According to them, the oppressive behavior and excessive naked abuse and misuse of power by the police in extorting confession by compelling the accused to speak under the untold pain by using third degree methods with diabolical barbarity in utter violation of human rights, cannot be lost sight of or consigned to oblivion and the courts would not be justified by showing a volte-face and turning a blind eye to the above reality and drawing a legal presumption that the confession might have been obtained by a police officer not lower in rank than a Superintendent of Police in terms of Section 15(1) only in accordance with the legally permissible procedure. They castigated the conduct of the police officers in whisking away the accused either on arrest or on obtaining custody from the court to an unknown destination or unannounced premises for custodial interrogation in order to get compulsory self-incriminating statement as a source of proof to be produced before a court of law.

....

248. As we have repeatedly pointed out supra, if it is shown to the court that a confession has been extorted by illegal means such as inducement, threat or promise as contemplated under Section 24 of the Evidence Act the confession thus obtained from an accused person would become irrelevant and cannot be used in a criminal proceeding as against the maker. It may be recalled that Sections 330* and 331* of the Indian Penal Code provide punishment to one who voluntarily causes hurt or grievous hurt as the case may be to extort the confession or any information which may lead to the detection of an offence or misconduct.

249. Thus the Constitution as well as the statutory procedural law and law of Evidence condemn the conduct of any official in extorting a confession or information under compulsion by using any third degree methods.

250. In this connection, we would like to reproduce the view of the National Police Commission (Fourth Report June 1980) with regard to the admissibility of confession made to a police officer as evidence, which is to the following effect:

> 27. 33 ... This total ban on the entry of a confessional statement recorded by a police officer into the area of judicial proceedings has

placed the police at a great disadvantage as compared to several other enforcement agencies who also handle investigation work leading to prosecution in court. This provision in the Evidence Act which was enacted in 1872 bears relevance to the then situation in which the police were practically the only enforcement agency available to the Government and they had acquired notoriety for the adoption of several gross malpractice involving torture and other pressure tactics of an extreme nature to obtain confessions from accused persons. More than 100 years have rolled by since then. We are aware that the police are still not totally free from adopting questionable practices while interrogating accused persons, but one cannot possibly deny that the greater vigilance now exercised by the public and the press, growing awareness of citizens about their individual rights under the law and increasing earnestness and commitment of the senior levels of command in the police structure to put down such malpractice have all tended to reduce the prevalence of such practices in the police to a lesser degree than before.... After a careful consideration of all aspects of this much debated question we feel that the stage has arrived now for us to take a small positive step towards removing this stigma on the police and make it possible for a confession made before a police officer to enter the area of judicial proceedings, if not as substantive evidence, at least as a document that could be taken into consideration by the court to aid it in inquiry or trial in the same manner as now provided in regard to case diaries under Section 172(2)* CrPC and the confession of a co-accused under Section 30 of the Evidence Act. We are also of the view that this approach to the evidentiary admissibility and value of a confession made before a police officer should apply not only to the police but to all persons in authority before whom a confession may be made. If the Evidence Act reflects this approach to confessions as a class, it would largely remove the present feeling of the police that they have been unjustly discriminated against in law.

251. Whatever may be said for and against the submission with regard to the admissibility of a confession made before a police officer, we cannot avoid but saying that we with the years of experience both at the Bar and on the Bench have frequently dealt with cases of atrocity and brutality practiced by some overzealous police officers resorting to inhuman, barbaric, archaic and drastic method of treating the suspects in their anxiety to collect evidence by hook or by crook and wrenching a decision in their favour. We remorsefully like to state that on few occasions even custodial deaths caused during interrogation are brought to our notice. We are very much distressed and deeply concerned about the oppressive behavior and the most degrading and despicable practice

adopted by some of the police officers even though no general and sweeping condemnation can be made.

252. In this connection, we feel it would be appropriate to extract the views expressed by National Judicial Commission (Fourth Report) discountenancing the conduct of police in practicing the third degree methods:

> Nothing is so dehumanising as the conduct of police in practicing torture of any kind on a person in their custody. Police image in the estimate of the public has badly suffered by the prevalence of this practice in varying degrees over several years. We note with concern the inclination of even some of the supervisory ranks to countenance the practice in a bid to achieve quick results by short-cut methods. Even well meaning officers are sometimes drawn towards third degree methods because of the expectation of some complainants in individual cases that the suspects named by them should be questioned by the police with some kind of pressure ...

253. Though we at the first impression thought of sharing the view of the learned counsel that it would be dangerous to make a statement given to a police officer admissible (notwithstanding the legal position making the confession of an accused before the police admissible in some advanced countries like United Kingdom, United States of America, Australia and Canada etc.) having regard to the legal competence of the legislature to make the law prescribing a different mode of proof, the meaningful purpose and object of the legislation, the gravity of terrorism unleashed by the terrorists and disruptionists endangering not only the sovereignty and integrity of the country but also the normal life of the citizens, and the reluctance of even the victims as well as the public in coming forward, at the risk of their life, to give evidence hold that the impugned section cannot be said to be suffering from any vice of unconstitutionality. In fact, if the exigencies of certain situations warrant such a legislation then it is constitutionally permissible as ruled in a number of decisions of this Court, provided none of the fundamental rights under Chapter III of the Constitution is infringed.

254. In view of the legal position vesting authority on higher police officer to record the confession hitherto enjoyed by the judicial officer in the normal procedure, we state that there should be no breach of procedure and the accepted norms of recording the confession which should reflect only the true and voluntary statement and there should be no room for hypercriticism that the authority has obtained an invented confession as a source of proof irrespective of the truth and creditability as it could be ironically put that when a Judge remarked, "Am I not to hear the truth," the prosecution giving a startling answer, "No, Your Lordship is to hear only the evidence."

255. As the Act now stands after its amendment consequent upon the deletion of Section 21(1)(c), a confession made by a person before a police officer can

be made admissible in the trial of such person not only as against the person but also against the co-accused, abettor or conspirator provided that the co-accused, abettor or conspirator is charged and tried in the same case together with the accused, namely, the maker of the confession. The present position is in conformity with Section 30 of the Evidence Act.

256. Under Section 21(1)(d), in a prosecution for an offence under subsection (1) of Section 3*, if it is proved that the accused had made a confession of the offence to any person other than a police officer, the Designated Court could raise a presumption that the accused had committed such offence unless the contrary is proved. By Act 43 of 1993, clause (d) of Section 21(1) has now been omitted. The resultant position is that no presumption can be raised by the Designated Court against the accused as to offenses under Section 3 on the basis of Section 21.

257. As per Section 15(1), a confession can either be reduced into writing or recorded on any mechanical device like cassettes, tapes or sound tracks from which sounds or images can be reproduced. As rightly pointed out by the learned counsel since the recording of evidence on mechanical device can be tampered, tailored, tinkered, edited and erased etc., we strongly feel that there must be some severe safeguards which should be scrupulously observed while recording a confession under Section 15(1) so that the possibility of extorting any false confession can be prevented to some appreciable extent.

258. Sub-section (2) of Section 15 enjoins a statutory obligation on the part of the police officer recording the confession to explain to the person making it that he is not bound to make a confession and to give a statutory warning that if he does so it may be used as evidence against him.

259. Rule 15 of the TADA Rules imposes certain conditions on the police officer with regard to the mode of recording the confession and requires the police officer to make a memorandum at the end of the confession to the effect that he has explained to the maker that he was not bound to make the confession and that the confession, if made by him, would be used as against him and that he recorded the confession only on being satisfied that it was voluntarily made. Rule 15(5) requires that every confession recorded under Section 15 should be sent forthwith either to the Chief Metropolitan Magistrate or the Chief Judicial Magistrate having jurisdiction over the area in which such confession has been recorded and the Magistrate should forthwith forward the recorded confession received by him to the Designated Court taking cognizance of the offence.

260. For the foregoing discussion, we hold that Section 15 is not liable to be struck down since that section does not offend either Article 14 or Article 21 of the Constitution.

261. Notwithstanding our final conclusion made in relation to the intendment of Section 15, we would hasten to add that the recording of a confession by a Magistrate under Section 164 of the Code is not excluded by any exclusionary

provision in the TADA Act, contrary to the Code but on the other hand the police officer investigating the case under the TADA Act can get the confession or statement of a person indicted with any offence under any of the provisions of the TADA Act recorded by any Metropolitan Magistrate, Judicial Magistrate, Executive Magistrate or Special Executive Magistrate of whom the two latter Magistrates are included in Section 164(1) by sub-section (3) of Section 20* of the TADA Act and empowered to record confession.

262. The net result is that any confession or statement of a person under the TADA Act can be recorded either by a police officer not lower in rank than of a Superintendent of Police, in exercise of the powers conferred under Section 15 or by a Metropolitan Magistrate or Judicial Magistrate or Executive Magistrate or Special Executive Magistrate who are empowered to record any confession under Section 164(1) in view of sub-section (3) of Section 20 of the TADA Act. As we will be elaborately dealing with Section 20(3) in the later part of this judgment, we do not like to go into detail any more.

263. However, we would like to lay down following guidelines so as to ensure that the confession obtained in the pre-indictment interrogation by a police officer not lower in rank than a Superintendent of Police is not tainted with any vice but is in strict conformity with the well-recognised and accepted a esthetic principles and fundamental fairness:

(1) The confession should be recorded in a free atmosphere in the same language in which the person is examined and as narrated by him;

(2) The person from whom a confession has been recorded under Section 15(1) of the Act, should be produced before the Chief Metropolitan Magistrate or the Chief Judicial Magistrate to whom the confession is required to be sent under Rule 15(5) along with the original statement of confession, written or recorded on mechanical device without unreasonable delay;

(3) The Chief Metropolitan Magistrate or the Chief Judicial Magistrate should scrupulously record the statement, if any, made by the accused so produced and get his signature and in case of any complaint of torture, the person should be directed to be produced for medical examination before a Medical Officer not lower in rank than of an Assistant Civil Surgeon;

(4) Notwithstanding anything contained in the Code of Criminal Procedure, 1973, no police officer below the rank of an Assistant Commissioner of Police in the Metropolitan cities and elsewhere of a Deputy Superintendent of Police or a police officer of equivalent rank, should investigate any offence punishable under this Act of 1987.

This is necessary in view of the drastic provisions of this Act. More so when the Prevention of Corruption Act, 1988 under Section 17* and the Immoral Traffic Prevention Act, 1956 under Section 13*, authorise only a police officer of a specified rank to investigate the offenses under those specified Acts.

(5) The police officer if he is seeking the custody of any person for pre-indict-ment or pretrial interrogation from the judicial custody, must file an affidavit sworn by him explaining the reason not only for such custody but also for the delay, if any, in seeking the police custody.

(6) In case the person taken for interrogation, on receipt of the statutory warn-ing that he is not bound to make a confession and that if he does so, the said statement may be used against him as evidence, asserts his right to silence, the police officer must respect his right of assertion without making any compul-sion to give a statement of disclosure.

The Central Government may take note of these guidelines and incorporate them by appropriate amendments in the Act and the Rules.

264. Though it is entirely for the court trying the offence to decide the ques-tion of admissibility or reliability of a confession in its judicial wisdom strictly adhering to the law, it must, while so deciding the question should satisfy itself that there was no trap, no track and no importune seeking of evidence during the custodial interrogation and all the conditions required are fulfilled.

265. In order to ensure higher level of scrutiny and applicability of TADA Act, there must be a screening Committee or a Review Committee constituted by the Central Government consisting of the Home Secretary, Law Secretary and other secretaries concerned of the various Departments to review all the TADA cases instituted by the Central Government as well as to have a quarterly ad-ministrative review, reviewing the States' action in the application of the TADA provisions in the respective. States, and the incidental questions arising in rela-tion thereto.

Similarly, there must be a Screening or Review Committee at the State level con-stituted by the respective States consisting of the Chief Secretary, Home Secretary, Law Secretary, Director General of Police (Law and Order) and other officials as the respective Government may think it fit, to review the action of the enforcing authorities under the Act and screen the cases registered under the provisions of the Act and decide the further course of action in every matter and so on.

Section 16 of 1987 Act ...

273. It is the further contention of the counsel that the remaining sub-sections of Section 16, save sub-section (1) of that section, empower a court to keep back from the defence the names and addresses of the witnesses without which the accused cannot prepare his defence or successfully defend himself at the trial. The object of the cross-examination, according to them, in such circum-stances, becomes futile and impotent. In continuation, it has been urged that Section 16(2) and (3) of Act 1987 empower the Designated Court to take measures for keeping the identity and address of witnesses secret and to issue directions for securing that their identity is not disclosed and that these provi-sions turn a trial under the provisions of TADA into a farce.

274. Mr Tarkunde states that it is true that in some cases the safety of witnesses requires the non-disclosure of the identity of the witnesses, but at the same time the cross-examination of witnesses is liable to be largely ineffective if their identity is not known to the accused and his counsel. He suggests that a proper course must be that when the Designated Court finds that the identity of witnesses cannot safely be disclosed, the trial should be dropped and the accused may, if the authority so decides, be detained under the preventive detention law.

275. With reference to the arguments relating to sub-section (2) of Section 16, it has been submitted by the learned Additional Solicitor General that the Legislature has merely regulated the right of fair trial and the right of accused. to effectively defend himself keeping in view the requirements of the situation prevailing in terrorists affected areas where the witnesses are living in a reign of terror and are unwilling to depose against the terrorists in courts for fear of retribution or reprisal. [He stated] that the right of cross-examination is neither absolute nor a constitutional right.... According to him, the person accused should know; firstly the nature of accusation made, secondly he should be given an opportunity to state his case and thirdly, that the tribunal should act in good faith; beyond that there is nothing more.

....

277. Under the Code of Criminal Procedure, whether it is a trial before a Court of Session or a trial or warrant cases by Magistrates there are specific provisions prescribing the mode of recording evidence with the right of cross-examination of any witness by the accused.... Both under the sessions trial and trial of warrant cases, the accused is given a discretionary right of deferring the cross examination of any witness or recalling any witness for further cross-examination ...

278.... It is the jurisprudence of law that cross-examination is an acid-test of the truthfulness of the statement made by a witness on oath in examination-in-chief, the objects of which are: (1) to destroy or weaken the evidentiary value of the witness of his adversary; (2) to elicit facts in favour of the cross-examining lawyer's client from the mouth of the witness of the adversary party; (3) to show that the witness is unworthy of belief by impeaching the credit of the said witness; and the questions to be addressed in the course of cross-examination are to test his veracity; to discover who he is and what is his position in life; and to shake his credit by injuring his character.

279. The identity of the witness is necessary in the normal trial of cases to achieve the above objects and the right of confrontation is one of the fundamental guarantees so that he could guard himself from being victimised by any false and invented evidence that may be tendered by the adversary party.

280. Under the provisions of this Act, the right of cross-examination is not taken away but the identity, and addresses of the witnesses are permitted to be

withheld. The submission of the counsel attacking sub-sections (2) and (3) of Section 16 is that the withholding or the issuance of any direction not to disclose the identity, names and addresses of the witnesses prevents the accused from having a fair trial to which right he is otherwise legitimately entitled to. As we have already pointed out that in the normal course, this difficulty does not arise. In fact when the copies of the documents on which the prosecution proposes to rely upon are furnished to the accused with a memo of evidence under Section 173* of the Code, he is informed of the names and addresses of the witnesses.

281. Notwithstanding the provisions of the Evidence Act and the procedure prescribed under the Code, there is no imposition of constitutional or statutory constraint against keeping the identity and address of any witness secret if some extraordinary circumstances or imperative situations warrant such nondisclosure of identity and address of the witnesses.

282. There are provisions in some local laws ... the constitutional validity of which has been approved as well as observations of this court in various decisions touching the question under consideration....

284. In Hira Nath Mishra v. Principal, Rajendra Medical College, Ranchi, a complaint was made by some girl students residing in the girls hostel of the College, alleging that the appellants with some others in a late night had entered into the compound of the girls hostel and walked without clothes on them. In respect of this allegation, an Enquiry Committee was constituted and that Committee recorded the statement of some of the girl students but not in presence of the appellants and finally was of the view that the students deserved deterrent punishment and recommended expulsion from the hostel. The appellants—the students—questioned the order on many grounds, the chief contention of which was that the rules of natural justice had not been followed before the order was passed since the inquiry had been held behind their back; the witnesses who tendered evidence against them were not examined in their presence and there was no opportunity to cross-examine the witnesses with a view to test their veracity. Rejecting this contention, this Court held thus:

> The very reasons for which the girls were not examined in the presence of the appellants, prevailed on the authorities not to give a copy of the report to them. It would have been unwise to do so ...

> Rules of natural justice cannot remain the same applying to all conditions. We know of statutes in India like the Goonda[k] Acts which permit evidence being collected behind the back of the goonda and the goonda being merely asked to represent against the main charges aris-

---

k. EDITOR's NOTE: In India, the term "goonda" is applied to violent professional street criminals.

ing out of the evidence collected. Care is taken to see that the witnesses who gave statements would not be identified. In such cases there is no question of the witnesses being called and the goonda being given an opportunity to cross-examine the witnesses. The reason is obvious. No witness will come forward to give evidence in the presence of the goonda. However unsavory the procedure may appear to a judicial mind, these are facts of life which are to be faced.

In this connection, the observation made by Chandrachud, C.J.... which is as follows, "Whatever it is, Parliament has not made any provision in the National Security Act, under which the detenu could claim the right of cross-examination and the matter must rest there."

We are therefore of the opinion that, in the proceedings before the Advisory Board, the detenu has no right to cross-examine either the persons on the basis of whose statement the order of detention is made or the detaining authority.

286. Under Section 16(2) of the 1987 Act, the Designated Court is given only a discretionary authority to keep the identity and address of any witness secret on the following three contingencies:

(1) On an application made by a witness in any proceedings before it; or (2) on an application made by the Public Prosecutor in relation to such witness; or (3) on its own motion.

287. Sub-section (3) classifies only the measures to be taken by the Designated Court while exercising its discretion under sub-section (2). If neither the witness nor the Public Prosecutor has made an application in that behalf nor the court has taken any decision of its own then the identity and addresses of the witnesses have to be famished to the accused. The measures are to be taken by the Designated Court under any one of the above contingencies so that a witness or witnesses may not be subjected to any harassment for having spoken against the accused.

288. Generally speaking, when the accused persons are of bad character, the witnesses are unwilling to come forward to depose against such persons, fearing harassment at the hands of those accused. The persons who are put for trial under this Act are terrorists and disruptionists. Therefore, the witnesses will all the more be reluctant and unwilling to depose at the risk of their life. The Parliament having regard to such extraordinary circumstances has thought it fit that the identity and addresses of the witnesses be not disclosed in any one of the above contingencies.

289. In this context, reference may be made to Section 228-A* of the Indian Penal Code as per which the disclosure of the identity of the victims of certain offences, as contemplated under sub-section (1) of that section is punishable but subject to sub-section (2). However, when the witnesses are examined in

the presence of the accused then the accused may have the chances of knowing the identity of the witnesses if they are already known to the defence. But if the witnesses are unknown to the defence then there is no possibility of knowing the identity of the witnesses even after they enter into the witness box. During a trial after examination of the witnesses in chief the accused have got a right of deferring the cross-examination and calling the witnesses for cross-examination on some other day. If the witnesses are known to the accused they could collect the material to cross-examine at the time of cross-examination in such circumstances. Whatever may be the reasons for non-disclosure of the witnesses, the fact remains that the accused persons to be put up for trial under this Act which provides severe punishments, will be put to disadvantage to effective cross-examining and exposing the previous conduct and character of the witnesses.

290. Therefore, in order to ensure the purpose and object of the cross-examination, we feel that ... the identity, names and addresses of the witnesses may be disclosed before the trial commences; but we would like to qualify it observing that it should be subject to an exception that the court for weighty reasons in its wisdom may decide not to disclose the identity and addresses of the witnesses especially of the potential witnesses whose life may be in danger.

....

363. Before formulating our conclusions, we would like to express our opinion on the role of the police in the implementation of these Acts.

....

365. It is heart-rending to note that day in and day out we come across with the news of blood-curdling incidents of police brutality and atrocities, alleged to have been committed, in utter disregard and in all breaches of humanitarian law and universal human rights as well as in total negation of the constitutional guarantees and human decency. We are undoubtedly committed to uphold human rights even as a part of long standing heritage and as enshrined in our constitutional law. We feel that this perspective needs to be kept in view by every law enforcing authority because the recognition of the inherent dignity and of the equal and inalienable rights of the citizens is the foundation of freedom, justice and peace in the world. If the human rights are outraged, then the court should set its face against such violation of human rights by exercising its majestic judicial authority.

366. The protection that the citizens enjoy under the Rule of Law are the quintessence of two thousand years of human struggling from Adam. It is not commonly realised how easily this may be lost. There is no known method of retaining them but by eternal vigilance. There is no institution to which the duty can be delegated except to the judiciary. If the law enforcing authority becomes a law breaker, it breeds contempt for law, it invites every man to become a law unto himself and ultimately it invites anarchy.

367. Many a time in human history, great societies have crumbled into oblivion through their failure to realise the significance of crisis situations operating within them. True, ours is a country which stands tallest even in troubled times, the country that clings to fundamental principles of human rights, the country that cherishes its constitutional heritage and rejects simple solutions that compromise the values that lie at the root of our democratic system. Each generation of mankind has considered its (sic own) perplexities and concerns to be unique and consequently their fundamental demands are more the cry for justice the longing for peace and the felt need for security.

368. The above are to maintain the higher rhythms of pulsating democratic life in a constitutional order. TO SUM UP ...

(9) Section 15 of the TADA Act is neither violative of Article 14 nor of Article 21. But the Central Government may take note of certain guidelines which we have suggested and incorporate them by appropriate amendments in the Act and the Rules made thereunder; ... (11) Sub-sections (2) and (3) of Section 16 are not liable to be struck down. However, in order to ensure the purpose and object of cross-examination, we uphold the view of the Full Bench of the Punjab and Haryana High Court in ... holding,"the identity, names and addresses of the witnesses may be disclosed before the trial commences," but subject to an exception that the court for weighty reasons in its wisdom may decide not to disclose the identity and addresses of the witnesses especially of potential witnesses, whose life may be in danger....

Note

Ramaswamy, J., dissented from the foregoing opinion, arguing that section 15 of the TADA ought to be struck down because it posed too great a risk that confessions obtained under that section would be obtained through police coercion.

2. Right to Counsel

a. Hussainara Khatoon and Others (IV) v. Home Secretary, State of Bihar, Patna, 1979 A.I.R.(S.C.) 1369, 1979 (3) S.C.R. 532

Bhagwati, J.

[This case was brought on behalf of a large number of persons held in jail while awaiting trial in the State of Bihar. All of these persons had been held for a period equal to the maximum sentence that could be imposed on them, assuming sentences for different offenses ran concurrently, if they were in fact convicted. Some of these had been held longer than the maximum length of time to which they could be served even if sentences for different offenses ran consecutively. The Court's primary concern was providing relief for this extreme delay in bringing accused persons to trial. In earlier decisions in this litigation, the Court had held that such extreme delays in criminal trials violated Article 21 of the Constitution of India.]

...

6. Then there are several undertrial prisoners who are charged with offences which are bailable but who are still in jail presumably because no application for bail has been made on their behalf or being too poor they are unable to furnish bail. It is not uncommon to find that undertrial prisoners who are produced before the Magistrates are unaware of their right to obtain release on bail and on account of their poverty, they are unable to engage a lawyer who would apprise them of their right to apply for bail and help them to secure release on bail by making a proper application to the Magistrates in that behalf. Sometimes the Magistrates also refuse to release the undertrial prisoners produced before them on their personal bond but insist on monetary bail with sureties, which by reason of their poverty the undertrial prisoners are unable to furnish and which, therefore, effectively shuts out for them any possibility of release from pre-trial detention. This unfortunate situation cries aloud for introduction of an adequate and comprehensive legal service program, but so far, these cries do not seem to have evoked any response. We do not think it is possible to reach the benefits of the legal process to the poor, to protect them against injustice and to secure to them their constitutional and statutory rights unless there is a nation-wide legal service program to provide free legal services to them. It is now well settled ... that when Article 21 provides that no person shall be deprived of his life or liberty except in accordance with the procedure established by law, it is not enough that there should be some semblance of procedure provided by law, but the procedure under which a person may be deprived of his life or liberty should be "reasonable, fair and just." Now, a procedure which does not make available legal services to an accused person who is too poor to afford a lawyer and who would, therefore, have to go through the trial without legal assistance, cannot possible be regarded as "reasonable, fair and just." It is an essential ingredient of reasonable, fair and just procedure to a prisoner who is to seek his liberation through the court's process that he should have legal services available to him. This Court pointed out in M.H. Hoskot v. State of Maharahstra:

> Judicial justice, with procedural intricacies, legal submissions and critical examination of evidence, leans upon professional expertise; and a failure of equal justice under the law is on the cards where such supportive skill is absent for one side. Our judicature, molded by

Anglo-American models and our judicial process, engineered by kindred legal technology, compel the collaboration of lawyer-power for steering the wheels of equal justice under the law.

Free legal services to the poor and the needy is a essential element of any "reasonable, fair and just" procedure. It is not necessary to quote authoritative pronouncements by judges and jurists in support of the view that without the service of a lawyer an accused person would be denied "reasonable, fair and just" procedure. Black, J., observed in Gideon v. Wainwright, 372 US 335, 344, 83 S. Ct. 792, 9 L. Ed 2nd 799 (1963):

> Not only those precedents but also reason and reflection require us to recognise that in our adversary system of criminal justice, any person haled into court who is too poor to hire a lawyer cannot be assured a fair trial unless counsel is provided for him. This seems to us to be an obvious truth. Governments, both State and Federal quite properly spend vast sums of money to establish machinery to try defendants accused of crime. Lawyers to prosecute are everywhere deemed essential to protect the public's interest in an orderly society. Similarly, there are few defendants charged with crime who fail to hire the best lawyers they can get to prepare and present their defences. That government hires lawyers to prosecute and defendants who have the money hire lawyers to defend are the strongest indications of the widespread belief that lawyers in criminal courts are necessities, not luxuries. The right of one charged with crime to counsel may not be deemed fundamental and essential to fair trials in some countries, but is in ours. From the very beginning, our State and national constitutions and laws have laid great emphasis on procedural and substantive safeguards designed to assure fair trials before impartial tribunals in which every defendant stands equal before the law. This noble ideal cannot be realised if the poor man charged with crime has to face his accusers without a lawyer to assist him.

[The Court also quotes from the opinion of Douglas, J., in Argersinger v. Hamlin, 407 U.S. 25, 92 S.Ct. 2006, 35 L.Ed.2nd 530 (1972) at 535–36]

7. We may also refer to Article 39-A, the fundamental constitutional directive ...

This article also emphasises that free legal service is an unalienable element of "reasonable, fair and just" procedure for without it a person suffering from economic or other disabilities would be deprived of the opportunity for securing justice. The right to free legal to free legal services, is therefore, clearly an essential ingredient of "reasonable, fair and just" procedure for a person accused of an offence and it must be held implicit in the guarantee of Article 21. This is a constitutional right of every accused person who is unable to engage a lawyer and secure legal services on account of reasons such as poverty, indigence or incommunicado situation and the State is under a mandate to provide a lawyer to an accused person if the circumstances of the case and the needs of justice so require, provided of course the accused person does not object to the provision of such lawyer. We would, therefore, direct that on the next remand dates, when the undertrial prisoners, charged with bailable offences, are produced before the Magistrates, the State Government should provide them a lawyer at its own cost for the purpose of making an application for bail, provided that no objection is raised to such lawyer on behalf of such undertrial prisoners.... The State Government will report to the High Court of Patna its compliance with this direction within a period of six weeks from today.

...

9. We may also take this opportunity of impressing upon the Government of India as also the State Governments, the urgent necessity of introducing a dynamic and comprehensive legal service program with a view to reaching justice to the common man. Today, unfortunately, in our country the poor are priced out of the judicial system with the result that they are losing faith in the capacity of our legal system to bring about changes in their life conditions and to deliver justice to them. The poor in their contact with the legal system have always been on the wrong side of the line. They have always come across "law for the poor" rather than "law of the poor." The law is regarded by them as something mysterious and forbidding—always taking something away from them and not as a positive and constructive social device for changing the social economic order and improving their life conditions by conferring rights and benefits on them. The result it that the legal system has lost its credibility for the weaker section of the community. It is, therefore, necessary that we should inject equal justice into legality and that can be done only by dynamic and activist scheme of legal services....

We would strongly recommend to the Government of India and the State Government that it is high time that a comprehensive legal service program is introduced in the country. That is not only a mandate of equal justice implicit in Article 14 and right to life and liberty conferred by Article 21, but also the compulsion of the constitutional directive embodied in Article 39-A....

Notes

1. Sheela Barse v. State of Maharashtra, 1983 A.I.R.(S.C.) 378, 1983 (2) S.C.R. 337, is to the same effect as the main case. In 1987, the Parliament of India enacted the Legal Services Authority Act; the Act went into effect in 1995. While the Act was intended to improve access to legal services for, among others, indigent criminal defendants, lack of access to legal services for those defendants apparently continues to be a serious problem. In "The Dynamics of

Access to Justice," published in *The Hindu* of May 29, 2007, V.R. Krishna Iyer, formerly a justice of the Supreme Court of India, decried the difficulties of the indigent in obtaining representation. Further, according to the website of the Press Information Bureau of the Government of India (http://pib.nic.in/ archieve/others/2006/may2006/2years_upa_gov_may2006/law_justice_2years_ upa_gov_may2006.asp) , from the time the Legal Services Authority Act went into effect on November 9, 1995 through the end of 2005, 135,310 persons in custody benefitted from free legal aid—a very small number, considering the period of time involved and the size of the population of India.

2. Nandini Satpathy v. Dani (P.L.) and Another, 1978 A.I.R.(S.C.) 1025, 1978 (2) S.C.C. 424, is important for the light it throws on the rights to counsel and to avoid self-incrimination. In that case Satpathy, a prominent politician, was being investigated for corruption. She was ordered to report to the police station where inquiries were being conducted; while section 160* of the Code of Criminal Procedure permits an investigating officer to require such attendance, it contains a proviso excepting women from the requirement of attending at a police station. While at the police station, Satpathy refused to answer certain questions propounded to her on the ground that they had a "tendency to expose her to a criminal charge"—an explicit exception to the duty to answer truthfully imposed by section 161* of the Code on persons being examined by the police. She then was charged with violating section 179** of the Penal Code, which provides:

> Whoever, being legally bound to state the truth on any subject to any public servant, refuses to answer any question demanded of him touching that subject by such public servant in the exercise of the legal powers of such public servant, shall be punished with simple imprisonment for a term which may extend to six months, or with fine which may extend to one thousand rupees, or with both.

Satpathy then argued that applying section 179 to her on these facts would violate her right to be free from compelled self-incrimination under Article 20(3) of the Constitution. In a somewhat confusing opinion, the court held that the rights conferred by section 161 and article 20(3) applied to any person who was the subject of a criminal investigation, not simply to testimony in court. The court also held, however, that the compulsion which would violate article 20(3) meant some greater degree of duress than was presented simply by the risk that a person would be prosecuted under section 179. Apparently, that is, there is no flat right to refuse to answer police questions under the Constitution of India. However, on the facts of the case, the court held that requiring Satpathy to be interrogated at the police station in violation of the proviso to section 160 qualified as compulsion adequate to trigger the constitutional right. The court also held that the police ought to permit an accused to have the assistance of counsel at any "near-custodial" interrogation, though the court seemed to see this holding as a matter of prudence rather than as a constitutional requirement.

D. The United States

1. Self-Incrimination; Right to Counsel; Police Interrogation

a. *Miranda v. State of Arizona, 384 U.S. 436, 86 S. Ct. 1602, 16 L. Ed. 2d 694 (1966)*

Mr. Chief Justice WARREN delivered the opinion of the Court.

The cases before us raise questions which go to the roots of our concepts of American criminal jurisprudence: the restraints society must observe consistent with the Federal Constitution in prosecuting individuals for crime. More specifically, we deal with the admissibility of statements obtained from an individual who is subjected to custodial police interrogation and the necessity for procedures which assure that the individual is accorded his privilege under the Fifth Amendment to the Constitution not to be compelled to incriminate himself.

...

We start here ... with the premise that our holding is not an innovation in our jurisprudence, but is an application of principles long recognized and applied in other settings[,] ... an explication of basic rights that are enshrined in our Constitution—that "No person ... shall be compelled in any criminal case to be a witness against himself," and that "the accused shall ... have the Assistance of Counsel"—rights which were put in jeopardy in that case through official overbearing. These precious rights were fixed in our Constitution only after centuries of persecution and struggle....

... It [is] necessary to insure that what was proclaimed in the Constitution [has] not become but a "form of words, ..."

Our holding will be spelled out with some specificity in the pages which follow but briefly stated it is this: the prosecution may not use statements, whether exculpatory or inculpatory, stemming from custodial interrogation of the defendant unless it demonstrates the use of procedural safeguards effective to secure the privilege against self-incrimination. By custodial interrogation, we mean questioning initiated by law enforcement officers after a person has been taken into custody or otherwise deprived of his freedom of action in any significant way....

I

The constitutional issue we decide in each of these cases is the admissibility of statements obtained from a defendant questioned while in custody or otherwise deprived of his freedom of action in any significant way. In each, the defendant was questioned by police officers, detectives, or a prosecuting attorney in a room in which he was cut off from the outside world. In none of these cases was the defendant given a full and effective warning of his rights at the outset of the interrogation process. In all the cases, the questioning elicited oral admissions, and in three of them, signed statements as well which were admitted at their trials. They all thus share salient features—incommunicado interrogation of individuals in a police-dominated atmosphere, resulting in self-incriminating statements without full warnings of constitutional rights.

An understanding of the nature and setting of this in-custody interrogation is essential to our decisions today. The difficulty in depicting what transpires at such interrogations stems from the fact that in this country they have largely taken place incommunicado. From extensive factual studies undertaken in the early 1930's ... it is clear that police violence and the 'third degree' flourished at that time. In a series of cases decided by this Court long after these studies, the police resorted to physical brutality—beatings, hanging, whipping—and to sustained and protracted questioning incommunicado in order to extort confessions.... The use of physical brutality and violence is not, unfortunately, relegated to the past or to any part of the country ...

[Such cases] are undoubtedly the exception now, but they are sufficiently widespread to be the object of concern. Unless a proper limitation upon custodial interrogation is achieved—such as these decisions will advance—there can be no assurance that practices of this nature will be eradicated in the foreseeable future....

Again we stress that the modern practice of in-custody interrogation is psychologically rather than physically oriented. As we have stated before, "[...] this Court has recognized that coercion can be mental as well as physical, and that the blood of the accused is not the only hallmark of an unconstitutional inquisition." Blackburn v. State of Alabama, 361 U.S. 199, 206, 80 S.Ct. 274, 4 L.Ed.2d 242 (1960). Interrogation still takes place in privacy. Privacy results in secrecy and this in turn results in a gap in our knowledge as to what in fact goes on in the interrogation rooms. A valuable source of information about present police practices, however, may be found in various police manuals and texts which document procedures employed with success in the past, and which recommend various other effective tactics. These texts are used by law enforcement agencies themselves as guides. It should be noted that these texts professedly present the most enlightened and effective means presently used to obtain statements through custodial interrogation. By considering these texts and other data, it is possible to describe procedures observed and noted around the country.

[The court describes procedures suggested in such manuals—that the police display an air of confidence in the suspect's guilt, suggesting that the suspect was not really blameworthy in committing the crime in order to induce admissions. They also suggest persistent interrogation, allowing the suspect breaks only for food, sleep and natural functions. Another tactic is suggesting a legal excuse for the suspect's act and then, upon the suspect making an admission, pointing to evidence inconsistent with the excuse in order to elicit further statements. Likewise, the manuals suggest "good cop, bad cop" approaches, or the use of deceit, with the police falsely stating that other evidence points to the accused, or that there is evidence that the accused committed additional crimes. With respect to suspects who refuse to discuss the matter or ask for an attorney or relatives, the examiner is to concede the suspect's right to silence, which should disappoint suspects expecting the interrogator to react unfavorably and impress the suspect with the fairness of the interrogator. Then, however, the interrogator is advised to point out the incriminating significance of the suspect's refusal to talk If the suspect still wishes to speak to a relative or an attorney, the manuals advise the interrogator to suggest that the suspect first tell the him the truth; if the suspect requests an attorney, the interrogator may suggest saving the expense, particularly if he is innocent of the offense under investigation, stating that the interrogator only wants the truth, and the suspect needs no lawyer if he is telling the truth.]

... [T]he setting prescribed by the manuals and observed in practice becomes clear. In essence, it is this: To be alone with the subject is essential to prevent distraction and to deprive him of any outside support. The aura of confidence in his guilt undermines his will to resist. He merely confirms the preconceived story the police seek to have him describe. Patience and persistence, at times relentless questioning, are employed. To obtain a confession, the interrogator must "patiently maneuver himself or his quarry into a position from which the desired objective may be attained." When normal procedures fail to produce the needed result, the police may resort to deceptive stratagems such as giving false legal advice. It is important to keep the subject off balance, for example, by trading on his insecurity about himself or his surroundings. The police then persuade, trick, or cajole him out of exercising his constitutional rights.

Even without employing brutality, the "third degree" or ... specific stratagems ... the very fact of custodial interrogation exacts a heavy toll on individual liberty and trades on the weakness of individuals. This fact may be illustrated simply by referring to three confession cases decided by this Court ... In Townsend v. Sain, 372 U.S. 293, 83 S.Ct. 745, 9 L.Ed.2d 770 (1963), the defendant was a 19-year-old heroin addict, described as a "near mental defective," id., at 307–310. The defendant in Lynumn v. State of Illinois, 372 U.S. 528, 83

S.Ct. 917, 9 L.Ed.2d 922 (1963), was a woman who confessed to the arresting officer after being importuned to "cooperate" in order to prevent her children from being taken by relief authorities. This Court as in those cases reversed the conviction of a defendant in Haynes v. State of Washington, 373 U.S. 503, 83 S.Ct. 1336, 10 L.Ed.2d 513 (1963), whose persistent request during his interrogation was to phone his wife or attorney. In other settings, these individuals might have exercised their constitutional rights. In the incommunicado police-dominated atmosphere, they succumbed.

In the cases before us today, given this background, we concern ourselves primarily with this interrogation atmosphere and the evils it can bring. In No. 759, Miranda v. Arizona, the police arrested the defendant and took him to a special interrogation room where they secured a confession. In No. 760, Vignera v. New York, the defendant made oral admissions to the police after interrogation in the afternoon, and then signed an inculpatory statement upon being questioned by an assistant district attorney later the same evening. In No. 761, Westover v. United States, the defendant was handed over to the Federal Bureau of Investigation by local authorities after they had detained and interrogated him for a lengthy period, both at night and the following morning. After some two hours of questioning, the federal officers had obtained signed statements from the defendant. Lastly, in No. 584, California v. Stewart, the local police held the defendant five days in the station and interrogated him on nine separate occasions before they secured his inculpatory statement.

In these cases, we might not find the defendants' statements to have been involuntary in traditional terms. Our concern for adequate safeguards to protect precious Fifth Amendment rights is, of course, not lessened in the slightest. In each of the cases, the defendant was thrust into an unfamiliar atmosphere and run through menacing police interrogation procedures. The potentiality for compulsion is forcefully apparent, for example, in Miranda, where the indigent Mexican defendant was a seriously disturbed individual with pronounced sexual fantasies, and in Stewart, in which the defendant was an indigent Los Angeles Negro who had dropped out of school in the sixth grade. To be sure, the records do not evince overt physical coercion or patent psychological ploys. The fact remains that in none of these cases did the officers undertake to afford appropriate safeguards at the outset of the interrogation to insure that the statements were truly the product of free choice.

It is obvious that such an interrogation environment is created for no purpose other than to subjugate the individual to the will of his examiner. This atmosphere carries its own badge of intimidation. To be sure, this is not physical intimidation, but it is equally destructive of human dignity. The current practice of incommunicado interrogation is at odds with one of our Nation's most cherished principles—that the individual may not be compelled to incriminate himself.

Unless adequate protective devices are employed to dispel the compulsion inherent in custodial surroundings, no statement obtained from the defendant can truly be the product of his free choice.

From the foregoing, we can readily perceive an intimate connection between the privilege against self-incrimination and police custodial questioning. It is fitting to turn to history and precedent underlying the Self-Incrimination Clause to determine its applicability in this situation.

II

We sometimes forget how long it has taken to establish the privilege against self-incrimination, the sources from which it came and the fervor with which it was defended. Its roots go back into ancient times....

Thus we may view the historical development of the privilege as one which groped for the proper scope of governmental power over the citizen. As a "noble principle often transcends its origins," the privilege has come rightfully to be recognized in part as an individual's substantive right, a "right to a private enclave where he may lead a private life. That right is the hallmark of our democracy." United States v. Grunewald, 233 F.2d 556, 579, 581–582 (Frank, J., dissenting), rev'd, 353 U.S. 391 (1957). We have recently noted that the privilege against self-incrimination—the essential mainstay of our adversary system—is founded on a complex of values ... All these policies point to one overriding thought: the constitutional foundation underlying the privilege is the respect a government—state or federal—must accord to the dignity and integrity of its citizens. To maintain a "fair state-individual balance," to require the government "to shoulder the entire load," 8 Wigmore, Evidence 317 (McNaughton rev. 1961), to respect the inviolability of the human personality, our accusatory system of criminal justice demands that the government seeking to punish an individual produce the evidence against him by its own independent labors, rather than by the cruel, simple expedient of compelling it from his own mouth. Chambers v. State of Florida, 309 U.S. 227, 235–238, 60 S.Ct. 472, 84 L.Ed. 716 (1940). In sum, the privilege is fulfilled only when the person is guaranteed the right "to remain silent unless he chooses to speak in the unfettered exercise of his own will."

The question in these cases is whether the privilege is fully applicable during a period of custodial interrogation. In this Court, the privilege has consistently been accorded a liberal construction.... We are satisfied that all the principles embodied in the privilege apply to informal compulsion exerted by law-enforcement officers during in-custody questioning. An individual swept from familiar surroundings into police custody, surrounded by antagonistic forces, and subjected to the techniques of persuasion described above cannot be otherwise than under compulsion to speak. As a practical matter, the compulsion to speak in the isolated setting of the police station may well be greater than in courts or other official investigations, where there are often impartial observers to guard against intimidation or trickery.

This question, in fact, could have been taken as settled in federal courts almost 70 years ago, when, in Bram v. United States, 168 U.S. 532, 542, 18 S.Ct. 183, 42 L.Ed. 568 (1897), this Court held:

> In criminal trials, in the courts of the United States, wherever a question arises whether a confession is incompetent because not voluntary, the issue is controlled by that portion of the fifth amendment … commanding that no person "shall be compelled in any criminal case to be a witness against himself."

In Bram, the Court … set down the Fifth Amendment standard for compulsion which we implement today:

> Much of the confusion which has resulted from the effort to deduce from the adjudged cases what would be a sufficient quantum of proof to show that a confession was or was not voluntary has arisen from a misconception of the subject to which the proof must address itself. The rule is not that, in order to render a statement admissible, the proof must be adequate to establish that the particular communications contained in a statement were voluntarily made, but it must be sufficient to establish that the making of the statement was voluntary; that is to say, that, from the causes which the law treats as legally sufficient to engender in the mind of the accused hope or fear in respect to the crime charged, the accused was not involuntarily impelled to make a statement when but for the improper influences he would have remained silent.

168 U.S. at 549.

The Court has adhered to this reasoning. In 1924, Mr. Justice Brandeis wrote for a unanimous Court in reversing a conviction resting on a compelled confession, Ziang Sung Wan v. United States, 266 U.S. 1, 45 S.Ct. 1, 69 L.Ed.2d 131 (1924). He stated:

> In the federal courts, the requisite of voluntariness is not satisfied by establishing merely that the confession was not induced by a promise or a threat. A confession is voluntary in law if, and only if, it was, in fact, voluntarily made. A confession may have been given voluntarily, although it was made to police officers, while in custody, and in answer to an examination conducted by them. But a confession obtained by compulsion must be excluded whatever may have been the character of the compulsion, and whether the compulsion was applied in a judicial proceeding or otherwise. Bram v. United States, 168 U.S. 532.

266 U.S., at 14–15.

In addition to the expansive historical development of the privilege and the sound policies which have nurtured its evolution, judicial precedent thus clearly establishes its application to incommunicado interrogation. In fact, the Government concedes this point as well established in No. 761, Westover v. United States, stating: "We have no doubt ... that it is possible for a suspect's Fifth Amendment right to be violated during in-custody questioning by a law-enforcement officer."

... [W]e have had little occasion in the past quarter century to reach the constitutional issues in dealing with federal interrogations....

Our decision in Malloy v. Hogan, 378 U.S. 1, 84 S.Ct. 1489, 12 L.Ed.2d 653 (1964), necessitates an examination of the scope of the privilege in state cases as well. In Malloy, we squarely held the privilege applicable to the States, and held that the substantive standards underlying the privilege applied with full force to state court proceedings. There ... we applied the existing Fifth Amendment standards to the case before us. Aside from the holding itself, the reasoning in Malloy made clear what had already become apparent—that the substantive and procedural safeguards surrounding admissibility of confessions in state cases had become exceedingly exacting, reflecting all the policies embedded in the privilege, 378 U.S., at 7–8. The voluntariness doctrine in the state cases, as Malloy indicates, encompasses all interrogation practices which are likely to exert such pressure upon an individual as to disable him from making a free and rational choice. The implications of this proposition were elaborated in our decision in Escobedo v. State of Illinois, 378 U.S. 478, 84 S.Ct. 1758, 12 L.Ed.2d 977 (1964) decided one week after Malloy applied the privilege to the States.

Our holding there stressed the fact that the police had not advised the defendant of his constitutional privilege to remain silent at the outset of the interrogation, and we drew attention to that fact at several points in the decision, 378 U.S., at 483, 485, 491. This was no isolated factor, but an essential ingredient in our decision. The entire thrust of police interrogation there, as in all the cases today, was to put the defendant in such an emotional state as to impair his capacity for rational judgment. The abdication of the constitutional privilege—the choice on his part to speak to the police—was not made knowingly or competently because of the failure to apprise him of his rights; the compelling atmosphere of the in-custody interrogation, and not an independent decision on his part, caused the defendant to speak.

A different phase of the Escobedo decision was significant in its attention to the absence of counsel during the questioning. There, as in the cases today, we sought a protective device to dispel the compelling atmosphere of the interrogation. In Escobedo, however, the police did not relieve the defendant of the anxieties which they had created in the interrogation rooms. Rather, they denied his request for the assistance of counsel, 378 U.S., at 481, 488, 491. This heightened his dilemma, and made his later statements the product of this compulsion. The denial of the defendant's request for his attorney thus undermined his ability to exercise the privilege—to remain silent if he chose or to speak without any intimidation, blatant or subtle. The presence of counsel, in all the cases before us today, would be the adequate protective device necessary to make the process of police interrogation conform to the dictates of the privilege. His presence would insure that statements made in the government-established atmosphere are not the product of compulsion.

It was in this manner that Escobedo explicated another facet of the pre-trial privilege, noted in many of the Court's prior decisions: the protection of rights at trial. That counsel is present when statements are taken from an individual during interrogation obviously enhances the integrity of the fact-finding processes in court. The presence of an attorney, and the warnings delivered to the individual, enable the defendant under otherwise compelling circumstances to tell his story without fear, effectively, and in a way that eliminates the evils in the interrogation process. Without the protections flowing from adequate warning and the rights of counsel, "all the careful safeguards erected around the giving of testimony, whether by an accused or any other witness, would become empty formalities in a procedure where the most compelling possible evidence of guilt, a confession, would have already been obtained at the unsupervised pleasure of the police." Mapp v. Ohio, 367 U.S. 643, 685, 81 S.Ct. 1684, 6 L.Ed.2d 1081 (1961) (Harlan, J., dissenting).

III

Today, then, there can be no doubt that the Fifth Amendment privilege is available outside of criminal court proceedings and serves to protect persons in all settings in which their freedom of action is curtailed in any significant way from being compelled to incriminate themselves. We have concluded that without proper safeguards the process of in-custody interrogation of persons suspected or accused of crime contains inherently compelling pressures which work to undermine the individual's will to resist and to compel him to speak where he would not otherwise do so freely. In order to combat these pressures and to permit a full opportunity to exercise the privilege against self-incrimination, the accused must be adequately and effectively apprised of his rights and the exercise of those rights must be fully honored.

It is impossible for us to foresee the potential alternatives for protecting the privilege which might be devised by Congress or the States in the exercise of their creative rule-making capacities. Therefore we cannot say that the Constitution necessarily requires adherence to any particular solution for the inherent compulsions of the interrogation process as it is presently conducted. Our decision in no way creates a constitutional straitjacket which will handicap sound efforts at reform, nor is it intended to have this effect. We encourage Congress and the States to continue their laudable search for increasingly effective ways of protecting the rights of the individual while promoting efficient enforcement of our criminal laws. However, unless we are shown other procedures which are at least as effective in apprising accused persons of their right of silence and in assuring a continuous opportunity to exercise it, the following safeguards must be observed.

At the outset, if a person in custody is to be subjected to interrogation, he must first be informed in clear and unequivocal terms that he has the right to remain silent. For those unaware of the privilege, the warning is needed simply to make them aware of it—the threshold requirement for an intelligent decision as to its exercise. More important, such a warning is an absolute prerequisite in overcoming the inherent pressures of the interrogation atmosphere. It is not just the subnormal or woefully ignorant who succumb to an interrogator's imprecations, whether implied or expressly stated, that the interrogation will continue until a confession is obtained or that silence in the face of accusation is itself damning and will bode ill when presented to a jury. Further, the warning will show the individual that his interrogators are prepared to recognize his privilege should he choose to exercise it.

In accord with our decision today, it is impermissible to penalize an individual for exercising his Fifth Amendment privilege when he is under police custodial interrogation. The prosecution may not, therefore, use at trial the fact that he stood mute or claimed his privilege in the face of accusation.

The Fifth Amendment privilege is so fundamental to our system of constitutional rule and the expedient of giving an adequate warning as to the availability of the privilege so simple, we will not pause to inquire in individual cases whether the defendant was aware of his rights without a warning being given. Assessments of the knowledge the defendant possessed, based on information as to his age, education, intelligence, or prior contact with authorities, can never be more than speculation; a warning is a clearcut fact. More important, whatever the background of the person interrogated, a warning at the time of the interrogation is indispensable to overcome its pressures and to insure that the individual knows he is free to exercise the privilege at that point in time.

The warning of the right to remain silent must be accompanied by the explanation that anything said can and will be used against the individual in court. This warning is needed in order to make him aware not only of the privilege, but also of the consequences of forgoing it. It is only through an awareness of these consequences that there can be any assurance of real understanding and intelligent exercise of the privilege. Moreover, this warning may serve to make the individual more acutely aware that he is faced with a phase of the adversary system—that he is not in the presence of persons acting solely in his interest.

The circumstances surrounding in-custody interrogation can operate very quickly to overbear the will of one merely made aware of his privilege by his interrogators. Therefore, the right to have counsel present at the interrogation is indispensable to the protection of the Fifth Amendment privilege under the system we delineate today. Our aim is to assure that the individual's right to choose between silence and speech remains unfettered throughout the interrogation process. A once-stated warning, delivered by those who will conduct the interrogation, cannot itself suffice to that end among those who most require knowledge of their rights. A mere warning given by the interrogators is not alone sufficient to accomplish that end. Prosecutors themselves claim that the admonishment of the right to remain silent without more "will benefit only the recidivist and the professional." Even preliminary advice given to the accused by his own attorney can be swiftly overcome by the secret interrogation process. Thus, the need for counsel to protect the Fifth Amendment privilege comprehends not merely a right to consult with counsel prior to questioning, but also to have counsel present during any questioning if the defendant so desires.

The presence of counsel at the interrogation may serve several significant subsidiary functions as well. If the accused decides to talk to his interrogators, the assistance of counsel can mitigate the dangers of untrustworthiness. With a lawyer present the likelihood that the police will practice coercion is reduced, and if coercion is nevertheless exercised the lawyer can testify to it in court. The presence of a lawyer can also help to guarantee that the accused gives a fully accurate statement to the police and that the statement is rightly reported by the prosecution at trial.

An individual need not make a pre-interrogation request for a lawyer. While such request affirmatively secures his right to have one, his failure to ask for a lawyer does not constitute a waiver. No effective waiver of the right to counsel during interrogation can be recognized unless specifically made after the warnings we here delineate have been given. The accused who does not know his rights and therefore does not make a request may be the person who most needs counsel....

In Carnley v. Cochran, 369 U.S. 506, 513, 82 S.Ct. 884, 8 L.Ed.2d 70 (1962), we stated: "(I)t is settled that where the assistance of counsel is a constitutional requisite, the right to be furnished counsel does not depend on a request." This proposition applies with equal force in the context of providing counsel to protect an accused's Fifth Amendment privilege in the face of interrogation. Although the role of counsel at trial differs from the role during interrogation, the differences are not relevant to the question whether a request is a prerequisite.

Accordingly we hold that an individual held for interrogation must be clearly informed that he has the right to consult with a lawyer and to have the lawyer with him during interrogation under the system for protecting the privilege we delineate today. As with the warnings of the right to remain silent and that anything stated can be used in evidence against him, this warning is an absolute prerequisite to interrogation. No amount of circumstantial evidence that the person may have been aware of this right will suffice to stand in its stead. Only through such a warning is there ascertainable assurance that the accused was aware of this right.

If an individual indicates that he wishes the assistance of counsel before any interrogation occurs, the authorities cannot rationally ignore or deny his request on the basis that the individual does not have or cannot afford a retained attorney. The financial ability of the individual has no relationship to the scope of the rights involved here. The privilege against self-incrimination secured by the Constitution applies to all individuals. The need for counsel in order to protect the privilege exists for the indigent as well as the affluent. In fact, were we to limit these constitutional rights to those who can retain an attorney, our decisions today would be of little significance. The cases before us as well as the vast majority of confession cases with which we have dealt in the past involve those unable to retain counsel. While authorities are not required to relieve the accused of his poverty, they have the obligation not to take advantage of indigence in the administration of justice. Denial of counsel to the indigent at the time of interrogation while allowing an attorney to those who can afford one would be no more supportable by reason or logic than the similar situation at trial and on appeal struck down in Gideon v. Wainwright, 372 U.S. 335 ...

In order fully to apprise a person interrogated of the extent of his rights under this system then, it is necessary to warn him not only that he has the right to consult with an attorney, but also that if he is indigent a lawyer will be appointed to represent him. Without this additional warning, the admonition of the right to consult with counsel would often be understood as meaning only that he can consult with a lawyer if he has one or has the funds to obtain one. The warning of a right to counsel would be hollow if not couched in terms that would convey to the indigent—the person most often subjected to interrogation—the knowledge that he too has a right to have counsel present. As with the warnings of the right to remain silent and of the general right to counsel, only by effective and express explanation to the indigent of this right can there be assurance that he was truly in a position to exercise it.

Once warnings have been given, the subsequent procedure is clear. If the individual indicates in any manner, at any time prior to or during questioning, that he wishes to remain silent, the interrogation must cease. At this point he has shown that he intends to exercise his Fifth Amendment privilege; any statement taken after the person invokes his privilege cannot be other than the product of compulsion, subtle or otherwise. Without the right to cut off questioning, the setting of in-custody interrogation operates on the individual to overcome free choice in producing a statement after the privilege has been once invoked. If the individual states that he wants an attorney, the interrogation must cease until an attorney is present. At that time, the individual must have an opportunity to confer with the attorney and to have him present during any subsequent questioning. If the individual cannot obtain an attorney and he indicates that he wants one before speaking to police, they must respect his decision to remain silent.

This does not mean, as some have suggested, that each police station must have a "station house lawyer" present at all times to advise prisoners. It does mean, however, that if police propose to interrogate a person they must make known to him that he is entitled to a lawyer and that if he cannot afford one, a lawyer will be provided for him prior to any interrogation. If authorities conclude that they will not provide counsel during a reasonable period of time in which investigation in the field is carried out, they may refrain from doing so without violating the person's Fifth Amendment privilege so long as they do not question him during that time.

If the interrogation continues without the presence of an attorney and a statement is taken, a heavy burden rests on the government to demonstrate that the defendant knowingly and intelligently waived his privilege against self-incrimination and his right to retained or appointed counsel. Escobedo v. State of Illinois, 378 U.S. 478, 490, n. 14. This Court has always set high standards of proof for the waiver of constitutional rights and we reassert these standards as applied to in custody interrogation. Since the State is responsible for establishing the isolated circumstances under which the interrogation takes place and has the only means of making available corroborated evidence of warnings given during incommunicado interrogation, the burden is rightly on its shoulders.

An express statement that the individual is willing to make a statement and does not want an attorney followed closely by a statement could constitute a waiver. But a valid waiver will not be presumed simply from the silence of the accused after warnings are given or simply from the fact that a confession was in fact eventually obtained ... Moreover, where in-custody interrogation is involved, there is no room for the contention that the privilege is waived if the individual answers some questions or gives some information on his own prior to invoking his right to remain silent when interrogated.

Whatever the testimony of the authorities as to waiver of rights by an accused, the fact of lengthy interrogation or incommunicado incarceration before a statement is made is strong evidence that the accused did not validly waive his rights. In these circumstances the fact that the individual eventually made a statement is consistent with the conclusion that the compelling influence of the interrogation finally forced him to do so. It is inconsistent with any notion of a voluntary relinquishment of the privilege. Moreover, any evidence that the accused was threatened, tricked, or cajoled into a waiver will, of course, show that the defendant did not voluntarily waive his privilege. The requirement of warnings and waiver of rights is a fundamental with respect to the Fifth Amendment privilege and not simply a preliminary ritual to existing methods of interrogation.

The warnings required and the waiver necessary in accordance with our opinion today are, in the absence of a fully effective equivalent, prerequisites to the admissibility of any statement made by a defendant. No distinction can be drawn between statements which are direct confessions and statements which amount to "admissions" of part or all of an offense. The privilege against self-incrimination protects the individual from being compelled to incriminate himself in any manner; it does not distinguish degrees of incrimination. Similarly, for precisely the same reason, no distinction may be drawn between inculpatory statements and statements alleged to be merely "exculpatory." If a statement made were in fact truly exculpatory it would, of course, never be used by the prosecution. In fact, statements merely intended to be exculpatory by the defendant are often used to impeach his testimony at trial or to demonstrate untruths in the statement given under interrogation and thus to prove guilt by implication. These statements are incriminating in any meaningful sense of the word and may not be used without the full warnings and effective waiver required for any other statement. In Escobedo itself, the defendant fully intended his accusation of another as the slayer to be exculpatory as to himself.

The principles announced today deal with the protection which must be given to the privilege against self-incrimination when the individual is first subjected to police interrogation while in custody at the station or otherwise deprived of his freedom of action in any significant way. It is at this point that our adversary system of criminal proceedings commences, distinguishing itself at the outset from the inquisitorial system recognized in some countries. Under the system of warnings we delineate today or under any other system which may be devised and found effective, the safeguards to be erected about the privilege must come into play at this point.

Our decision is not intended to hamper the traditional function of police officers in investigating crime. When an individual is in custody on probable cause, the police may, of course, seek out evidence in the field to be used at trial against him. Such investigation may include inquiry of persons not under restraint. General on-the-scene questioning as to facts surrounding a crime or other general questioning of citizens in the fact-finding process is not affected by our holding. It is an act of responsible citizenship for individuals to give whatever information they may have to aid in law enforcement. In such situations the compelling atmosphere inherent in the process of in-custody interrogation is not necessarily present.

In dealing with statements obtained through interrogation, we do not purport to find all confessions inadmissible. Confessions remain a proper element in law enforcement. Any statement given freely and voluntarily without any compelling influences is, of course, admissible in evidence. The fundamental import of the privilege while an individual is in custody is not whether he is allowed to talk to the police without the benefit of warnings and counsel, but whether he can be interrogated. There is no requirement that police stop a person who enters a police station and states that he wishes to confess to a crime, or a person who calls the police to offer a confession or any other statement he desires to make. Volunteered statements of any kind are not barred by the Fifth Amendment and their admissibility is not affected by our holding today.

To summarize, we hold that when an individual is taken into custody or otherwise deprived of his freedom by the authorities in any significant way and is subjected to questioning, the privilege against self-incrimination is jeopardized. Procedural safeguards must be employed to protect the privilege and unless other fully effective means are adopted to notify the person of his right of silence and to assure that the exercise of the right will be scrupulously honored, the following measures are required. He must be warned prior to any questioning that he has the right to remain silent, that anything he says can be used against him in a court of law, that he has the right to the presence of an attorney, and that if he cannot afford an attorney one will be appointed for him prior to any questioning if he so desires. Opportunity to exercise these rights must be afforded to him throughout the interrogation. After such warnings have been given, and such opportunity afforded him, the individual may knowingly and intelligently waive these rights and agree to answer questions or make a statement. But unless and until such warnings and waiver are demonstrated by the prosecution at trial, no evidence obtained as a result of interrogation can be used against him.

IV

A recurrent argument made in these cases is that society's need for interrogation outweighs the privilege. This argument is not unfamiliar to this Court. The whole thrust of our foregoing discussion demonstrates that the Constitution has prescribed the rights of the individual when confronted with the power of government when it provided in the Fifth Amendment that an individual cannot be compelled to be a witness against himself. That right cannot be abridged....

If the individual desires to exercise his privilege, he has the right to do so. This is not for the authorities to decide. An attorney may advise his client not to talk to police until he has had an opportunity to investigate the case, or he may wish to be present with his client during any police questioning. In doing so an attorney is merely exercising the good professional judgment he has been taught. This is not cause for considering the attorney a menace to law enforcement. He is merely carrying out what he is sworn to do under his oath—to protect to the extent of his ability the rights of his client. In fulfilling this responsibility the attorney plays a vital role in the administration of criminal justice under our Constitution.

In announcing these principles, we are not unmindful of the burdens which law enforcement officials must bear, often under trying circumstances. We also fully recognize the obligation of all citizens to aid in enforcing the criminal laws. This Court, while protecting individual rights, has always given ample latitude to law enforcement agencies in the legitimate exercise of their duties. The limits we have placed on the interrogation process should not constitute an undue interference with a proper system of law enforcement. As we have noted, our decision does not in any way preclude police from carrying out their traditional investigatory functions. Although confessions may play an important role in some convictions, the cases before us present graphic examples of the overstatement of the "need" for confessions. In each case authorities conducted interrogations ranging up to five days in duration despite the presence, through standard investigating practices, of considerable evidence against each defendant.

It is also urged that an unfettered right to detention for interrogation should be allowed because it will often redound to the benefit of the person questioned. When police inquiry determines that there is no reason to believe that the person has committed any crime, it is said, he will be released without need for further formal procedures. The person who has committed no offense, however, will be better able to clear himself after warnings with counsel present than without. It can be assumed that in such circumstances a lawyer would advise his client to talk freely to police in order to clear himself.

Custodial interrogation, by contrast, does not necessarily afford the innocent an opportunity to clear themselves. A serious consequence of the present practice of the interrogation alleged to be beneficial for the innocent is that many arrests "for investigation" subject large numbers of innocent persons to detention and interrogation. In one of the cases before us, No. 584, California v. Stewart, police held four persons, who were in the defendant's house at the time of the arrest, in jail for five days until defendant confessed. At that time they were finally released, police stated that there was "no evidence to connect them with any crime." Available statistics on the extent of this practice where it is condoned indicate that these four are far from alone in being subjected to arrest, prolonged detention, and interrogation without the requisite probable cause. Over the years the Federal Bureau of Investigation has compiled an exemplary record of effective law enforcement while advising any suspect or arrested person, at the outset of an interview, that he is not required to make a statement, that any statement may be used against him in court, that the individual may obtain the services of an attorney of his own choice and, more recently, that he has a right to free counsel if he is unable to pay....

The practice of the FBI can readily be emulated by state and local enforcement agencies. The argument that the FBI deals with different crimes than are dealt with by state authorities does not mitigate the significance of the FBI experience.

The experience in some other countries also suggests that the danger to law enforcement in curbs on interrogation is overplayed. [The Court notes that, in England, a suspect must be warned by a police officer as soon as he has evidence that affords reasonable grounds for suspicion; any statement made by the accused must be given without questioning by police; and the individual's right to consult with an attorney during this period is expressly recognized. Scotland bars most confessions obtained through police interrogation. In India and Ceylon, confessions made to the police but not in the presence of a magistrate are excluded. And under the Uniform Code of Military Justice of the United States, no suspect may be interrogated without first being warned of his right not to make a statement and that any statement he makes may be used against him, nor may a suspect be denied the right to consult counsel during interrogation.] There appears to have been no marked detrimental effect on criminal law enforcement in these jurisdictions as a result of these rules. Conditions of law enforcement in our country are sufficiently similar to permit reference to this experience as assurance that lawlessness will not result from warning an individual of his rights or allowing him to exercise them. Moreover, it is consistent with our legal system that we give at least as much protection to these rights as is given in the jurisdictions described. We deal in our country with rights grounded in a specific requirement of the Fifth Amendment of the Constitution, whereas other jurisdictions arrived at their conclusions on the basis of principles of justice not so specifically defined.

It is also urged upon us that we withhold decision on this issue until state legislative bodies and advisory groups have had an opportunity to deal with these problems by rule making. We have already pointed out that the Constitution does not require any specific code of procedures for protecting the privilege against self-incrimination during custodial interrogation. Congress and the States are free to develop their own safeguards for the privilege, so long as they are fully as effective as those described above in informing accused persons of their right of silence and in affording a continuous opportunity to exercise it. In any event, however, the issues presented are of constitutional dimensions and must be determined by the courts. The admissibility of a statement in the face of a claim that it was obtained in violation of the defendant's constitutional rights is an issue the resolution of which has long since been undertaken by this Court. Judicial solutions to problems of constitutional dimension have evolved decade by decade. As courts have been presented with the need to enforce constitutional rights, they have found means of doing so. That was our responsibility when *Escobedo* was before us and it is our responsibility today. Where rights secured by the Constitution are involved, there can be no rule making or legislation which would abrogate them.

V

Because of the nature of the problem and because of its recurrent significance in numerous cases, we have to this point discussed the relationship of the Fifth

Amendment privilege to police interrogation without specific concentration on the facts of the cases before us. We turn now to these facts to consider the application to these cases of the constitutional principles discussed above. In each instance, we have concluded that statements were obtained from the defendant under circumstances that did not meet constitutional standards for protection of the privilege.

No. 759. Miranda v. Arizona.

[Miranda was arrested at his home and taken to a Phoenix police station in connection with the investigation of a kidnapping and rape. He was there identified by the complaining witness. He was then questioned by two police officers, who admitted at trial that Miranda was not advised that he had a right to have an attorney present. After two hours, the officers emerged from the interrogation room with a written confession signed by Miranda. At his trial before a jury, the written confession was admitted into evidence over the objection of defense counsel, and the officers testified to a prior oral confession made by Miranda during the interrogation. Miranda was found guilty of kidnapping and rape. On appeal, the Supreme Court of Arizona affirmed, emphasizing heavily the fact that Miranda did not specifically request counsel.]

We reverse. From the testimony of the officers and by the admission of respondent, it is clear that Miranda was not in any way apprised of his right to consult with an attorney and to have one present during the interrogation, nor was his right not to be compelled to incriminate himself effectively protected in any other manner. Without these warnings the statements were inadmissible. The mere fact that he signed a statement which contained a typed-in clause stating that he had "full knowledge" of his "legal rights" does not approach the knowing and intelligent waiver required to relinquish constitutional rights.

No. 760. Vignera v. New York.

[Vignera was picked up by New York police on October 14, 1960, in connection with the robbery of a Brooklyn dress shop. He was taken to a police station, where under interrogation he confessed committing the robbery to a detective. While at the police station, Vignera was identified by two witnesses as the robber of the dress shop. At about 3 p.m. he was formally arrested. At 11 p.m. Vignera was questioned by an assistant district attorney in the presence of a hearing reporter who transcribed the questions and Vignera's answers. The transcription contained no statement of any warnings given by the assistant district attorney. At Vignera's trial for robbery, the detective testified as to the oral confession. When the defense sought to question him on cross-examination as to whether Vignera was warned of his right to counsel prior to interrogation, the prosecution objected and the trial judge sustained the objection, thereby preventing the defense from making any showing that no warnings had been given. The transcription of the statement taken was also introduced in evidence. The trial judge's charge to the jury included the statement that the confession was not void or invalidated because Vignera was not advised of his rights. The New York appellate courts affirmed.]

We reverse. The foregoing indicates that Vignera was not warned of any of his rights before the questioning by the detective and by the assistant district attorney. No other steps were taken to protect these rights. Thus he was not effectively apprised of his Fifth Amendment privilege or of his right to have counsel present and his statements are inadmissible.

No. 761. Westover v. United States.

[At about 9:45 p.m. on March 20, 1963, Westover was arrested by Kansas City police as a suspect in two Kansas City robberies. A report was also received from the FBI that he was wanted on a felony charge in California. He was placed in a line-up at a police station on the local charges, and at about 11:45 p.m., he was booked. Kansas City police interrogated Westover on the night of his arrest and again throughout the morning of the next day. Shortly before noon they informed the FBI that they had finished interrogating Westover and that the FBI could proceed to interrogate him. There is nothing in the record to indicate that Westover was ever given any warning as to his rights by local police. At noon, agents of the FBI continued the interrogation in a private interview room of the Kansas City Police Department with respect to robberies of a savings and loan association and a bank in Sacramento, California. After two or two and one-half hours, Westover signed confessions to each of the robberies which one of the agents had prepared during the interrogation. At trial an agent testified, and a paragraph on each of the statements stated, that Westover had been advised that he did not have to make a statement, that any statement he made could be used against him, and that he had the right to see an attorney. Westover was tried by a jury in federal court and convicted of the California robberies. His statements were introduced at trial. On appeal, the conviction was affirmed.]

We reverse. On the facts of this case we cannot find that Westover knowingly and intelligently waived his right to remain silent and his right to consult with counsel prior to the time he made the statement. At the time the FBI agents began questioning Westover, he had been in custody for over 14 hours and had been interrogated at length during that period. The FBI interrogation began immediately upon the conclusion of the interrogation by Kansas City police and was conducted in local police headquarters. Although the two law enforcement authorities are legally distinct and the crimes for which they interrogated Westover were different, the impact on him was that of a continuous period of questioning. There is no evidence of any warning given prior to the FBI interrogation nor is there any evidence of an articulated waiver of rights after the FBI commenced its interrogation. The record simply shows that the defendant did in fact confess a short time after being turned over to the FBI following interrogation by local police. Despite the fact that the FBI agents gave warnings at the outset of their interview, from Westover's point of view the warnings came at the end of the interrogation process. In these circumstances an intelligent waiver of constitutional rights cannot be assumed.

We do not suggest that law enforcement authorities are precluded from questioning any individual who has been held for a period of time by other authorities and interrogated by them without appropriate warnings. A different case would be presented if an accused were taken into custody by the second authority, removed both in time and place from his original surroundings, and then adequately advised of his rights and given an opportunity to exercise them. But here the FBI interrogation was conducted immediately following the state interrogation in the same police station—in the same compelling surroundings. Thus, in obtaining a confession from Westover the federal authorities were the beneficiaries of the pressure applied by the local in-custody interrogation. In these circumstances the giving of warnings alone was not sufficient to protect the privilege.

No. 584. California v. Stewart.

[During a Los Angeles police investigation of a series of purse-snatch robberies in which one of the victims had died of injuries inflicted by her assailant, Stewart was identified as the endorser of checks taken in one of the robberies. Police officers went to Stewart's house and arrested him. A consent search of the house turned up items taken from the robbery victims. At the time of Stewart's arrest, police also arrested Stewart's wife and three other persons who were visiting him, all of whom were jailed and interrogated. Stewart was placed in a cell at a police station and was interrogated nine times over five days. Except for a confrontation with an accusing witness during the first interrogation session, Stewart was isolated with his interrogators. Stewart admitted that he had robbed the deceased victim during the ninth session, and was then brought before a magistrate for the first time. Since there was no evidence to connect them with any crime, the police then released the other four persons arrested with him. The record was silent as to whether Stewart was advised of his right to remain silent or his right to counsel. In a number of instances, however, the interrogating officers were asked to recount everything that was said during the interrogations. None indicated that Stewart was ever advised of his rights. Stewart was charged with kidnapping to commit robbery, rape, and murder. At his trial, transcripts of the first interrogation and the confession at the last interrogation were introduced in evidence. The jury found Stewart guilty of robbery and first degree murder and fixed the penalty as death. On appeal, the Supreme Court of California reversed, holding that under the decision in Escobedo, Stewart should have been advised of his right to remain silent and of his right to counsel and that it would not presume in the face of a silent record that the police advised Stewart of his rights.]

We affirm. In dealing with custodial interrogation, we will not presume that a defendant has been effectively apprised of his rights and that his privilege against self-incrimination has been adequately safeguarded on a record that does not show that any warnings have been given or that any effective alternative has been employed. Nor can a knowing and intelligent waiver of these rights be assumed on a silent record. Furthermore, Stewart's steadfast denial of the alleged offenses through eight of the nine interrogations over a period of five days is subject to no other construction than that he was compelled by persistent interrogation to forgo his Fifth Amendment privilege.

Therefore, in accordance with the foregoing, the judgments of the Supreme Court of Arizona in No. 759, of the New York Court of Appeals in No. 760, and of the Court of Appeals for the Ninth Circuit in No. 761 are reversed. The judgment of the Supreme Court of California in No. 584 is affirmed. It is so ordered.

(dissenting opinions omitted)

Notes

1. In Escobedo, the Court had held that use of a person's statements against him at a criminal trial violates his Sixth Amendment right to assistance of counsel, made applicable to the states by the due process clause of the Fourteenth Amendment, if the statements were elicited after the investigation had begun to focus on the person and he been taken into custody, but had requested and been denied access to his lawyer and had not been warned of his right to silence. Gideon v. Wainwright held that a person charged with a felony and unable to afford an attorney had the right to have counsel appointed for him by the government under the Sixth Amendment as made applicable to the states by the Fourteenth Amendment. In Griffin v. California, 380 U.S. 609, 85 S.Ct. 1229, 14 L.Ed.2d 106 (1965), the Court held that the Fifth Amendment's right against self-incrimination forbade either a prosecutor or the court from commenting to the jury on a defendant's failure to testify at trial, though the court qualified this rule in Lockett v. Ohio, 438 U.S. 586, 98 S.Ct. 2954, 57 L.Ed.2d 973 (1978), holding the prosecutor was permitted to refer to the state's case as uncontradicted where defense counsel had outlined the defense in the opening statement, and had stated that the defendant would testify, but the defendant did not take the stand. Also, United States v. Robinson, 485 U.S. 25, 108 S.Ct. 864, 99 L.Ed.2d 23 (1988) held that, where the defense had commented during trial that the government had never allowed defendant to explain his position, the prosecutor was allowed to state that the defendant could have testified and given his explanation.

2. Prior to its decisions interpreting the Due Process clause of the Fourteenth Amendment as incorporating the requirements of the Fifth and Sixth Amendments, the Court read the Due Process clause as forbidding practices by state

and local police characterized as "revolting to the sense of justice," Brown v. United States, 297 U.S. 286, 56 S. Ct. 461, 80 L. Ed. 682 (1936). Thus, for example, Brown itself held that a confession procured by hanging and whipping a suspect until he admitted guilt could not be admitted at trial consistent with the requirements of due process. And Chambers v. Florida, 309 U.S. 227, 60 S. Ct. 472, 84 L. Ed. 716 (1940), held that the confession of a suspect held for five days without charge, in a room surrounded by guards, with the confession obtained after an all-night session of questioning in an atmosphere of mob violence must be seen as involuntary and therefore as inadmissable under the Due Process clause.

3. Of course, even if the Miranda warnings are given and a suspect agrees to answer questions anyway, subsequent police conduct could render a confession induced by that conduct involuntary. The cases described in the foregoing note therefore remain relevant. On the other hand, the court has upheld certain police tactics as not vitiating the voluntariness of confessions obtained after the Miranda warnings had been given. Thus, the Court upheld the admission of a confession in Frazier v. Cupp, 394 U.S. 731, 89 S. Ct. 1420, 22 L. Ed. 2d 684 (1969) where, after receiving the Miranda warnings, the suspect confessed after the police had stated falsely that an accomplice had confessed to the crime, and after further questioning following the police statement. The Court held that the confession could not be called involuntary, even in light of this false statement, in light of the totality of the circumstances, 394 U.S. at 739. Again, in Fare v. Michael C., 442 U.S. 725, 99 S. Ct. 2560, 61 L. Ed. 2d 197 (1979), the Court held that indications by police officers that it would be to the suspect's benefit to cooperate did not, in light of all the circumstances, render the suspect's confession involuntary, 442 U.S. at 727.

2. Right to Confront Witnesses

a. Michael D. Crawford, Petitioner v. Washington, 541 U.S. 36, 124 S.Ct. 1354, 158 L.Ed.2d 177 (2004)

Justice Scalia delivered the opinion of the Court.

Petitioner Michael Crawford stabbed a man who allegedly tried to rape his wife, Sylvia. At his trial, the State played for the jury Sylvia's tape-recorded statement to the police describing the stabbing, even though he had no opportunity for cross-examination. The Washington Supreme Court upheld petitioner's conviction after determining that Sylvia's statement was reliable. The question presented is whether this procedure complied with the Sixth Amendment's guarantee that, "[i]n all criminal prosecutions, the accused shall enjoy the right ... to be confronted with the witnesses against him."

I

On August 5, 1999, Kenneth Lee was stabbed at his apartment. Police arrested petitioner later that night. After giving petitioner and his wife Miranda warnings, detectives interrogated each of them twice. Petitioner eventually confessed that he and Sylvia had gone in search of Lee because he was upset over an earlier incident in which Lee had tried to rape her. The two had found Lee at his apartment, and a fight ensued in which Lee was stabbed in the torso and petitioner's hand was cut.

Petitioner gave the following account of the fight:

"Q. Okay. Did you ever see anything in [Lee's] hands?

"A. I think so, but I'm not positive.

"Q. Okay, when you think so, what do you mean by that?

"A. I coulda swore I seen him goin' for somethin' before, right before everything happened. He was like reachin', fiddlin' around down here and stuff ... and I just ... I don't know, I think, this is just a possibility, but I think, I think that he pulled somethin' out and I grabbed for it and that's how I got cut ... but I'm not positive. I, I, my mind goes blank when things like this happen. I mean, I just, I remember things wrong, I remember things that just doesn't, don't make sense to me later." App. 155 (punctuation added).

Sylvia generally corroborated petitioner's story about the events leading up to the fight, but her account of the fight itself was arguably different—particularly with respect to whether Lee had drawn a weapon before petitioner assaulted him:

"Q. Did Kenny do anything to fight back from this assault?

"A. (pausing) I know he reached into his pocket ... or somethin' ... I don't know what.

"Q. After he was stabbed?

"A. He saw Michael coming up. He lifted his hand ... his chest open, he might [have] went to go strike his hand out or something and then (inaudible).

"Q. Okay, you, you gotta speak up.

"A. Okay, he lifted his hand over his head maybe to strike Michael's hand down or something and then he put his hands in his ... put his right hand in his right pocket ... took a step back ... Michael proceeded to stab him ... then his hands were like ... how do you explain this ... open arms ... with his hands open and he fell down ... and we ran (describing subject holding hands open, palms toward assailant).

"Q. Okay, when he's standing there with his open hands, you're talking about Kenny, correct?

"A. Yeah, after, after the fact, yes.

"A. (pausing) um um (no)." Id., at 137 (punctuation added).

The State charged petitioner with assault and attempted murder. At trial, he claimed self-defense. Sylvia did not testify because of the state marital privilege, which generally bars a spouse from testifying without the other spouse's consent ... In Washington, this privilege does not extend to a spouse's out-of-court statements admissible under a hearsay exception, ... so the State sought to introduce Sylvia's tape-recorded statements to the police as evidence that the stabbing was not in self-defense. Noting that Sylvia had admitted she led petitioner to Lee's apartment and thus had facilitated the assault, the State invoked the hearsay exception for statements against penal interest, ...

Petitioner countered that, state law notwithstanding, admitting the evidence would violate his federal constitutional right to be "confronted with the witnesses against him." Amdt. 6. According to our description of that right in Ohio v. Roberts, 448 U.S. 56, 65 L.Ed.2d 597, 100 S.Ct. 2531 (1980), it does not bar admission of an unavailable witness's statement against a criminal defendant if the statement bears "adequate 'indicia of reliability.'" Id., at 66, 65 L.Ed.2d 597, 100 S.Ct. 2531. To meet that test, evidence must either fall within a "firmly rooted hearsay exception" or bear "particularized guarantees of trustworthiness." Ibid. The trial court here admitted the statement on the latter ground, offering several reasons why it was trustworthy: Sylvia was not shifting blame but rather corroborating her husband's story that he acted in self-defense or "justified reprisal"; she had direct knowledge as an eyewitness; she was describing recent events; and she was being questioned by a "neutral" law enforcement officer. App. 76-77. The prosecution played the tape for the jury and relied on it in closing, arguing that it was "damning evidence" that "completely refutes [petitioner's] claim of self-defense." Tr. 468 (Oct. 21, 1999). The jury convicted petitioner of assault.

The Washington Court of Appeals reversed. It applied a nine-factor test to determine whether Sylvia's statement bore particularized guarantees of trustworthiness, and noted several reasons why it did not: The statement contradicted one she had previously given; it was made in response to specific questions; and at one point she admitted she had shut her eyes during the stabbing. The court considered and rejected the State's argument that Sylvia's statement was reliable because it coincided with petitioner's to such a degree that the two "interlocked." The court determined that, although the two statements agreed about the events leading up to the stabbing, they differed on the issue crucial to petitioner's self-defense claim: "[Petitioner's] version asserts that Lee may have had something in his hand when he stabbed him; but Sylvia's version has Lee grabbing for something only after he has been stabbed." App. 32.

The Washington Supreme Court reinstated the conviction, unanimously concluding that, although Sylvia's statement did not fall under a firmly rooted hearsay exception, it bore guarantees of trustworthiness: "'[W]hen a codefendant's confession is virtually identical [to, i.e., interlocks with,] that of a defendant, it may be deemed reliable.'" 147 Wash. 2d 424, 437, 54 P. 3d 656, 663 (2002).... The court explained:

"Although the Court of Appeals concluded that the statements were contradictory, upon closer inspection they appear to overlap....

"[B]oth of the Crawfords' statements indicate that Lee was possibly grabbing for a weapon, but they are equally unsure when this event may have taken place. They are also equally unsure how Michael received the cut on his hand, leading the court to question when, if ever, Lee possessed a weapon. In this respect they overlap.

"[N]either Michael nor Sylvia clearly stated that Lee had a weapon in hand from which Michael was simply defending himself. And it is this omission by both that interlocks the statements and makes Sylvia's statement reliable." 147 Wash. 2d, at 438–439, 54 P. 3d, at 664 (internal quotation marks omitted).

We granted certiorari to determine whether the State's use of Sylvia's statement violated the Confrontation Clause. 540 U.S. 964, 157 L. Ed. 2d 309, 124 S. Ct. 460 (2003).

II

The Sixth Amendment's Confrontation Clause provides that, "[i]n all criminal prosecutions, the accused shall enjoy the right ... to be confronted with the witnesses against him." We have held that this bedrock procedural guarantee applies to both federal and state prosecutions. Pointer v. Texas, 380 U.S. 400, 406, 13 L. Ed. 2d 923, 85 S. Ct. 1065 (1965). As noted above, Roberts says that an unavailable witness's out-of-court statement may be admitted so long as it has adequate indicia of reliability—i.e., falls within a "firmly rooted hearsay exception" or bears "particularized guarantees of trustworthiness." 448 U.S., at 66, 13 L. Ed. 2d 923, 85 S. Ct. 1065. Petitioner argues that this test strays from the original meaning of the Confrontation Clause and urges us to reconsider it.

A

The Constitution's text does not alone resolve this case. One could plausibly read "witnesses against" a defendant to mean those who actually testify at trial, ... those whose statements are offered at trial, see 3 J. Wigmore, Evidence §1397, p 104 (2d ed. 1923) (hereinafter Wigmore), or something in-between, ... We must therefore turn to the historical background of the Clause to understand its meaning.

The right to confront one's accusers is a concept that dates back to Roman times. See Coy v. Iowa, 487 U.S. 1012, 1015, 101 L. Ed. 2d 857, 108 S. Ct. 2798 (1988); Herrmann & Speer, Facing the Accuser: Ancient and Medieval Precursors of the Confrontation Clause, 34 Va. J. Int'l L. 481 (1994). The founding generation's immediate source of the concept, however, was the common law. English common law has long differed from continental civil law in regard to the manner in which witnesses give testimony in criminal trials. The common-law tradition is one of live testimony in court subject to adversarial testing, while the civil law condones examination in private by judicial officers. See 3 W. Blackstone, Commentaries on the Laws of England 373–374 (1768).

Nonetheless, England at times adopted elements of the civil-law practice. Justices of the peace or other officials examined suspects and witnesses before trial. These examinations were sometimes read in court in lieu of live testimony, a practice that "occasioned frequent demands by the prisoner to have his 'accusers,' i.e. the witnesses against him, brought before him face to face." 1 J. Stephen, History of the Criminal Law of England 326 (1883). In some cases, these demands were refused. See 9 W. Holdsworth, History of English Law 216–217, 228 (3d ed. 1944) ...

Pretrial examinations became routine under two statutes passed during the reign of Queen Mary in the 16th century, 1 & 2 Phil. & M., c. 13 (1554), and 2 & 3 id., c. 10 (1555). These Marian bail and committal statutes required justices of the peace to examine suspects and witnesses in felony cases and to certify the results to the court. It is doubtful that the original purpose of the examinations was to produce evidence admissible at trial. See J. Langbein, Prosecuting Crime in the Renaissance 21–34 (1974). Whatever the original purpose, however, they came to be used as evidence in some cases, see 2 M. Hale, Pleas of the Crown 284 (1736), resulting in an adoption of continental procedure. See 4 Holdsworth, supra, at 528–530.

The most notorious instances of civil-law examination occurred in the great political trials of the 16th and 17th centuries. One such was the 1603 trial of Sir Walter Raleigh for treason. Lord Cobham, Raleigh's alleged accomplice, had implicated him in an examination before the Privy Council and in a letter. At Raleigh's trial, these were read to the jury. Raleigh argued that Cobham had lied to save himself: "Cobham is absolutely in the King's mercy; to excuse me cannot avail him; by accusing me he may hope for favour." 1 D. Jardine, Criminal Trials 435 (1832). Suspecting that Cobham would recant, Raleigh demanded that the judges call him to appear, arguing that "[t]he Proof of the Common Law is by witness and jury: let Cobham be here, let him speak it. Call my accuser before my face...." 2 How. St. Tr., at 15–16. The judges refused, id., at 24, and, despite Raleigh's protestations that he was being tried "by the Spanish Inquisition," id., at 15, the jury convicted, and Raleigh was sentenced to death.

One of Raleigh's trial judges later lamented that " 'the justice of England has never been so degraded and injured as by the condemnation of Sir Walter Raleigh.' " 1 Jardine, supra, at 520. Through a series of statutory and judicial reforms, English law developed a right of confrontation that limited these abuses. For example, treason statutes required witnesses to confront the accused "face to face" at his arraignment. E.g., 13 Car. 2, c. 1, §5 (1661); see 1 Hale, supra, at 306. Courts, meanwhile, developed relatively strict rules of unavailability, admitting examinations only if the witness was demonstrably unable to testify in person. See Lord Morley's Case, 6 How. St. Tr. 769, 770–771 (H. L. 1666); ... Several authorities also stated that a suspect's confession could be admitted only against himself, and not against others he implicated. See 2 W. Hawkins, Pleas of the Crown c. 46, §3, pp. 603–604 (T. Leach 6th ed. 1787); 1 Hale, supra, at 585, n (k); ...

One recurring question was whether the admissibility of an unavailable witness's pretrial examination depended on whether the defendant had had an opportunity to cross-examine him. In 1696, the Court of King's Bench answered this question in the affirmative, in the widely reported misdemeanor libel case of King v Paine, 5 Mod. 163, 87 Eng. Rep. 584. The court ruled that, even though a witness was dead, his examination was not admissible where "the defendant not being present when [it was] taken before the mayor ... had lost the benefit of a cross-examination." Id., at 165, 87 Eng. Rep., at 585. The question was also debated at length during the infamous proceedings against Sir John Fenwick on a bill of attainder. Fenwick's counsel objected to admitting the examination of a witness who had been spirited away, on the ground that Fenwick had had no opportunity to cross-examine. See Fenwick's Case, 13 How. St. Tr. 537, 591–592 (H. C. 1696) (Powys) ("[T]hat which they would offer is something that Mr. Goodman hath sworn when he was examined ... ; sir J. F. not being present or privy, and no opportunity given to cross-examine the person; and I conceive that cannot be offered as evidence ..."); id., at 592 (Shower) ("[N]o deposition of a person can be read, though beyond sea, unless in cases where the party it is to be read against was privy to the examination, and might have cross-examined him.... [O]ur constitution is, that the person shall see his accuser"). The examination was nonetheless admitted on a closely divided vote after several of those present opined that the common-law rules of procedure did not apply to parliamentary attainder proceedings—one speaker even admitting that the evidence would normally be inadmissible. See id., at 603–604 (Williamson); id., at 604–605 (Chancellor of the Exchequer); id., at 607; 3 Wigmore §1364, at 22–23, n 54. Fenwick was condemned, but the proceedings "must have burned into the general consciousness the vital importance of the rule securing the right of cross-examination." Id., §1364, at 22; cf. Carmell v. Texas, 529 U.S. 513, 526–530, 146 L. Ed. 2d 577, 120 S. Ct. 1620 (2000).

Paine had settled the rule requiring a prior opportunity for cross-examination as a matter of common law, but some doubts remained over whether the Marian statutes prescribed an exception to it in felony cases. The statutes did not identify the circumstances under which examinations were admissible, see 1 & 2 Phil. & M., c. 13 (1554); 2 & 3 id., c. 10 (1555), and some inferred that no prior opportunity for cross-examination was required.... Many who expressed this view acknowledged that it meant the statutes were in derogation of the common law....

Nevertheless, by 1791 (the year the Sixth Amendment was ratified), courts were applying the cross-examination rule even to examinations by justices of the peace in felony cases.... Early 19th-century treatises confirm that requirement.... When Parliament amended the statutes in 1848 to make the requirement explicit, see 11 & 12 Vict., c. 42, §17, the change merely "introduced in terms" what was already afforded the defendant "by the equitable construction of the law." Queen v Beeston, 29 Eng. L. & Eq. R. 527, 529 (Ct. Crim. App. 1854) (Jervis, C. J.).

B

Controversial examination practices were also used in the Colonies. Early in the 18th century, for example, the Virginia Council protested against the Governor for having "privately issued several commissions to examine witnesses against particular men ex parte," complaining that "the person accused is not admitted to be confronted with, or defend himself against his defamers." A Memorial Concerning the Maladministrations of His Excellency Francis Nicholson, reprinted in 9 English Historical Documents 253, 257 (D. Douglas ed. 1955). A decade before the Revolution, England gave jurisdiction over Stamp Act offenses to the admiralty courts, which followed civil-law rather than common-law procedures and thus routinely took testimony by deposition or private judicial examination. See 5 Geo. 3, c. 12, §57 (1765); Pollitt, The Right of Confrontation: Its History and Modern Dress, 8 J. Pub. L. 381, 396–397 (1959). Colonial representatives protested that the Act subverted their rights "by extending the jurisdiction of the courts of admiralty beyond its ancient limits" Resolutions of the Stamp Act Congress §8th (Oct. 19, 1765), reprinted in Sources of Our Liberties 270, 271 (R. Perry & J. Cooper eds. 1959). John Adams, defending a merchant in a high-profile admiralty case, argued: "Examinations of witnesses upon Interrogatories, are only by the Civil Law. Interrogatories are unknown at common Law, and Englishmen and common Lawyers have an aversion to them if not an Abhorrence of them." Draft of Argument in Sewall v. Hancock (1768–1769), in 2 Legal Papers of John Adams 194, 207 (K. Wroth & H. Zobel eds. 1965).

Many declarations of rights adopted around the time of the Revolution guaranteed a right of confrontation. See ... 1 B. Schwartz, The Bill of Rights: A Documentary History 235, 265, 278, 282, 287, 323, 342, 377 (1971). The proposed Federal Constitution, however, did not. At the Massachusetts ratifying convention, Abraham Holmes objected to this omission precisely on the ground that it would lead to civil-law practices: "The mode of trial is altogether indetermined; ... whether [the defendant] is to be allowed to confront the witnesses, and have the advantage of cross-examination, we are not yet told.... [W]e shall find Congress possessed of powers enabling them to institute judicatories little less inauspicious than a certain tribunal in Spain, ... the Inquisition." 2 Debates on the Federal Constitution 110–111 (J. Elliot 2d ed. 1863). Similarly, a prominent Antifederalist writing under the pseudonym Federal Farmer criticized the use of "written evidence" while objecting to the omission of a vicinage right: "Nothing can be more essential than the cross examining [of] witnesses, and generally before the triers of the facts in question.... [W]ritten evidence ... [is] almost useless; it must be frequently taken ex parte, and but very seldom leads to the proper discovery of truth." R. Lee, Letter IV by the Federal Farmer (Oct. 15, 1787), reprinted in 1 Schwartz, supra, at 469, 473. The First Congress responded by including the Confrontation Clause in the proposal that became the Sixth Amendment.

Early state decisions shed light upon the original understanding of the common-law right. State v. Webb, 2 N. C. 103 (1794) (per curiam), decided a mere three years after the adoption of the Sixth Amendment, held that depositions could be read against an accused only if they were taken in his presence. Rejecting a broader reading of the English authorities, the court held: "[I]t is a rule of the common law, founded on natural justice, that no man shall be prejudiced by evidence which he had not the liberty to cross examine." Id., at 104.

Similarly, in State v. Campbell, 30 S.C.L. 124 (1844), South Carolina's highest law court excluded a deposition taken by a coroner in the absence of the accused. It held: "[I]f we are to decide the question by the established rules of the common law, there could not be a dissenting voice. For, notwithstanding the death of the witness, and whatever the respectability of the court taking the depositions, the solemnity of the occasion and the weight of the testimony, such depositions are ex parte, and, therefore, utterly incompetent." Id., at 125. The court said that one of the "indispensable conditions" implicitly guaranteed by the State Constitution was that "prosecutions be carried on to the conviction of the accused, by witnesses confronted by him, and subjected to his personal examination." Ibid.

Many other decisions are to the same effect. Some early cases went so far as to hold that prior testimony was inadmissible in criminal cases even if the accused had a previous opportunity to cross-examine.... Most courts rejected that view, but only after reaffirming that admissibility depended on a prior opportunity for cross-examination.... Nineteenth-century treatises confirm the rule ...

III

This history supports two inferences about the meaning of the Sixth Amendment.

A

First, the principal evil at which the Confrontation Clause was directed was the civil-law mode of criminal procedure, and particularly its use of ex parte examinations as evidence against the accused. It was these practices that the Crown deployed in notorious treason cases like Raleigh's; that the Marian statutes invited; that English law's assertion of a right to confrontation was meant to prohibit; and that the founding-era rhetoric decried. The Sixth Amendment must be interpreted with this focus in mind.

Accordingly, we once again reject the view that the Confrontation Clause applies of its own force only to in-court testimony, and that its application to out-of-court statements introduced at trial depends upon "the law of Evidence for the time being." 3 Wigmore § 1397, at 101; accord, Dutton v. Evans, 400 U.S. 74, 94, 27 L. Ed. 2d 213, 91 S. Ct. 210 (1970) (Harlan, J., concurring in result). Leaving the regulation of out-of-court statements to the law of evidence would render the Confrontation Clause powerless to prevent even the most flagrant inquisitorial practices. Raleigh was, after all, perfectly free to confront those who read Cobham's confession in court.

This focus also suggests that not all hearsay implicates the Sixth Amendment's core concerns. An off-hand, overheard remark might be unreliable evidence and thus a good candidate for exclusion under hearsay rules, but it bears little resemblance to the civil-law abuses the Confrontation Clause targeted. On the other hand, ex parte examinations might sometimes be admissible under modern hearsay rules, but the Framers certainly would not have condoned them.

The text of the Confrontation Clause reflects this focus. It applies to "witnesses" against the accused—in other words, those who "bear testimony." 1 N. Webster, An American Dictionary of the English Language (1828). "Testimony," in turn, is typically "[a] solemn declaration or affirmation made for the purpose of establishing or proving some fact." Ibid. An accuser who makes a formal statement to government officers bears testimony in a sense that a person who makes a casual remark to an acquaintance does not. The constitutional text, like the history underlying the common-law right of confrontation, thus reflects an especially acute concern with a specific type of out-of-court statement.

Various formulations of this core class of "testimonial" statements exist: "ex parte in-court testimony or its functional equivalent—that is, material such as affidavits, custodial examinations, prior testimony that the defendant was unable to cross-examine, or similar pretrial statements that declarants would reasonably expect to be used prosecutorially," Brief for Petitioner 23; "extrajudicial statements ... contained in formalized testimonial materials, such as affidavits, depositions, prior testimony, or confessions," White v. Illinois, 502 U.S. 346, 365, 116 L. Ed. 2d 848, 112 S. Ct. 736 (1992) (Thomas, J., joined by Scalia, J., concurring in part and concurring in judgment); "statements that were made under circumstances which would lead an objective witness reasonably to believe that the statement would be available for use at a later trial," Brief for National Association of Criminal Defense Lawyers et al. as Amici Curiae 3. These formulations all share a common nucleus and then define the Clause's coverage at various levels of abstraction around it. Regardless of the precise articulation, some statements qualify under any definition—for example, ex parte testimony at a preliminary hearing.

Statements taken by police officers in the course of interrogations are also testimonial under even a narrow standard. Police interrogations bear a striking resemblance to examinations by justices of the peace in England. The statements are not sworn testimony, but the absence of oath was not dispositive. Cobham's examination was unsworn, see 1 Jardine, Criminal Trials, at 430, yet Raleigh's trial has long been thought a paradigmatic confrontation violation, see, e.g., Campbell, 30 S.C.L., at 130. Under the Marian statutes, witnesses were typically put on oath, but suspects were not. See 2 Hale, Pleas of the Crown, at 52. Yet Hawkins and others went out of their way to caution that such unsworn confessions were not admissible against anyone but the confessor. See supra, at 45, 158 L.Ed. 2d, at 189.

That interrogators are police officers rather than magistrates does not change the picture either. Justices of the peace conducting examinations under the Marian statutes were not magistrates as we understand that office today, but had an essentially investigative and prosecutorial function. See 1 Stephen, Criminal Law of England, at 221; Langbein, Prosecuting Crime in the Renaissance, at 34–45. England did not have a professional police force until the 19th century, see 1 Stephen, supra, at 194–200, so it is not surprising that other government officers performed the investigative functions now associated primarily with the police. The involvement of government officers in the production of testimonial evidence presents the same risk, whether the officers are police or justices of the peace.

In sum, even if the Sixth Amendment is not solely concerned with testimonial hearsay, that is its primary object, and interrogations by law enforcement officers fall squarely within that class.

B

The historical record also supports a second proposition: that the Framers would not have allowed admission of testimonial statements of a witness who did not appear at trial unless he was unavailable to testify, and the defendant had had a prior opportunity for cross-examination. The text of the Sixth Amendment does not suggest any open-ended exceptions from the confrontation requirement to be developed by the courts. Rather, the "right ... to be confronted with the witnesses against him," Amdt. 6, is most naturally read as a reference to the right of confrontation at common law, admitting only those exceptions established at the time of the founding. See Mattox v. United States, 156 U.S. 237, 243, 39 L. Ed. 409, 15 S. Ct. 337 (1895); .... As the English authorities above reveal, the common law in 1791 conditioned admissibility of an absent witness's examination on unavailability and a prior opportunity to cross-examine. The Sixth Amendment therefore incorporates those limitations. The numerous early state decisions applying the same test confirm that these principles were received as part of the common law in this country.

We do not read the historical sources to say that a prior opportunity to cross-examine was merely a sufficient, rather than a necessary, condition for admissibility of testimonial statements. They suggest that this requirement was dispositive, and not merely one of several ways to establish reliability. This is not to deny, as the Chief Justice notes, that "[t]here were always exceptions to the general rule of exclusion" of hearsay evidence. Post, at 73, 158 L. Ed. 2d, at 206. Several had become well established by 1791. See 3 Wigmore § 1397, at 101; Brief for United States as Amicus Curiae 13, n 5. But there is scant evidence that exceptions were invoked to admit testimonial statements against the accused in a criminal case. Most of the hearsay exceptions covered statements that by their nature were not testimonial—for example, business records or statements in furtherance of a conspiracy. We do not infer from these that the Framers thought exceptions would apply even to prior testimony. Cf. Lilly v. Virginia, 527 U.S. 116, 134, 144 L. Ed. 2d 117, 119 S. Ct. 1887 (1999) (plurality opinion) ("[A]ccomplices' confessions that inculpate a criminal defendant are not within a firmly rooted exception to the hearsay rule").

IV

Our case law has been largely consistent with these two principles. Our leading early decision, for example, involved a deceased witness's prior trial testimony. Mattox v. United States, 156 U.S. 237, 39 L. Ed. 409, 15 S. Ct. 337 (1895). In allowing the statement to be admitted, we relied on the fact that the defendant had had, at the first trial, an adequate opportunity to confront the witness: "The substance of the constitutional protection is preserved to the prisoner in the advantage he has once had of seeing the witness face to face, and of subjecting him to the ordeal of a cross-examination. This, the law says, he shall under no circumstances be deprived of...." Id., at 244, 39 L. Ed. 409, 15 S. Ct. 337.

Our later cases conform to Mattox's holding that prior trial or preliminary hearing testimony is admissible only if the defendant had an adequate opportunity to cross-examine.... Even where the defendant had such an opportunity, we excluded the testimony where the government had not established unavailability of the witness.... We similarly excluded accomplice confessions where the defendant had no opportunity to cross-examine.... In contrast, we considered reliability factors beyond prior opportunity for cross-examination when the hearsay statement at issue was not testimonial....

Even our recent cases, in their outcomes, hew closely to the traditional line. Ohio v. Roberts, 448 U.S., at 67–70, 65 L. Ed. 2d 597, 100 S. Ct. 2531, admitted testimony from a preliminary hearing at which the defendant had examined the witness. Lilly v Virginia, supra, excluded testimonial statements that the defendant had had no opportunity to test by cross-examination. And Bourjaily v. United States, 483 U.S. 171, 181–184, 97 L. Ed. 2d 144, 107 S. Ct. 2775 (1987), admitted statements made unwittingly to an FBI informant after applying a more general test that did not make prior cross-examination an indispensable requirement.[1]

Lee v. Illinois, 476 U.S. 530, 90 L. Ed. 2d 514, 106 S. Ct. 2056 (1986), on which the State relies, is not to the contrary. There, we rejected the State's attempt to admit an accomplice confession. The State had argued that the confession was admissible because it "interlocked" with the defendant's. We dealt with the argument by rejecting its premise, holding that "when the discrepancies between the statements are not insignificant, the codefendant's confession may not be admitted." Id., at 545, 90 L. Ed. 2d 514, 106 S. Ct. 2056. Respondent argues that "[t]he logical inference of this statement is that when the discrepancies between the statements are insignificant, then the codefendant's statement may be admitted." Brief for Respondent 6. But this is merely a possible inference, not an inevitable one, and we do not draw it here. If Lee had meant authoritatively to announce an exception—previously unknown to this Court's jurisprudence—for interlocking confessions, it would not have done so in such an oblique manner. Our only precedent on interlocking confessions had addressed the entirely different question whether a limiting instruction cured prejudice to codefendants from admitting a defendant's own confession against him in a joint trial. See Parker v. Randolph, 442 U.S. 62, 69–76, 60 L. Ed. 2d 713, 99 S. Ct. 2132 (1979) (plurality opinion), abrogated by Cruz v. New York, 481 U.S. 186, 95 L. Ed. 2d 162, 107 S. Ct. 1714 (1987).

Our cases have thus remained faithful to the Framers' understanding: statements of witnesses absent from trial have been admitted only where the declarant is unavailable, and only where the defendant has had a prior opportunity to cross-examine.

---

1. One case arguably in tension with the rule requiring a prior opportunity for cross-examination when the proffered statement is testimonial is White v. Illinois, 502 U.S. 346, 116 L. Ed. 2d 848, 112 S. Ct. 736 (1992), which involved, inter alia, statements of a child victim to an investigating police officer admitted as spontaneous declarations. Id., at 349–35, 1116 L. Ed. 2d 848, 112 S. Ct. 736. It is questionable whether testimonial statements would ever have been admissible on that ground in 1791; to the extent the hearsay exception for spontaneous declarations existed at all, it required that the statements be made "immediat[ely] upon the hurt received, and before [the declarant] had time to devise or contrive any thing for her own advantage." Thompson v Trevanion, Skin. 402, 90 Eng. Rep. 179 (K. B. 1694). In any case, the only question presented in White was whether the Confrontation Clause imposed an unavailability requirement on the types of hearsay at issue. See 502 U.S., at 348–349, 116 L. Ed. 2d 848, 112 S. Ct. 736. The holding did not address the question whether certain of the statements, because they were testimonial, had to be excluded even if the witness was unavailable. We "[took] as a given ... that the testimony properly falls within the relevant hearsay exceptions." Id., at 351, n. 4, 116 L. Ed. 2d 848, 112 S. Ct. 736.

V

Although the results of our decisions have generally been faithful to the original meaning of the Confrontation Clause, the same cannot be said of our rationales. Roberts conditions the admissibility of all hearsay evidence on whether it falls under a "firmly rooted hearsay exception" or bears "particularized guarantees of trustworthiness." 448 U.S., at 66, 65 L. Ed. 2d 597, 100 S. Ct. 2531. This test departs from the historical principles identified above in two respects. First, it is too broad: It applies the same mode of analysis whether or not the hearsay consists of ex parte testimony. This often results in close constitutional scrutiny in cases that are far removed from the core concerns of the Clause. At the same time, however, the test is too narrow: It admits statements that do consist of ex parte testimony upon a mere finding of reliability. This malleable standard often fails to protect against paradigmatic confrontation violations.

Members of this Court and academics have suggested that we revise our doctrine to reflect more accurately the original understanding of the Clause.... They offer two proposals: First, that we apply the Confrontation Clause only to testimonial statements, leaving the remainder to regulation by hearsay law — thus eliminating the overbreadth referred to above. Second, that we impose an absolute bar to statements that are testimonial, absent a prior opportunity to cross-examine — thus eliminating the excessive narrowness referred to above.

In White, we considered the first proposal and rejected it. 502 U.S., at 352–353, 116 L. Ed. 2d 848, 112 S. Ct. 736. Although our analysis in this case casts doubt on that holding, we need not definitively resolve whether it survives our decision today, because Sylvia Crawford's statement is testimonial under any definition. This case does, however, squarely implicate the second proposal.

A

Where testimonial statements are involved, we do not think the Framers meant to leave the Sixth Amendment's protection to the vagaries of the rules of evidence, much less to amorphous notions of "reliability." Certainly none of the authorities discussed above acknowledges any general reliability exception to the common-law rule. Admitting statements deemed reliable by a judge is fundamentally at odds with the right of confrontation. To be sure, the Clause's ultimate goal is to ensure reliability of evidence, but it is a procedural rather than a substantive guarantee. It commands, not that evidence be reliable, but that reliability be assessed in a particular manner: by testing in the crucible of cross-examination. The Clause thus reflects a judgment, not only about the desirability of reliable evidence (a point on which there could be little dissent), but about how reliability can best be determined. Cf. 3 Blackstone, Commentaries, at 373 ("This open examination of witnesses ... is much more conducive to the clearing up of truth"); M. Hale, History and Analysis of the

Common Law of England 258 (1713) (adversarial testing "beats and bolts out the Truth much better").

The Roberts test allows a jury to hear evidence, untested by the adversary process, based on a mere judicial determination of reliability. It thus replaces the constitutionally prescribed method of assessing reliability with a wholly foreign one. In this respect, it is very different from exceptions to the Confrontation Clause that make no claim to be a surrogate means of assessing reliability. For example, the rule of forfeiture by wrongdoing (which we accept) extinguishes confrontation claims on essentially equitable grounds; it does not purport to be an alternative means of determining reliability. See Reynolds v. United States, 98 U.S. 145, 158–159, 25 L. Ed. 244 (1879).

The Raleigh trial itself involved the very sorts of reliability determinations that Roberts authorizes. In the face of Raleigh's repeated demands for confrontation, the prosecution responded with many of the arguments a court applying Roberts might invoke today: that Cobham's statements were self-inculpatory, 2 How. St. Tr., at 19, that they were not made in the heat of passion, id., at 14, and that they were not "extracted from [him] upon any hopes or promise of Pardon," id., at 29. It is not plausible that the Framers' only objection to the trial was that Raleigh's judges did not properly weigh these factors before sentencing him to death. Rather, the problem was that the judges refused to allow Raleigh to confront Cobham in court, where he could cross-examine him and try to expose his accusation as a lie.

Dispensing with confrontation because testimony is obviously reliable is akin to dispensing with jury trial because a defendant is obviously guilty. This is not what the Sixth Amendment prescribes.

B

The legacy of Roberts in other courts vindicates the Framers' wisdom in rejecting a general reliability exception. The framework is so unpredictable that it fails to provide meaningful protection from even core confrontation violations.

Reliability is an amorphous, if not entirely subjective, concept. There are countless factors bearing on whether a statement is reliable; the nine-factor balancing test applied by the Court of Appeals below is representative. See, e.g., People v. Farrell, 34 P. 3d 401, 406–407 (Colo. 2001) (eight-factor test). Whether a statement is deemed reliable depends heavily on which factors the judge considers and how much weight he accords each of them. Some courts wind up attaching the same significance to opposite facts. For example, the Colorado Supreme Court held a statement more reliable because its inculpation of the defendant was "detailed," id., at 407, while the Fourth Circuit found a statement more reliable because the portion implicating another was "fleeting," United States v. Photogrammetric Data Servs., Inc., 259 F.3d 229, 245

(2001). The Virginia Court of Appeals found a statement more reliable because the witness was in custody and charged with a crime (thus making the statement more obviously against her penal interest), see Nowlin v. Commonwealth, 40 Va. App. 327, 335–338, 579 S. E. 2d 367, 371–372 (2003), while the Wisconsin Court of Appeals found a statement more reliable because the witness was not in custody and not a suspect, see State v. Bintz, 2002 WI App. 204, P13, 257 Wis. 2d 177, 187, 650 N.W.2d 913, 918. Finally, the Colorado Supreme Court in one case found a statement more reliable because it was given "immediately after" the events at issue, Farrell, supra, at 407, while that same court, in another case, found a statement more reliable because two years had elapsed, Stevens v. People, 29 P. 3d 305, 316 (2001).

The unpardonable vice of the Roberts test, however, is not its unpredictability, but its demonstrated capacity to admit core testimonial statements that the Confrontation Clause plainly meant to exclude. Despite the plurality's speculation in Lilly, 527 U.S., at 137, 144 L. Ed. 2d 117, 119 S. Ct. 1887, that it was "highly unlikely" that accomplice confessions implicating the accused could survive Roberts, courts continue routinely to admit them.... One recent study found that, after Lilly, appellate courts admitted accomplice statements to the authorities in 25 out of 70 cases—more than one-third of the time. Kirst, Appellate Court Answers to the Confrontation Questions in Lilly v. Virginia, 53 Syracuse L. Rev. 87, 105 (2003). Courts have invoked Roberts to admit other sorts of plainly testimonial statements despite the absence of any opportunity to cross-examine....

To add insult to injury, some of the courts that admit untested testimonial statements find reliability in the very factors that make the statements testimonial. As noted earlier, one court relied on the fact that the witness's statement was made to police while in custody on pending charges—the theory being that this made the statement more clearly against penal interest and thus more reliable. Nowlin, supra, at 335–338, 579 S. E. 2d, at 371–372. Other courts routinely rely on the fact that a prior statement is given under oath in judicial proceedings.... That inculpating statements are given in a testimonial setting is not an antidote to the confrontation problem, but rather the trigger that makes the Clause's demands most urgent. It is not enough to point out that most of the usual safeguards of the adversary process attend the statement, when the single safeguard missing is the one the Confrontation Clause demands.

C

Roberts' failings were on full display in the proceedings below. Sylvia Crawford made her statement while in police custody, herself a potential suspect in the case. Indeed, she had been told that whether she would be released "depend[ed] on how the investigation continues." App. 81. In response to often leading questions from police detectives, she implicated her husband in Lee's stabbing and at least arguably undermined his self-defense claim. Despite all this, the trial court admitted her statement, listing several reasons why it was reliable. In its opinion reversing, the Court of Appeals listed several other reasons why the statement was not reliable. Finally, the State Supreme Court relied exclusively on the interlocking character of the statement and disregarded every other factor the lower courts had considered. The case is thus a self-contained demonstration of Roberts' unpredictable and inconsistent application.

Each of the courts also made assumptions that cross-examination might well have undermined. The trial court, for example, stated that Sylvia Crawford's statement was reliable because she was an eyewitness with direct knowledge of the events. But Sylvia at one point told the police that she had "shut [her] eyes and ... didn't really watch" part of the fight, and that she was "in shock." App. 134. The trial court also buttressed its reliability finding by claiming that Sylvia was "being questioned by law enforcement, and, thus, the [questioner] is ... neutral to her and not someone who would be inclined to advance her interests and shade her version of the truth unfavorably toward the defendant." Id., at 77. The Framers would be astounded to learn that ex parte testimony could be admitted against a criminal defendant because it was elicited by "neutral" government officers. But even if the court's assessment of the officer's motives was accurate, it says nothing about Sylvia's perception of her situation. Only cross-examination could reveal that.

The State Supreme Court gave dispositive weight to the interlocking nature of the two statements—that they were both ambiguous as to when and whether Lee had a weapon. The court's claim that the two statements were equally ambiguous is hard to accept. Petitioner's statement is ambiguous only in the sense that he had lingering doubts about his recollection: "A. I coulda swore I seen him goin' for somethin' before, right before everything happened.... [B]ut I'm not positive." Id., at 155. Sylvia's statement, on the other hand, is truly inscrutable, since the key timing detail was simply assumed in the leading question she was asked: "Q. Did Kenny do anything to fight back from this assault?" Id., at 137. Moreover, Sylvia specifically said Lee had nothing in his hands after he was stabbed, while petitioner was not asked about that.

The prosecutor obviously did not share the court's view that Sylvia's statement was ambiguous—he called it "damning evidence" that "completely refutes [petitioner's] claim of self-defense." Tr. 468 (Oct. 21, 1999). We have no way of knowing whether the jury agreed with the prosecutor or the court. Far from obviating the need for cross-examination, the "interlocking" ambiguity of the two statements made it all the more imperative that they be tested to tease out the truth.

We readily concede that we could resolve this case by simply reweighing the "reliability factors" under Roberts and finding that Sylvia Crawford's statement falls short. But we view this as one of those rare cases in which the result below is so improbable that it reveals a fundamental failure on our part to interpret the Constitution in a way that secures its intended constraint on judicial discretion. Moreover, to reverse the Washington Supreme Court's decision after conducting ou own reliability analysis would perpetuate, not avoid, what the Sixth Amendment condemns. The Constitution prescribes a procedure for determining the reliability of testimony in criminal trials, and we, no less than the state courts, lack authority to replace it with one of our own devising.

We have no doubt that the courts below were acting in utmost good faith when they found reliability. The Framers, however, would not have been content to indulge this assumption. They knew that judges, like other government officers, could not always be trusted to safeguard the rights of the people; the likes of the dread Lord Jeffreys were not yet too distant a memory. They were loath to leave too much discretion in judicial hands. Cf. U.S. Const., Amdt. 6 (criminal jury trial); Amdt. 7 (civil jury trial); Ring v. Arizona, 536 U.S. 584, 611–612, 153 L. Ed. 2d 556, 122 S. Ct. 2428 (2002) (Scalia, J., concurring). By replacing categorical constitutional guarantees with open-ended balancing tests, we do violence to their design. Vague standards are manipulable, and, while that might be a small concern in run-of-the-mill assault prosecutions like this one, the Framers had an eye toward politically charged cases like Raleigh's—great state trials where the impartiality of even those at the highest levels of the judiciary might not be so clear. It is difficult to imagine Roberts' providing any meaningful protection in those circumstances.

* * *

Where nontestimonial hearsay is at issue, it is wholly consistent with the Framers' design to afford the States flexibility in their development of hearsay law—as does Roberts, and as would an approach that exempted such statements from Confrontation Clause scrutiny altogether. Where testimonial evidence is at issue, however, the Sixth Amendment demands what the common law required: unavailability and a prior opportunity for cross-examination. We leave for another day any effort to spell out a comprehensive definition of "testimonial." Whatever else the term covers, it applies at a minimum to prior testimony at a preliminary hearing, before a grand jury, or at a former trial; and to police interrogations. These are the modern practices with closest kinship to the abuses at which the Confrontation Clause was directed.

In this case, the State admitted Sylvia's testimonial statement against petitioner, despite the fact that he had no opportunity to cross-examine her. That alone is sufficient to make out a violation of the Sixth Amendment. Roberts notwithstanding, we decline to mine the record in search of indicia of reliability. Where testimonial statements are at issue, the only indicium of reliability sufficient to satisfy constitutional demands is the one the Constitution actually prescribes: confrontation.

The judgment of the Washington Supreme Court is reversed, and the case is remanded for further proceedings not inconsistent with this opinion.

It is so ordered.

(concurring opinion omitted)

Chapter Four

Capital Punishment

A. Japan

1. Judgment upon the Case Concerning That an Appeals Court Judgment That Maintained the Sentence of Life Imprisonment in the First Instance Court Judgment Was Quashed Because the Sentence Period Was Considered Inappropriate; Keishu Vol.53, No.9, at 1160; Case Number: 1997 (A) No.479 (Second Petty Bench, December 10, 1999)

References: Article 411 of the Code of Criminal Procedure; Articles 11 and 240 of the Penal Code

Main text of the judgment:

The portion regarding the defendant in the second instance court judgment shall be quashed

...

Reasons:

...

1. This case is a matter wherein the defendant, who was given a sentence of life imprisonment for the crime of burglary and murder, committed burglary and murder, forgery of private sealed documents, act of forgery, and fraud while on parole. That is, the defendant conspired with defendant B, who was a colleague from his former workplace, and planned to murder C, who he knew (who was then 87 years old), and steal money and goods, and manipulated the woman and took her into the mountains, gave her a forceful blow to the back

of her head with a rock and made her lose consciousness, tied a vinyl rope, which he had ready, around her neck and bound her and strangled her, stole her Japanese bank passbook and other items, and returned to her [home] to search for money and goods (first instance court judgment, decision one, burglary and murder), and furthermore the defendant alone acted or conspired with a female acquaintance to defraud and withdraw almost 310,000 yen in cash in about three transactions from, among others, banks by using this Japanese bank passbook (private sealed documents, act of forgery, and fraud in 1 to 3 under no. 2 of this judgment).

2. The second instance court decision rendered the following judgment on the weight of the sentence upon the defendant.

> With respect to the burglary and murder in this case, there were no extenuating circumstances in his motives, and the developments that led to the murder were premeditated and malicious, and the manner of the murder was cold-blooded and brutal, and this court cannot not find the result of these developments to be tragic, and the second son of the victim, who is the deceased's family, has requested the maximum sentence be given to the defendant, and the impact of this case upon society is major. The defendant was given a sentence of life imprisonment for the crime of burglary and murder, and committed all of these crimes while out on parole from this sentence, and played the primary role in the crime of the burglary and murder in this case, and also after these crimes the defendant committed the crime of, among others, fraud in this case, and in light of the fact that the defendant continued to live a degenerate life, this court finds that the criminal and anti-society nature of this defendant are clear. Summarizing the above points, the crimes were very malicious, and the Defendant is fully responsible for the crimes, and there is justified reason for the prosecutor to opine that the defendant should be given the maximum sentence, however, ... this court can endorse the weight of the sentence in this judgment that rendered the defendant a [sentence of] life in prison.

3. Of the reasons in the First Instance court judgment as reasons not to elect the death penalty, the three following points were considered and endorsed by the second instance court. Firstly, the burglary and murder in this case was premeditated, however, the defendant made decisions to commit the crimes consecutively as he considered the situation of the victim, and search for a location to commit the crime by trial and error, and therefore there was little premeditation to commit these crimes by the defendant. Secondly, the defendant confessed to the crimes immediately after the arrest, and himself realized afterwards at all times his full responsibility for the crimes, and is prepared to receive the maximum sentence, and when this court considers the fact that his

behavior while he served the previous sentence was respectable and he was allowed a relatively early parole, this court cannot absolutely state that the defendant cannot be reformed or rehabilitated. Thirdly, in the cases decided in the
past ten years, all defendants who were given a sentence of life imprisonment
and committed a burglary and murder while out on parole were all given the
sentence of the death penalty, however, when this case is compared to these
other cases, the extenuating circumstances of the defendant are greater since
the crimes were not as malicious, with respect to the brutality and tenacity of
the method of murder and criminal history.

4. The death penalty is the maximum and most severe sentence available, and
there is no question that the court must apply this penalty carefully. However,
as indicated by a precedent … under the current law and regulation on the system of the death penalty, upon review by the court of the maliciousness, moti-
vation, and type of crime, particularly the brutality and tenacity of the method
of murder, and the seriousness of the result, particularly the number of victims murdered, pain and suffering upon the deceased's family, impact on society, age of the criminal, criminal history, and all extenuating circumstances,
such as those after the crime, if the court finds the responsibility for the crimes
to be full, and finds the maximum sentence is unavoidable from a prevention
viewpoint and balanced viewpoint regarding crimes, the court shall have no
option but to elect the death penalty.

(Summary) When this is considered in this case, as described above, the burglary and murder in this case was a case wherein an elderly woman was taken
away from her home and strangled in the mountains, and her money and
goods were stolen. The nature of the crime committed and results are very
serious, and the victimization of the deceased's family is serious, and this
court cannot ignore the impact this crime had on society. The motive of the
defendant to commit this crime was the defendant's Pachinko habit, which
led to him borrowing money from loan sharks, having difficulty making repayments, and seeking a solution. There is no area for the court to show
sympathy. The method of murder was the defendant gave a blow to the head
of the victim with a rock and made her lose consciousness, he then tied a
vinyl string to her neck and the two big men each pulled an end of the string
at full force and strangled her, and the dead body was thrown from over a
cliff and left there to hide traces of the crime, and when these points are also
considered, the court must acknowledge that this crime was brutal and cold-
blooded. With respect to the relationship of the defendant to defendant B,
the defendant played a lead role from the start to the finish in all of the actions and the burglary and murder plan, and the defendant later used the
Japanese bank passbook to commit the crime of fraud in this case. Furthermore, after committing the crime of the burglary and murder in this case,
the defendant prevented B from his wish to surrender to the police, and con-

tinued his lifestyle of Pachinko addiction without holding down a serious job, therefore the extenuating circumstances after the crime were not satisfactory to the court. Furthermore, the defendant was carrying out his sentence of life imprisonment for the crime of burglary and murder, and was released on parole when he again committed burglary and murder, and the court considers this point to be nothing but a very malicious act. In particular, in the prior burglary and murder, the defendant came to have great difficulty with the repayments on loans accumulated from car races, and threatened a housewife who he was friendly with in the neighborhood with a kitchen knife ... and stole cash, and he then murdered this woman whom he knew and covered his criminal acts and decided to run, and with respect to the point that the defendant took advantage of the relationship and got close to the women he knew to repay the loans from his gambling and committed the crime in a premeditated manner, the court finds significant similarity to his earlier crimes. Therefore, the court must find that the criminal and anti-society nature of the defendant who committed the burglary and murder in this case while out on parole for the prior matter cannot be looked upon lightly.

When the points above are considered in total, the number of victims murdered in this case was one, however, the crime committed by the defendant was a very serious crime, and unless there are particularly extenuating circumstances, the court has no choice but render a decision of the death penalty.

5. With respect to this, the second instance court decision, and the first instance court decision that endorse this decision, the defendant argues that there are the three extenuating circumstances described above.

With respect to the first point that there was little premeditation, it is true that the defendants when they discussed this prior to the crime did not go as far as to make plans in detail regarding when and where to murder the victim, and the defendants decided to commit the murder after visiting the home of the victim, and upon confirming whether there was money or goods to steal, and furthermore, this court finds evidence that the defendants searched the scene of the murder after the defendants took the victim away from her home. However, the defendants had made preparations, for example, they discussed and decided on the basic points prior to the crime that they would strangle the victim using string and steal money and goods, and then purchased vinyl string and work gloves ... to use in the crime, and created a stronger knot from this string by bundling the string. After they visited the victim's house, to confirm whether the victim had cash, they entered a separate room feigning illness and peeked in her Japanese bank passbook, and asked if he could borrow money from the victim and survey her finances, and was crafty. Furthermore, after the defendants took the victim away from her house, the defendants continued to search for a long period for a suitable crime scene without revealing the intention to murder, and accomplished the crime. With such circumstances under consideration, it is unreasonable for this court to assess that there was little premeditation in the burglary and murder in this case.

With respect to the second point that the defendant may be reformed and rehabilitated, it is true that the defendant made a complete confession to all of the crimes in this case at a relatively early stage after the arrest, and this point was maintained in the trials of both the first instance court and the second instance court, and the defendant stated that he is prepared for the maximum sentence. Furthermore, the behavior of the defendant in prison in serving the sentence for the crime above was respectable, and the court also finds evidence that the defendant made efforts earlier on to assimilate soundly back into society when he was paroled. However, the defendant started his life after parole in a fortunate environment wherein he received support from family, and soon developed a Pachinko habit and borrowed money many times, and in the end he committed the burglary and murder in this case. In addition, the defendant has taken no action to alleviate the pain and suffering caused upon the family of the victim. Given this fact, this court cannot logically take into consideration, among others, the primary facts that the defendant had confessed and has indicated remorse.

The third point, that is, in comparison with a prior and existing case wherein a person, who committed the crime of burglary and murder while he was released on parole and to whom a sentence of life without parole was given, was given the death penalty, and with respect to the point that there were less major malicious activities conducted by the defendant, as the death penalty was selected in such cases at the trial for all Supreme Court cases wherein the judgment was rendered after July 8, 1983, this court cannot assess that, in these cases, the circumstances of the defendant as described above, even when compared to cases wherein there was only one victim who was murdered, the degree of maliciousness was overall sufficiently low to avoid the election of the death penalty.

6. The second instance court judgment had then endorsed the weight of the sentence in the first instance court judgment that rendered the judgment of life imprisonment upon the defendant, as a result of an erred assessment of the facts that were to be considered to determine the weight of the sentence, however, this court finds that the weight on this sentence is improper, and there will be serious injustice if this judgment is not quashed.

Therefore, the portion on the defendant in the second instance court judgment shall be quashed under Code of Criminal Procedure Article 411(ii), and with the seriousness of this matter under consideration, in order to perform a very careful deliberation on whether there were other extenuating circumstances for the court to consider, the court has decided to remand this case to the original court under the Code of Criminal Procedure Article 413*, and all justices unanimously agreed on this opinion, and decided as set forth in the main text of the judgment.

(This translation is provisional and subject to revision.)

(* Translated by Judicial Research Foundation)

B. The European Human Rights System

Note on the Death Penalty in Europe

Protocol No. 6 to the Convention for the Protection of Human Rights and Fundamental Freedoms[l] requires those states ratifying it to abolish the death penalty except in time of war.[m] Of the 46 members of the Council of Europe, only Russia has not ratified this protocol, though even Russia has signed it.[n] Russia has, however, observed a moratorium on the death penalty since 1996.[o]

As might be supposed from the foregoing, opposition to the death penalty is very strong in Europe. For example, see the following press release quoting the President of the Council of Europe Parliamentary Assembly:

> **"Capital punishment must be totally removed in all countries which strive to uphold democracy, the rule of law and human rights," says PACE President**
>
> Strasbourg, 10.10.2006—"Capital punishment must be totally removed once and for all from the legislation of all countries which strive to uphold democracy, the rule of law and human rights," the President of the Council of Europe Parliamentary Assembly (PACE), René van der Linden, said today to mark the World Day Against the Death Penalty.

---

l. Protocol No. 6 to the Convention for the Protection of Human Rights and Fundamental Freedoms concerning the abolition of the death penalty as amended by Protocol No. 11, ETS 114 (1983).

m. *Id.*, arts. 1, 2.

n. Protocol No. 6 to the Convention for the Protection of Human Rights and Fundamental Freedoms Concerning the Abolition of the Death Penalty, CETS No. 114, status of ratifications as of 12/21/2006, seen at Council of Europe Website, http://conventions. coe.int/Treaty/Commun/ChercheSig.asp?NT=114&CM=7&DF=12/21/2006&CL=ENG, last visited December 21, 2006.

o. Parliamentary Assembly of the Council of Europe, Position of the Parliamentary Assembly as regards the Council of Europe member and observer states which have not abolished the death penalty, Recommendation 1760 (2006).

"The death penalty has been abolished in all our member states, with just one exception, the Russian Federation", Mr van der Linden said. He urged the Russian authorities to show, vis-à-vis public opinion in their country, the same determination and persuasiveness displayed by the other Council of Europe member states, which had the political will and courage to abolish the death penalty despite the potential unpopularity of the measure. "The sentence of life imprisonment of the only surviving Beslan terrorist was a clear signal of Russia's respect of a de facto moratorium on the death penalty, but I hope that this moratorium could soon result in a de jure abolition of the death penalty," he said.

At the same time, he warned against all attempts to launch discussion on the re-introduction of the death penalty in Europe.

He also recalled that at its June 2006 session, the Assembly had noted with concern that the separatist territories, not recognised internationally, of Abkhazia, South Ossetia and the Dnestr Moldavian Republic do not observe the abolition of the death penalty by Georgia and Moldova respectively. "The Assembly believes that the death penalty should be abolished in these territories and that the sentences of all prisoners currently on death row in Abkhazia and the Dnestr Moldavian Republic should be immediately commuted to terms of imprisonment in order to put an end to the cruel and inhuman treatment of those who have been kept on death row for years in a state of uncertainty as to their ultimate fate," he stressed.

In respect of countries having observer status with the Council of Europe, he referred to earlier PACE Resolutions 1349 (2003) and 1253 (2001), in which the Assembly calls on Japan and the United States to place an immediate moratorium on executions and to take the necessary steps to abolish the death penalty. "The Assembly finds it inadmissible that these appeals have gone unheeded and that both Japan and the United States continue to apply the death penalty and violate their fundamental obligation to uphold human rights."

He finally called on all countries in the world which have not yet abolished the death penalty to follow the lead given by the 46-nation Council of Europe, a de facto "death-penalty-free zone".

Council of Europe Press Release 575 (2006).

C. India

1. Bachan Singh v. State of Punjab, 1980 A.I.R.(S.C.) 898, 1980 (2) S.C.C. 684

SARKARIA, J. This reference to the Constitution Bench raises a question in regard to the constitutional validity of death penalty for murder provided in Section 302, Penal Code, and the sentencing procedure embodied in sub-section (3) of S. 354 of the Code of Criminal Procedure, 1973.

2. The reference has arisen in these circumstances: Bachan Singh, appellant in Criminal Appeal No. 273 of 1979, was tried and convicted and sentenced to death under Section 302, Indian Penal Code for the murders of Desa Singh, Durga Bai and Veeran Bai by the Sessions Judge. The High Court confirmed his death sentence and dismissed his appeal.

3. Bachan Singh's appeal by special leave, came up for hearing before a Bench of this Court (consisting of Sarkaria and Kailasam, JJ.). The only question for consideration in the appeal was, whether the facts found by the courts below would be "special reasons" for awarding the death sentence as required under S. 354(3) of the Code of Criminal Procedure, 1973.

4. Shri H. K. Puri, appearing as amicus curiae on behalf of the appellant, Bachan Singh ... contended that in view of the ratio of Rajendra Prasad v. State of U.P., 1979 (3) S.C.R. 646, the courts below were not competent to impose the extreme penalty of death on the appellant. It was submitted that neither the circumstance that the appellant was previously convicted for murder and committed these murders after he had served out the life sentence in the earlier case, nor the fact that these three murders were extremely heinous and inhuman, constitutes a "special reason" for imposing the death sentence within the meaning of Section 354(3) of the Code of Criminal Procedure, 1974. Reliance for this argument was placed on Rajendra Prasad (ibid) which, according to the counsel, was on facts very similar, if not identical, to that case.

5. Kailasam, J. was of opinion that the majority view in Rajendra Prasad taken by V. R. Krishna Iyer, J., who spoke for himself and D. A. Desai, J., was contrary to the judgment of the Constitution Bench in Jagmohan Singh v. State of Uttar Pradesh, 1973 (2) S.C.R. 541, inter alia, on these aspects:

(i) In Rajendra Prasad, V. R. Krishna Iyer, J. observed:

> The main focus of our judgment is on this poignant gap in "human rights jurisprudence" within the limits of the Penal Code, impregnated by the Constitution. To put it pithily, a world order voicing the worth of the human person, a cultural legacy charged with compas-

sion, an interpretative liberation from colonial callousness to life and liberty, a concern for social justice as setting the sights of individual justice, interest with the inherited text of the Penal Code to yield the goals desiderated [sic] by the Preamble and Articles 14, 19 and 21.

6. According to Kailasam, J., the challenge to the award of the death sentence as violative of Arts. 19, 14 and 21, was repelled by the Constitution Bench in Jagmohan's case:

(ii) In Jagmohan's case, the Constitution Bench held:

> The impossibility of laying down standards (in the matter of sentencing) is at the very core of criminal law as administered in India which invests the Judges with a very wide discretion in the matter of fixing the degree of punishment and that this discretion in the matter of sentence is liable to be corrected by superior courts.... The exercise of judicial discretion on well recognised principles is, in the final analysis, the safest possible safeguard for the accused.

In Rajendra Prasad, the majority decision characterised the above observations in Jagmohan as "incidental observations without concentration on the sentencing criteria," and said that they are not the ratio of the decision, adding "Judgments are not Bible for every line to be venerated."

(iii) In Rajendra Prasad, the plurality observed:

> It is constitutionally permissible to swing a criminal out of corporeal existence only if the security of State and society, public order and the interests of the general public compel that course as provided in Article 19(2) to (6).

This view again, according to Kailsam, J., is inconsistent with the law laid down by the Constitution Bench in Jagmohan, wherein it was held that deprivation of life is constitutionally permissible if that is done according to "procedure established by law."

(iv) In Rajendra Prasad, the majority has further opined:

> The only correct approach is to read into Section 302, I.P.C. and Section 354(3), Criminal P.C., the human rights and humane trends in the Constitution. So examined, the right to life and the fundamental freedoms is deprived when he is hanged to death, his dignity is defiled when his neck is noosed and strangled.

7. Against the above, Kailasam, J. commented: The only change after the Constitution Bench delivered its judgment is the introduction of Section 354(3) which requires special reasons to be given if the court is to award the death sentence. If without the restriction of stating sufficient reasons death sentence could be constitutionally awarded under the I.P.C. and Criminal P.C. as it stood before the amendment, it is difficult to perceive how by requiring special

reasons to be given the amended section would be unconstitutional unless the "sentencing sector is made restrictive and least vagarious."

(v) In Rajendra Prasad, the majority has held that:

> such extraordinary grounds alone constitutionally qualify as special reasons as leave no option to the court but to execute the offender if State and society are to survive. One stroke of murder hardly qualifies for this drastic requirement, however gruesome the killing or pathetic the situation, unless the inherent testimony oozing from that act is irresistible that the murderous appetite of the convict is too chronic and deadly, that ordered life in a given locality or society or in prison itself would be gone if this man were now or later to be at large. If he is an irredeemable murderer, like a bloodthirsty tiger, he has to quit his terrestrial tenancy.

8. According to Kailasam, J., what is extracted above, runs directly counter to and cannot be reconciled with the following observations in Jagmohan's case:

> But some (murders) at least are diabolical in conception and cruel in execution. In some others where the victim is a person of high standing in the country, society is liable to be rocked to its very foundation. Such murders cannot be simply washed away by finding alibis in the social maladjustment of the murderer. Prevalence of such crimes speaks, in the opinion of many, for the inevitability of death penalty not only by way of deterrence but as a token of emphatic disapproval by the society.... A very responsible body (Law Commission) has come to the conclusion after considering all the relevant factors. On the conclusions thus offered to us, it will be difficult to hold that capital punishment as such is unreasonable or not required in the public interest.

(vi) Kailasam, J. was further of the opinion that it is equally beyond the functions of a court to evolve "working rules for imposition of death sentence bearing the markings of enlightened flexibility and social sensibility" or to make law "by cross-fertilisation from sociology, history, cultural anthropology and current national perils and developmental goals and, above all, constitutional currents...."

This function, in his view, belongs only to Parliament. The Court must administer the law as it stands.

(vii) The learned Judge has further expressed that the view taken by V. R. Krishna Iyer, J. in Rajendra Prasad that "special reasons" necessary for imposing death penalty must relate not to the crime as such, but to the criminal is not warranted by the law as it stands today.

. . . .

10. In the meanwhile, several persons convicted of murders and sentenced to death, filed writ petitions ... under Article 32 of the Constitution directly chal-

lenging the constitutional validity of the death penalty provided in Section 302 of the Indian Penal Code for the offence of murder, and the sentencing procedure provided in Section 354(3) of the Code of Criminal Procedure, 1974. That is how, the matter has now come up before this larger Bench of five Judges.

....

17. The principal questions that fall to be considered in this case are:

(I) Whether death penalty provided for the offence of murder in Section 302, Penal Code is unconstitutional; (II) If the answer to the foregoing question be in the negative, whether the sentencing procedure provided in Section 354(3) of the Code of Criminal Procedure, 1973 (Act 2 of 1974) is unconstitutional on the ground that it invests the Court with unguided and untrammelled discretion and allows death sentence to be arbitrarily or freakishly imposed on a person found guilty of murder or any other capital offence punishable under the Indian Penal Code with death or, in the alternative, with imprisonment for life.

18. We will first take up Question No. I relating to the constitutional validity of Section 302, Penal Code.

Question No. I:

....

23. The first contention ... is that the provision of death penalty in Section 302, Penal Code offends Article 19 of the Constitution. It is submitted that the right to live is basic to the enjoyment of all the six freedoms guaranteed in Clauses (a) to (e) and (g) of Article 19(1) of the Constitution and death penalty puts an end to all these freedoms; that since death penalty serves no social purpose and its value as a deterrent remains unproven and it defiles the dignity of the individual so solemnly vouchsafed in the Preamble of the Constitution, its imposition must be regarded as an "unreasonable restriction" amounting to total prohibition, on the six freedoms guaranteed in Article 19(1).

....

25.... Broadly speaking, Article 19 is intended to protect the rights to the freedoms specifically enumerated in the six sub-clauses of Clause (1) against State action, other than in the legitimate exercise of its power to regulate these rights in the public interest relating to heads specified in Clauses (2) to (6). The six fundamental freedoms guaranteed under Art. 19(1) are not absolute rights. Firstly, they are subject to inherent restraints stemming from the reciprocal obligation of one member of a civil society to so use his rights as not to infringe or injure similar rights of another. This is on the principle sic uteri tuo ut alienum non laedas. Secondly, under Cls. (2) to (6) these rights have been expressly made subject to the power of the State to impose reasonable restrictions, which may even extend to prohibition, on the exercise of those rights.

26. The power, if properly exercised, is itself a safeguard of the freedoms guaranteed in Clause (1). The conferment of this power is founded on the fundamental truth that uncontrolled liberty entirely freed from restraint, degenerates into a license, leading to anarchy and chaos; that libertine pursuit of liberty, absolutely free, and free for all, may mean liberticide for all. "Liberty has, therefore," as Justice Patanjali Sastri put it, "to be limited in order to be effectively possessed."

27. It is important to note that whereas Article 21 expressly deals with the right to life and personal liberty, Article 19 does not. The right to life is not one of the rights mentioned in Article 19(1).

28. The first point under Question (I) to be considered is whether Article 19 is at all applicable for judging the validity of the impugned provision in Section 302, Penal Code.

29.... [T]he condition precedent for the applicability of Article 19 is that the activity which the impugned law prohibits and penalises, must be within the purview and protection of Article 19(1).... The argument that the provisions of the Penal Code, prescribing death sentence as an alternative penalty for murder have to be tested on the ground of Article 19, appears to proceed on the fallacy that the freedoms guaranteed by Article 19(1) are absolute freedoms and they cannot be curtailed by law imposing reasonable restrictions, which may amount to total prohibition. Such an argument was advanced before the Constitution Bench in the State of Bombay v. R. M. D. Chamarbaugwala, 1957 (1) S.C.R. 874 at p. 920.... Speaking for the Constitution Bench, S. R. Das, C.J. repelled this contention, in these terms:

> On this argument it will follow that criminal activities undertaken and carried on with a view to earning profit will be protected as fundamental rights until they are restricted by law. Thus there will be a guaranteed right to carry on a business of hiring out goondas to commit assault or even murder, or house-breaking, or selling obscene pictures, or trafficking in women and so on until the law curbs or stops such activities. This appears to us to be completely unrealistic and incongruous. We have no doubt that there are certain activities which can under no circumstance be regarded as trade or business or commerce although the usual forms and instruments are employed therein. To exclude those activities from the meaning of those words is not to cut down their meaning at all but to say only that they are not within the true meaning of those words.

This approach to the problem still holds the field. The observations in Chamarbaugwala, extracted above, were recently quoted with approval by V. R. Krishna Iyer, J., while delivering the judgment of the Bench in Fatehchand Himmatlal v. State of Maharashtra, 1977 A.I.R. (S.C.) 1825 at p. 1833.

30. In A. K. Gopalan v. The State of Madras, 1950 (1) S.C.R. 88, all the six learned Judges constituting the Bench held that punitive detention or impris-

onment awarded as punishment after conviction for an offence under the Indian Penal Code is outside the scope of Article 19, although this conclusion was reached by them by adopting more or less different approaches to the problem.

....

41. We have copiously extracted from the judgments in A. K. Gopalan's case, to show that all the propositions propounded, arguments and reasons employed or approaches adopted by the learned Judges in that case, in reaching the conclusion that the Indian Penal Code, particularly those of its provisions which do not have a direct impact on the rights conferred by Article 19(1), is not a law imposing restrictions on those rights, have not been overruled or rendered bad by the subsequent pronouncements of this Court.... Indeed, the reasoning ... that such a construction which treats every section of the Indian Penal Code as a law imposing "restriction" on the rights in Article 19(1), will lead to absurdity is unassailable. There are several offences under the Penal Code, such as theft, cheating, ordinary assault, which do not violate or affect "public order," but only "law and order." These offences injure only specific individuals as distinguished from the public at large. It is by now settled that "public order" means "even tempo of the life of the community." That being so, even all murders do not disturb or affect "public order...." Yet, no rational being can say that punishment of such murderers is not in the general public interest. It may be noted that general public interest is not specified as a head in Clauses (2) to (4) on which restriction on the rights mentioned in Clause (1) of the Article may be justified.

42. It is true, as was pointed out by Hidayatullah, J. (as he then was) in Dr. Ram Manohar Lohia's case 1966 (1) S.C.R. 709 and in several other decisions that followed it, that the real distinction between the areas of "law and order" and "public order" lies not merely in the nature or quality of the act, but in the degree and extent. Violent crimes similar in nature, but committed in different contexts and circumstances might cause different reactions.... Nonetheless, the fact remains that for such murders which do not affect "public order," even the provision for life imprisonment in Section 302, Indian Penal Code, as an alternative punishment, would not be justifiable under Cls. (2), (3) and (4) as a reasonable restriction in the interest of "public order." Such a construction must, therefore, be avoided. Thus construed, Article 19 will be attracted only to such laws, the provisions of which are capable of being tested under Cls. (2) to (5) of Art. 19.

....

45. In R. C. Cooper v. Union of India, 1970 (3) S.C.R. 530, 1970 A.I.R.(S.C.) 564 (popularly known as Bank Nationalization case), the majority adopted the twofold test for determining as to when a law violated fundamental rights, namely:

(1) It is not the object of the authority making the law impairing the right of a citizen, nor the form of action that determines the protection he can claim; (2) it is the effect of the law and of the action upon the right which attract the jurisdiction of the Court to grant relief. The direct operation of the act upon the rights forms the real test.

46. In Maneka Gandhi v. Union of India, 1978 (2) S.C.R. 621, 1978 A.I.R.(S.C.) 597, Bhagwati, J. explained the scope of the same test by saying that a law or an order made thereunder will be hit by Article 19, if the direct and inevitable consequence of such law or order is to abridge or take away any one or more of the freedoms guaranteed by Article 19(1). If the effect and operation of the statute by itself, upon a person's fundamental rights is remote or dependent upon "factors which may or may not come into play" then such statute is not ultra vires on the ground of its being violative of that fundamental right. Bhagwati, J. described this proposition as "the doctrine of intended and real effect"; while Chandrachud, J. (as he then was) called it "the test of proximate effect and operation of the statute."

. . . .

60. ... [A] comprehensive test which [sic] can be formulated, may be restated as under:

> Does the impugned law, in its pith and substance, whatever may be its form and object, deal with any of the fundamental rights conferred by Art. 19(1)? If it does, does it abridge or abrogate any of those rights? And even if it does not, in its pith and substance, deal with any of the fundamental rights conferred by Art. 19(1) is the direct and inevitable effect of the impugned law such as to abridge or abrogate any of those rights?

The mere fact that impugned law incidentally, remotely or collaterally has the effect of abridging or abrogating those rights, will not satisfy the test. If the answer to the above queries be in the affirmative, the impugned law in order to be valid, must pass the test of reasonableness under Article 19. But if the impact of the law on any of the rights under cl. (1) of Art. 19 is merely incidental, indirect, remote or collateral and is dependent upon factors which may or may not come into play, the anvil of Article 19 will not be available for judging its validity.

61. Now, let us apply this test to the provisions of the Penal Code, in question. Section 299 defines "culpable homicide" and Section 300 defines culpable homicide amounting to murder. Section 302 prescribes death or imprisonment for life as penalty for murder. It cannot reasonably or rationally, be contended that any of the rights mentioned in Article 19(1) of the Constitution confers the freedom to commit murder or, for the matter of that, the freedom to commit any offence whatsoever. Therefore, penal laws, that is to say, laws

which define offences and prescribe punishment for the commission of offences do not attract the application of Art. 19(1).... But the point of the matter is that, in pith and substance, penal laws do not deal with the subject matter of rights enshrined in Article 19(1). That again is not enough for the purpose of deciding upon the applicability of Article 19 because as the test formulated by us above shows, even if a law does not, in its pith and substance, deal with any of the fundamental rights conferred by Article 19(1), if the direct and inevitable effect of the law is such as to abridge or abrogate any of those right, Art. 19(1) shall have been attracted.... On this latter aspect of the matter, we are of the opinion that the deprivation of freedom consequent upon an order of conviction and sentence is not a direct and inevitable consequence of the penal law but is merely incidental to the order of conviction and sentence which may or may not come into play, that is to say, which may or may not be passed. Considering therefore the test formulated by us in its dual aspect, we are of the opinion that Section 302 of the Penal Code does not have to stand the test of Article 19(1) of the Constitution.

....

65. [In addressing the question whether, if it is assumed arguendo that penal statutes implicate Article 19, who would bear the burden of proving the constitutionality/unconstitutionality of the provision in question, the Court observes] ... [T]he recent decisions of this Court ... start with the initial presumption in favour of the constitutionality of the statute and throw the burden of rebutting that presumption on the party who challenges its constitutionality on the ground of Article 19.

....

67. Behind the view that there is a presumption of constitutionality of a statute and the onus to rebut the same lies on those who challenge the legislation, is the rationale of judicial restraint, a recognition of the limits of judicial review, a respect for the boundaries of legislative and judicial functions, and the judicial responsibility to guard the trespass from one side or the other....

....

70. Even where the burden is on the State to show that the restriction imposed by the impugned statute is reasonable and in public interest, the extent and the manner of discharge of the burden necessarily depends on the subject-matter of the legislation, the nature of the inquiry, and the scope and limits of judicial review....

71. In the instant case, the State has discharged its burden primarily by producing for the perusal of the Court, the 35th Report of the Law Commission, 1967, and the judgments of this Court in Jagmohan Singh and in several subsequent cases, in which it has been recognised that death penalty serves as a deterrent. It is, therefore, for the petitioners to prove and establish that the death

sentence for murder is so outmoded, unusual or excessive as to be devoid of any rational nexus with the purpose and object of the legislation.

72. The Law Commission of India, after making an intensive and extensive study of the subject of death penalty in India, published and submitted its 35th Report in 1967 to the Government. After examining, a wealth of evidential material and considering the arguments for and against its retention, that high-powered Body summed up its conclusions at page 354 of its Report, as follows:

> The issue of abolition or retention has to be decided on a balancing of the various arguments for and against retention. No single argument for abolition or retention can decide the issue. In arriving at any conclusion on the subject, the need for protecting society in general and individual human beings must be borne in mind.

> It is difficult to rule out the validity of the strength behind many of the arguments for abolition nor does the Commission treat lightly the argument based on the irrevocability of the sentence of death, the need for a modern approach, the severity of capital punishment and the strong feeling shown by certain sections of public opinion in stressing deeper questions of human values.

> Having regard, however, to the conditions in India, to the variety of the social up-bringing of its inhabitants, to the disparity in the level of morality and education in the country, to the vastness of its area, to diversity of its population and to the paramount need for maintaining law and order in the country at the present juncture, India cannot risk the experiment of abolition of capital punishment.

73. This Report was, also, considered by the Constitution Bench of this Court in Jagmohan. It was the main piece of evidence on the basis of which the challenge to the constitutional validity of Section 302 of the Penal Code, on the ground of its being violative of Article 19, was repelled. Parliament must be presumed to have considered these views of the Law Commission and the judgment of this Court in Jagmohan, and must also have been aware of the principles crystallised by judicial precedents in the matter of sentencing when it took up revision of the Code of Criminal Procedure in 1972–73, and inserted in it, Section 354(3) which indicates that death penalty can be awarded in exceptional cases for murder and for some other offences under the Penal Code for special reasons to be recorded.

74. Death penalty has been the subject of an age-old debate between Abolitionists and Retentionists....

75. The chief arguments of the Abolitionists, which have been substantially adopted by the learned counsel for the petitioners, are as under:

(a) The death penalty is irreversible. Decided upon according to fallible processes of law by fallible human beings, it can be—and actually has been—inflicted upon people innocent of any crime.

(b) There is no convincing evidence to show that death penalty serves any penological purpose:

(i) Its deterrent effect remains unproven. It has not been shown that incidence of murder has increased in countries where death penalty has been abolished, after its abolition.

(ii) Retribution in the sense of vengeance, is no longer an acceptable end of punishment.

(iii) On the contrary, reformation of the criminal and his rehabilitation is the primary purpose of punishment. Imposition of death penalty nullifies that purpose.

(c) Execution by whatever means and for whatever offence is a cruel, inhuman and degrading punishment.

76. It is proposed to deal with these arguments, as far as possible, in their serial order.

Regarding (a): It is true that death penalty is irrevocable and a few instances can be cited, including some from England, of persons who after their conviction and execution for murder, were discovered to be innocent. But this, according to the Retentionists is not a reason for abolition of the death penalty, but an argument for reform of the judicial system and the sentencing procedure. Theoretically, such errors of judgment cannot be absolutely eliminated from any system of justice, devised and worked by human beings, but their incidence can be infinitesimally reduced by providing adequate safeguards and checks. We will presently see, while dealing with the procedural aspect of the problem, that, in India, ample safeguards have been provided by law and the Constitution which almost eliminate the chances of an innocent person being convicted and executed for a capital offence.

Regarding (b): Whether death penalty serves any penological purpose.

77. Firstly, in most of the countries in the world, including India, a very large segment of the population, including notable penologists, judges, jurists, legislators and other enlightened people still believe that death penalty for murder and certain other capital offences does serve as a deterrent, and a greater deterrent than life imprisonment. We will set out very briefly, by way of sample, opinions of some of these distinguished persons.

78. In the first place, we will notice a few decisions of Courts wherein the deterrent value of death penalty has been judicially recognised [discussing cases].

....

80. In Jagmohan, also, this Court took due note of the fact that for certain types of murders, death penalty alone is considered as adequate deterrent [the

court cites numerous judicial opinions, both from India and other countries, as well as opinions by certain scholars, who assert the deterrent/incapacitive value of the death penalty.]

....

98. The Law Commission of India in its 35th Report, after carefully sifting all the materials collected by them recorded their views regarding the deterrent effect of capital punishment as follows:

> In our view capital punishment does act as a deterrent. We have already discussed in detail several aspects of this topic. We state below, very briefly, the main points that have weighed with us in arriving at this conclusion;
>
> (a) Basically, every human being dreads death.
>
> (b) Death, as a penalty, stands on a totally different level from imprisonment for life or any other punishment. The difference is one of quality, and not merely of degree.
>
> (c) Those who are specifically qualified to express an opinion on the subject, including particularly the majority of the replies received from State Governments, Judges, Members of Parliament and Legislatures and Members of the Bar and police officers—are definitely of the view that the deterrent object of capital punishment is achieved in a fair measure in India.
>
> (d) As to conduct of prisoners released from jail (after undergoing imprisonment for life), it would be difficult to come to a conclusion, without studies extending over a long period of years.
>
> (e) Whether any other punishment can possess all the advantages of capital punishment is a matter of doubt.
>
> (f) Statistics of other countries are inconclusive on the subject. If they are not regarded as proving the deterrent effect, neither can they be regarded as conclusively disproving it.

....

Retribution in the sense of reprobation whether a totally rejected concept of punishment

101. Even retribution in the sense of society's reprobation for the worst of crimes, i.e., murder, is not an altogether outmoded concept. This view is held by many distinguished sociologists, jurists and judges [quotes such views.].

....

104. Retribution and deterrence are not two divergent ends of capital punishment. They are convergent goals which ultimately merge into one. How these ends of punishment coalesce into one was described by the Law Commission of India, thus:

> The retributive object of capital punishment has been the subject-matter of sharp attack at the hands of the abolitionists. We appreciate that many persons would regard the instinct of revenge as barbarous. How far it should form part of the penal philosophy in modern times will always remain a matter of controversy. No useful purpose will be served by a discussion as to whether the instinct of retribution is or is not commendable. The fact remains, however, that whenever there is a serious crime, the society feels a sense of disapprobation. If there is any element of retribution in the law, as administered now, it is not the instinct of the man of jungle but rather a refined evolution of that instinct the feeling prevails in the public is a fact of which notice is to be taken. The law does not encourage it, or exploit it for any undesirable ends. Rather, by reserving the death penalty for murder, and thus visiting this gravest crime with the gravest punishment, the law helps the element of retribution merge into the element of deterrence. (Para 265(18), 35th Report)

[cites still more lawyers and judges on propriety of justifying capital punishment on grounds of retribution, and as necessary deterrent for politically motivated murders.]

....

119. In India, very few scientific studies in regard to crime and punishment in general, and capital punishment, in particular, have been made, for the petitioners referred us to Chap. VI, captioned "Capital Punishment", in the book, "Quantum of Punishment in Criminal Law in India", written by Dr. Kirpal Singh Chhabra, now on the staff of G.N. University, Amritsar. In this article, which was primarily meant as LL.D. thesis, the learned author concludes:

> On the basis of statistics both of India and abroad, U.N.O. findings and other weighty arguments, we can safely conclude that death penalty is not sustainable on merits. Innately it has no reformative element. It has been proved that death penalty as operative carries no deterrent value and crime of murder is governed by factors other than death penalty. Accordingly, I feel that the death penalty should be abolished.

120. It will be seen, in the first place, that the analysis by Dr. Chhabra in coming to the conclusion, that death penalty is of no penological value, is based on stale, incomplete and inadequate statistics. This is more particularly true of the

data relating to India, which does not cover the period subsequent to 1961. Secondly, the approach to the problem adopted by him, like the other Abolitionists referred to by him, is mainly, if not merely, statistical.

121. As already noticed, the proponents of the opposite view of capital punishment, point out that statistics alone are not determinative of the question whether or not death penalty serves any deterrent or other penological purpose. Firstly, statistics of deterred potential murderers are hard to obtain. Secondly, the approach adopted by the Abolitionists is oversimplified at the cost of other relevant but imponderable factors, the appreciation of which is essential to assess the true penological value of capital punishment. The number of such factors is infinitude, their character variable, duration transient and abstract formulation difficult. Conditions change from country to country and time to time. Due to the inconstancy of social conditions, it is not scientifically possible to assess with any degree of accuracy, as to whether the variation in the incidence of capital crime is attributable to the presence or absence of death penalty in the penal law of that country for such crimes. That is why statistical attempts to assess the true penological value of capital punishment, remain inconclusive.

122. Pursued beyond a certain point, both the Abolitionists and the Retentionists retreat into their own conceptual bunkers firmly entrenched in their respective "faiths". We need not take sides with either of them. There is always a danger in adhering too rigidly to concepts. As Prof. Brett has pointed out "all concepts are abstractions from reality, and that in the process of abstraction something of the reality is bound to be lost." (An Enquiry into Criminal Guilt by Prof. Peter Brett, 1963 Edn. Melbourne, p. 13). We must, therefore, view the problem against the perspective of the hard realities of the time and the conditions prevailing in the world, particularly in our own country.

123. A review of the world events of the last seven or eight years, as evident from Encyclopaedia Britannica Year Books and other material referred to by the learned counsel, would show that most countries in the world are in the grip of an ever-rising tide of violent crime. Murders for monetary gain or from misdirected political motives, robbery, rape, assault are on the increase. India is no exception. The Union of India has produced for our perusal a statement of facts and figures showing the incidence of violent crime, including murder, dacoity and robbery, in the various States of India, during the years 1965 to 1975. Another statement has been furnished showing the number of persons convicted of murder and other capital offences and sentenced to death in some of the States of India during the period 1974 to 1978. This statement however, is incomplete and inadequate. On account of that deficiency and for the general reasons set out above, it cannot, even statistically, show conclusively or with any degree of certainty, that capital punishment has no penological

worth. But the first statement does bring out clearly the stark reality that the crimes of murder, dacoity and robbery in India are since 1965 increasing.

124. Now, looking around at the world during the last decade, we may recall that in Furman v. Georgia (decided on June 29, 1976), the Supreme Court of the United States held by a majority, that the imposition and carrying out of the death penalty constitutes 'cruel and unusual' punishment, in violation of the Eighth and Fourteenth Amendments. Brennan and Marshall, JJ. (differing from the plurality) went to the extent of holding that death penalty was per se unconstitutional as it was a cruel and unusual punishment. In so holding, these learned Justices purported to adopt the contemporary standards of decency prevailing among the enlightened public of the United States. Justice Marshall ruled that "it was morally unacceptable to the people of the United States." This opinion of the learned Justices was sharply rebuffed by the people of the United States through their chosen representatives. Soon after the decision in Furman, bowing to the thrust of public opinion, the Legislatures of no less than 32 States, post-haste revised their penal laws and reinstituted death penalty for murder and certain other crimes. Public opinion polls then taken show that approximately 70 per cent of Americans have been in favour of death penalty.... In 1976, a Gallup Poll taken in the United States showed that more than 65 per cent of those polled preferred to have an operative death penalty.

125. Incidentally, the rejection by the people of the approach adopted by the two learned Judges in Furman, furnishes proof of the fact that judicial opinion does not necessarily reflect the moral attitudes of the people. At the same time, it is a reminder that Judges should not take upon themselves the responsibility of becoming oracles or spokesmen of public opinion. Not being representatives of the people, it is often better, as a matter of judicial restraint, to leave the function of assessing public opinion to the chosen representatives of the people in the legislature concerned.

126. Coming back to the review of the world crime situation, during the last decade, Saudi Arabia and some other countries have reinstated death penalty or enacted harsher punishments not only for murder but for some other crimes, also. In America, apart from 32 States which reinstated death penalty under revised laws after Furman, the legislatures of some of the remaining 15 States have either reinstituted or are considering to reintroduce death penalty. Currently, a federal legislation for reinstituting or prescribing capital punishment for a larger range of offences of homicide is under consideration of United States Congress. According to the report of the Amnesty International, in U.S.A., as on May 1, 1979, death penalty can be imposed for aggravated murder in 35 States. Attempts have been made in other countries, also to reintroduce death penalty. In Britain, in the wake of serious violent incidents of terrorism, a Bill was moved in Parliament to reintroduce capital punishment for murder and certain other offences. It was defeated by a free vote on April

19, 1979. Even so, no less than 243 members of Parliament had voted in favour of this measure. We have noted that Israel has also recently reintroduced death penalty for certain criminal "acts of inhuman cruelty." In People's Republic of China, a new legislation was adopted on July 1, 1979 by China's Parliament, according to Article 43 of which, death penalty can be imposed "for the most heinous crimes." In Argentina, the death penalty was reintroduced in 1976. Similarly, Belgium reintroduced death penalty and increased the number of crimes punishable with death. In France, in 1978, a movement in favour of abolition initiated by the French bishops failed to change the law under which death penalty is a valid sanction for murder and certain other offences. In Japan, death penalty is a legal sanction for 13 crimes. In Greece and Turkey, death penalty can be imposed for murder and other capital offences. In Malaysia and the Republic of Singapore under the Drugs Act of May, 1979, misuse of drugs is also punishable with death. Cuba introduced a new penal code in February, 1978, which provides punishment of death by shooting for crimes ranging from some types of murder and robbery to hijacking and rape.

127. In the U.S.S.R. (Russia) as many as 18 offenses are punishable with death....

[EDITOR'S NOTE: Since this opinion was written, Belgium, France, Greece, Turkey and Argentina have abolished the death penalty, and Russia has imposed a moratorium on its use.]

Our object in making the above survey is to bring out the hard fact that in spite of the Abolitionist movement, only 18 States (as on 30th May, 1979) in the world have abolished the death penalty for all offences, while 8 more have retained it for specific offences committed in time of war, only.... [EDITOR'S NOTE: As of 2006, 87 countries have abolished capital punishment.] This means, most of the countries in the modern world still retain death penalty as a legal sanction for certain specified offences. The countries which retain death penalty in their penal laws, such as, Russia, U.S.A., France, Belgium, Malaysia, China and Japan, etc., cannot, by any standard, be called uncivilized nations or immature societies.

128. Surveyors and students of world events and current trends believe that the reversal of the attitudes towards criminals and their judicial punishments in general, and capital punishment in particular, in several countries of the world, is partly due to the fact that milder sanctions or corrective processes, or even the alternative of imprisonment, have been found inadequate and wanting to stem the mounting tide of serious crime ...

129. Faced with the spectre of rising crime, people and sociologists alike, have started questioning the rehabilitation policy....

131. India also, as the statistics furnished by the respondent (Union of India) show, is afflicted by a rising rate of violent crime, particularly murder, armed

robbery and dacoity etc., and this has been the cause of much public concern. All attempts made by individual members to move Bills in the Parliament for abolition or restriction of the area of death penalty have ended in failure. At least four of such unsuccessful attempts were made after India won Independence, in 1949, 1958, 1961 and 1978. It may be noted that the last of these attempts was only to restrict the death penalty to a few types of murders specified in the Bill. Though it was passed by the Rajya Sabha after being recast, it has not been passed by Lok Sabha.

132. To sum up, the question whether or not death penalty serves any penological purpose is a difficult, complex and intractable issue. It has evoked strong, divergent views. For the purpose of testing the constitutionality of the impugned provision as to death penalty in Section 302, Penal Code on the ground of reasonableness in the light of Articles 19 and 21 of the Constitution, is not necessary for us to express any categorical opinion, one way or the other, as to which of these two antithetical views, held by the Abolitionists and Retentionists, is correct. It is sufficient to say that the very fact that persons of reason, learning and light are rationally and deeply divided in their opinion on this issue, is a ground among others, for rejecting the petitioner's argument that retention of death penalty in the impugned provision, is totally devoid of reason and purpose. If, notwithstanding the view of the Abolitionists to the contrary, a very large segment of people, the world over, including sociologists, legislators, jurists, judges and administrators still firmly believe in the worth and necessity of capital punishment for the protection of society, if in the perspective of prevailing crime conditions in India, contemporary public opinion channelized through the people's representatives in Parliament, has repeatedly in the last three decades, rejected all attempts, including the one made recently, to abolish or specifically restrict the area of death penalty, if death penalty is still a recognised legal sanction for murder or some types of murder in most of the civilised countries in the world, if the framers of the Indian Constitution were fully aware—as we shall presently show they were—of the existence of death penalty as punishment for murder, under the Indian Penal Code, if the 35th Report and subsequent Reports of the Law Commission suggesting retention of death penalty, and recommending revision of the Criminal Procedure Code and the insertion of the new Sections 235(2) and 354(3) in that Code providing for pre-sentence hearing and sentencing procedure on conviction for murder and other capital offences were before the Parliament and presumably considered by it when in 1972–1973 it took up revision of the Code of 1898 and replaced it by the Code of Criminal Procedure, 1973, it is not possible to hold that the provision of death penalty as an alternative punishment for murder, in Section 302, Penal Code is unreasonable and not in the public interest. We would, therefore, conclude that the impugned provision in Section 302, violates neither the letter nor the ethos of Article 19.

133. We will now consider the issue whether the impugned limb of the provision in Section 302, Penal Code contravenes Article 21 of the Constitution.

134. Before dealing with the contentions canvassed on the point, it will be proper to notice briefly the principles which should inform the interpretation of Art. 21.

135. In Maneka Gandhi's case, which was a decision by a Bench of seven learned Judges, it was held by Bhagwati, J. in his concurring judgment, that the expression "personal liberty" in Article 21 is of the widest amplitude and it covers a variety of rights which go to constitute the personal liberty of man and some of them have been raised to the status of distinct fundamental rights under Article 19. It was further observed that Articles 14, 19 and 21 are not to be interpreted in water-tight compartments, and consequently, a law depriving a person of personal liberty and prescribing a procedure for that purpose within the meaning of Article 21 has to stand the test of one or more of the fundamental rights conferred under Article 19 which may be applicable in a given situation, ex-hypothesi it must also be liable to be tested with reference to Article 14. The principle of reasonableness pervades all the three Articles, with the result, that the procedure contemplated by Art. 21 must be "right and just and fair" and not "arbitrary, fanciful or oppressive," otherwise, it should be no procedure at all and the requirement of Article 21 would not be satisfied.

136.... If [Article 21] is expanded in accordance with the interpretative principle indicated in Maneka Gandhi, it will read as follows:

> No person shall be deprived of his life or personal liberty except according to fair, just and reasonable procedure established by valid law.

In the converse positive form, the expanded Article will read as below:

> A person may be deprived of his life or personal liberty in accordance with fair, just and reasonable procedure established by valid law.

Thus expanded and read for interpretative purposes, Article 21 clearly brings out the implication that the Founding Fathers recognised the right of the State to deprive a person of his life or personal liberty in accordance with fair, just and reasonable procedure established by valid law. There are several other indications, also, in the Constitution which show that the Constitution-makers were fully cognizant of the existence of death penalty for murder and certain other offences in the Indian Penal code. Entries 1* and 2* in List III—Concurrent List—of the Seventh Schedule, specifically refer to the Indian Penal Code and the Code of Criminal Procedure as in force at the commencement of the Constitution. Article 72(1)(c)* specifically invests the President with power to suspend, remit or commute the sentence of any person convicted of any offence, and also "in all cases where the sentence is a sentence of death." Likewise, under Article 161*, the Governor of a State has been given power to suspend, remit or commute, inter alia, the sentence of death of any person convicted of murder or other capital offence relating to a matter to which the executive power of the State extends. Article 134*, in terms, gives a right of appeal to the Supreme Court to a person who is sentenced to death by the High Court, after reversal of his acquittal by the trial Court. Under the successive Criminal Procedure Codes which have been in force for about 100 years, a sentence of death is to be carried out by hanging. In view of the aforesaid constitutional postulates, by no stretch of imagination can it be said that death penalty under Section 302, Penal Code, either per se or because of its execution by hanging, constitutes an unreasonable, cruel or unusual punishment. By reason of the same constitutional postulates, it cannot be said that the framers of the Constitution considered death sentence for murder or the prescribed traditional mode of its execution as a degrading punishment which would defile "the dignity of the individual" within the contemplation of the Preamble to the Constitution.

On parity of reasoning, it cannot be said that death penalty for the offence of murder violates the basic structure of the Constitution.

[The court rejects the argument that Article 6* of the International Covenant on Civil and Political Rights, to which India is a party, requires abolition of the death penalty, reading that provision requiring only the same guarantees as the Indian Constitution.]

....

141. For all the foregoing reasons, we would answer the first main question in the negative. This takes us to Question No. II.

Question No. II.

142. Are the provisions of Section 354(3) of the Code of Criminal Procedure, 1973 unconstitutional? That is the question. The constitutional validity of Section 354(3) is assailed on these grounds:

(i)(a) Section 354(3) of the Code of Criminal Procedure, 1973, delegates to the Court the duty to legislate in the field of 'special reasons' for choosing between life and death, and (b) permits imposition of death penalty in an arbitrary and whimsical manner inasmuch as it does not lay down any rational principles or criteria for invoking this extreme sanction ...

(ii) If Section 354(3) is to be saved from the vice of unconstitutionality, the Court should so interpret it and define its scope that the imposition of death penalty comes to be restricted only to those types of grave murders and capital offences which imperil the very existence and security of the State. (Reliance for this argument has been placed on Rajendra Prasad's case....

143. As against this, the learned Solicitor General submits that the policy of the law in the matter of imposition of death sentence is writ large and clear in Section 354(3), namely, that life imprisonment is the rule and death sentence an exception; that the correct approach should be to apply this policy to the rele-

vant facts of the particular case, bearing on the question of sentence, and to find out if there are any exceptional reasons justifying imposition of the death penalty, as a departure from the normal rule.

144. It is submitted that conferment of such sentencing discretion on the courts, to be exercised judicially, in no sense, amounts to delegation of the legislative powers by Parliament.

145. Shri Sorabji further submits that there is no inherent impossibility in formulating broad guidelines consistent with the policy indicated by the legislature, for the exercise of the judicial functions under Section 354(3). He emphasises that only broad guidelines, as distinct from rigid rules, can be laid down by the Court. Since the discretion—proceeds the argument—is to be exercised judicially after taking into consideration all the aggravating and mitigating circumstances relating to the crime and the criminal in a particular case, and ample safeguards by way of appeal and reference to the superior courts against erroneous or arbitrary exercise of the sentencing discretion have been provided, Section 354(3) cannot be said to be violative of Articles 14, 19 and 21 or anything else in the Constitution.

146. Before embarking upon a discussion of the arguments advanced on both sides, it is necessary to have a peep into the history and legislative background of the procedural provisions relating to sentencing in the Code of Criminal Procedure.

....

151. Section 354(3) of the Code of Criminal Procedure, 1973, marks a significant shift in the legislative policy underlying the Code of 1898, as in force immediately before April 1, 1974, according to which both the alternative sentences of death or imprisonment for life provided for murder and for certain other capital offences under the Penal Code, were normal sentences. Now according to this changed legislative policy which is patent on the face of Section 354(3), the normal punishment for murder and six other capital offences under the Penal Code, is imprisonment for life (or imprisonment for a term of years) and death penalty is an exception....

152. In the context, we may also notice Section 235(2) of the Code of 1973, because it makes not only explicit, what according to the decision in Jagmohan's case was implicit in the scheme of the Code, but also bifurcates the trial by providing for two hearings, one at the pre-conviction stage and another at the pre-sentence stage.... Although sub-section (2) of Section 235 does not contain a specific provision as to evidence and provides only for hearing of the accused as to sentence, yet it is implicit in this provision that if a request is made in that behalf by either the prosecution or the accused, or by both, the Judge should give the party or parties concerned an opportunity of producing evidence or material relating to the various factors bearing on the question of sentence....

153. We may also notice Sections 432*, 433* and 433-A*, as they throw light as to whether life imprisonment as currently administered in India, can be considered an adequate alternative to the capital sentence even in extremely heinous cases of murder.

....

156.... Section 433-A restricts the power of remission and commutation conferred on the appropriate Government under Sections 432 and 433, so that a person who is sentenced to imprisonment for life or whose death sentence is commuted to imprisonment for life must serve actual imprisonment for a minimum of 14 years.

157. We may next notice other provisions of the extant Code (corresponding to Sections 374*, 375*, 376* and 377* of the repealed Code) bearing on capital punishment. Section 366(i)* of the Code requires the Court passing a sentence of death to submit the proceedings to the High Court, and further mandates that such a sentence shall not be executed unless it is confirmed by the High Court. On such a reference for confirmation of death sentence, the High Court is required to proceed in accordance with Sections 367* and 368*. Section 367 gives power to the High Court to direct further inquiry to be made or additional evidence to be taken. Section 368 empowers the High Court to confirm the sentence of death or pass any other sentence warranted by law; or to annul or alter the conviction or order a new trial or acquit the accused. Section 369* enjoins that in every case so submitted, the confirmation of the sentence, or any new sentence or order passed by the High Court, shall, when such court consists of two or more Judges, be made, passed and signed by at least two of them. Section 370* provides that where any such case is heard before a Bench of Judges and such Judges are equally divided in opinion, the case shall be referred to a third Judge.

158. In this fasciculus of sections relating to confirmation proceedings in the High Court, the Legislature has provided valuable safeguards of the life and liberty of the subject in cases of capital sentences. These provisions seek to ensure that where in a capital case, the life of the convicted person is at stake, the entire evidential material bearing on the innocence or guilt of the accused and the question of sentence must be scrutinised with utmost caution and care by a superior Court.

159. The High Court has been given very wide powers under these provisions to prevent any possible miscarriage of justice. In State of Maharashtra v. Sidhi, 1975 (3) S.C.R. 574, this Court reiterated, with emphasis, that while dealing with a reference for confirmation of a sentence of death, the High Court must consider the proceedings in all their aspects, reappraise, reassess and reconsider the entire facts and law and if necessary, after taking additional evidence, come to its own conclusions on the material on record in regard to the convic-

tion of the accused (and the sentence) independently of the view expressed by the Sessions Judge.

160. Similarly, where on appeal, the High Court reverses an acquittal, and convicts, Section 379* of the Code of 1973, gives him a right of appeal to Supreme Court. Finally, there is Article 136* of the Constitution under which the Supreme Court is empowered, in its discretion, to entertain an appeal of behalf of a person whose sentence of death awarded by the Sessions Judge is confirmed by the High Court.

161. In the light of the above conspectus, we will now consider the effect of the aforesaid legislative changes on the authority and efficacy of the propositions laid down by this Court in Jagmohan's case. These propositions may be summed up as under: (i) The general legislative policy that underlies the structure of our criminal law, principally contained in the Indian Penal Code and the Criminal Procedure Code, is to define an offence with sufficient clarity and to prescribe only the maximum punishment therefor, and to allow a very wide discretion to the Judge in the matter of fixing the degree of punishment.

With the solitary exception of Section 303,ᵖ the same policy permeates Section 302 and some other sections of the Penal Code, where the maximum punishment is the death penalty.

(ii)(a) No exhaustive enumeration of aggravating or mitigating circumstances which should be considered when sentencing an offender, is possible....

(b) The impossibility of laying down standards is at the very core of the criminal law as administered in India which invests the matter of fixing the degree of punishment.

(iii) The view taken by the plurality in Furman v. Georgia decided by the Supreme Court of the United States to the effect, that a law which gives uncontrolled and unguided discretion to the Jury (or the Judge) to choose arbitrarily between a sentence of death and imprisonment for a sentence of death and imprisonment for a capital offence, violates the Eighth Amendment, is not applicable in India. We do not have in our Constitution any provision like the Eighth Amendment, nor are we at liberty to apply the test of reasonableness with the freedom with which the Judges of the Supreme Court of America are accustomed to apply "the due process" clause. There are grave doubts about the expediency of transplanting Western experience in our country. Social con-

---

p. EDITOR's NOTE: Section 303 of the Indian Penal Code, reproduced in the Appendix, mandates the death sentence for persons who commit murder while sentenced to life in prison.

ditions are different and so also the general intellectual level. Arguments which would be valid in respect of one area of the world may not hold good in respect of another area.

(iv)(a) This discretion in the matter of sentence is to be exercised by the Judge judicially, after balancing all the aggravating and mitigating circumstances of the crime.

(b) The discretion is liable to be corrected by superior courts. The exercise of judicial discretion on well-recognised principles is, in the final analysis, the safest possible safeguard for the accused.

In view of the above, it will be impossible to say that there would be at all any discrimination, since crime as crime may appear to be superficially the same but the facts and circumstances of a crime are widely different. Thus considered, the provision in Section 302, Penal Code is not violative of Article 14 of the Constitution on the ground that it confers on the Judges an unguided and uncontrolled discretion in the matter of awarding capital punishment or imprisonment for life.

(v)(a) Relevant facts and circumstances impinging on the nature and circumstances of the crime can be brought before the Court at the preconviction stage, notwithstanding the fact that no formal procedure for producing evidence regarding such facts and circumstances had been specifically provided. Where counsel addresses the Court with regard to the character and standing of the accused, they are duly considered by the Court unless there is something in the evidence itself which belies him or the Public Prosecutor challenge the facts.

(b) It is to be emphasised that in exercising its discretion to choose either of the two alternative sentences provided in Section 302, Penal Code,

> the Court is principally concerned with the facts and circumstances whether aggravating or mitigating, which are connected with the particular crime under inquiry. All such facts and circumstances are capable of being proved in accordance with the provisions of the Indian Evidence Act in a trial regulated by the Cr.P.C. The trial does not come to an end until all the relevant facts are proved and the counsel on both sides have an opportunity to address the Court....

162. A study of the propositions set out above, will show that, in substance, the authority of none of them has been affected by the legislative changes since the decision in Jagmohan case [except for (iv)(a) and (v)(b).]

....

165. Attuned to the legislative policy delineated in Section 354(3) and 235(2), propositions (iv)(a) and (v)(b) in Jagmohan shall have to be recast and may be stated as below:

(a) The normal rule is that the offence of murder shall be punished with the sentence of life imprisonment. The court can depart from that rule and impose the sentence of death only if there are special reasons for doing so. Such reasons must be recorded in writing before imposing the death sentence.

(b) While considering the question of sentence to be imposed for the offence of murder under Section 302, Penal Code, the court must have regard to every relevant circumstance relating to the crime as well as the criminal. If the court finds, but not otherwise, that the offence is of an exceptionally depraved and heinous character and constitutes, on account of its design and the manner of its execution, a source of grave danger to the society at large, the court may impose the death sentence.

166. The soundness or application of the other propositions in Jagmohan and the premises on which they rest, are not affected in any way by the legislative changes since effected. On the contrary, these changes reinforce the reasons given in Jagmohan for holding that the impugned provisions of the Penal Code and the Criminal Procedure Code do not offend Articles 14 and 21 of the Constitution. Now, Parliament has in Section 354(3) given a broad and clear guideline which is to serve the purpose of lodestar to the court in the exercise of its sentencing discretion. Parliament has advisedly not restricted this sentencing discretion further, as, in its legislative judgment, it is neither possible nor desirable to do so. Parliament could not but be aware that since the Amending Act 26 of 1955*, death penalty has been imposed by courts on an extremely small percentage of persons convicted of murder—a fact which demonstrates that courts have generally exercised their discretion in inflicting this extreme penalty with great circumspection, caution and restraint. Cognizant of the past experience of the administration of death penalty in India, Parliament, in its wisdom, though it best and safe to leave the imposition of this gravest punishment in gravest cases of murder, to the judicial discretion of the courts which are manned by persons of reason, experience and standing in the profession. The exercise of this sentencing discretion cannot be said to be untrammelled and unguided. It is exercised judicially in accordance with well recognised principles crystallised by judicial decisions, directed along the broad contours of legislative policy towards the signposts enacted in Section 354(3).

167. The new Section 235(2) adds to the number of several other safeguards which were embodied in the Criminal Procedure Code of 1898 and have been re-enacted in the Code of 1973. Then, the errors in the exercise of this guided judicial discretion are liable to be corrected by the superior courts. The Procedure provided in Criminal Procedure Code for imposing capital punishment for murder and some other capital crimes under the Penal Code cannot, by any reckoning, be said to be unfair, unreasonable and unjust. Nor can it be said that this sentencing discretion, with which the courts are invested, amounts to delegation of its power of legislation by Parliament. The argument

to that effect is entirely misconceived. We would, therefore, reaffirm the view taken by this Court in Jagmohan and hold that the impugned provisions do not violate Articles 14, 19 and 21 of the Constitution.

168. Now, remains the question whether this Court can lay down standards or norms restricting the area of the imposition of death penalty to a narrow category of murders.

169. Dr. Chitale contends that the wide observations in Jagmohan as to the impossibility of laying down standards or norms in the matter of sentencing are too sweeping. It is submitted that soon after the decision in Furman, several States in U.S.A. amended their penal statutes and brought them in conformity with the requirements of Furman. Support has also been sought for this argument from Gregg v. Georgia wherein the Supreme Court of the United States held that the concerns expressed in Furman decision that death penalty may not be imposed in an arbitrary or capricious manner could be met by a carefully drafted statute ensuring that the sentencing authority was given adequate guidance and information for determining the appropriate sentence, a bifurcated sentencing proceeding being preferable as a general proposition.

170. If by "laying down standards," it is meant that "murder" should be categorised beforehand according to the degrees of its culpability and all the aggravating and mitigating circumstances should be exhaustively and rigidly enumerated so as to exclude all free play of discretion, the argument merits rejection.

171. As pointed out in Jagmohan, such "standardisation" is well-nigh impossible.

....

176. We must leave unto the Legislature, the things that are Legislature's.

"The highest judicial duty is to recognise the limits on judicial power and to permit the democratic processes to deal with matters falling outside of those limits."

As Judges, we have to resist the temptation to substitute our own value-choices for the will of the people. Since substituted judicial 'made-to-order' standards, howsoever painstakingly made, do not bear the people's imprimatur, they may not have the same authenticity and efficacy as the silent zones and green belts designedly marked out and left open by Parliament in its legislative planning for fair play of judicial discretion to take care of the variable, unpredictable circumstances of the individual cases, relevant to individualised sentencing.... In this sensitive highly controversial area of death penalty, with all its complexity, vast implications and manifold ramifications, even all the Judges sitting cloistered in this Court and acting unanimously, cannot assume the role which properly belongs to the chosen representatives of the people in Parliament, particularly when Judges have no divining rod to divine accurately the will of the people. In Furman the Hon'ble Judges claimed to articulate the contemporary standards of morality among the American people. But speaking through public referenda, Gallup Polls and the State legislatures, the American people sharply rebuffed them. We must draw a lesson from the same.

....

178. From what has been extracted above, it is clear that this Court should not venture to formulate rigid standards in an area in which the Legislature so warily treads. Only broad guide-lines consistent with the policy indicated by the legislature in Section 354(3) can be laid down. Before we come to this aspect of the matter, it will be fair to notice briefly the decisions of the Supreme Court of U.S.A. in Gregg v. Georgia and companion cases.

....

193. Critically examined, it is clear that the [American decisions] demonstrate the truth of what we have said earlier, that it is neither practicable nor desirable to imprison the sentencing discretion of judge or jury in the strait-jacket of exhaustive and rigid standards. Nevertheless, these decisions do show that it is not impossible to lay down broad guide-lines as distinguished from iron-cased standards, which will minimise the risk of arbitrary imposition of death penalty for murder and some other offences under the Penal Code.

....

195. In Jagmohan, this Court had held this sentencing discretion is to be exercised judicially on well recognised principles, after balancing all the aggravating and mitigating circumstances of the crime. By "well recognised principles" the court obviously meant the principles crystallised by judicial decisions illustrating as to what were regarded as aggravating or mitigating circumstances in those cases. The legislative changes since Jagmohan—as we have discussed already—do not have the effect of abrogating or nullifying those principles. The only effect is that the application of those principles is now to be guided by the paramount beacons of legislative policy discernible from Section 354(3) and 235(2), namely: (1) The extreme penalty can be inflicted only in gravest cases of extreme culpability; (2) In making choice of the sentence, in addition to the circumstances of the offence, due regard must be paid to the circumstances of the offender, also.

196. We will first notice some of the aggravating circumstances which, in the absence of any mitigating circumstances, have been regarded as an indication for imposition of extreme penalty.

197. Pre-planned, calculated, cold blooded murder has always been regarded as one of an aggravated kind ...

198.... In Rajendra Prasad however, the majority (of 2:1) has completely reversed the view that had been taken ... regarding the application of Section

354(3) on this point. According to it, after the enactment of Section 354(3), "murder most foul" is not the test. The shocking nature of the crime of the number of murders committed is also not the criterion. It was said that the focus has now completely shifted from the crime to the criminal. "Special reasons" necessary for imposing death penalty "must relate not to the crime as such but to the criminal."

199. With great respect, we find ourselves unable to agree to this enunciation. As we read Sections 354(3) and 235(2) and other related provisions of the Code of 1973, it is quite clear to us that for making the choice of punishment or for ascertaining the existence or absence of "special reasons" in that context, the court must pay due regard both to the crime and the criminal. What is the relative weight to be given to the aggravating and mitigating factors, depends on the fact and circumstances of the particular case. More often than not these two aspects are so interwined that it is difficult to give a separate treatment to each of them. This is so because "style is the man." In many cases, the extremely cruel or beastly manner of the commission of murder is itself a demonstrated index of the depraved character of the perpetrator. That is why it is not desirable to consider the circumstances of the crime and the circumstances of the criminal in two separate watertight compartments. In a sense, to kill is to be cruel and therefore all murders are cruel. But such cruelty may vary in its degree of culpability. And it is only when the culpability assumes the proportion of extreme depravity that "special reasons" can legitimately be said to exist.

200. Drawing upon the penal statutes of the states in U.S.A. framed after Furman v. Georgia, in general, and Clauses 2(a), (b), (c) and (d) of the Indian Penal Code (Amendment) Bill* passed in 1978 by the Rajya Sabha, in particular, Dr. Chitale has suggested these "aggravating circumstances":

> Aggravating circumstances: A court may, however, in the following cases imposed the penalty of death in its discretion:
>
> (a) if the murder has been committed after previous planning and involves extreme brutality; or
>
> (b) if the murder involves exceptional depravity; or
>
> (c) if the murder is of a member of any of the armed forces of the Union or of a member of any police force or of any public servant and was committed—
>
> > (i) while such member or public servant was on duty; or
> >
> > (ii) in consequence of anything done or attempted to be done by such member or public servant in the lawful discharge of his duty as such member or public servant whether at the time of murder he was such member or public servant, as the case may be, or had ceased to be such member or public servant; or

(d) if the murder is of a person who had acted in the lawful discharge of his duty ... or who had rendered assistance to a magistrate or a police officer demanding his aid or requiring his assistance ...

201. Stated broadly, there can be no objection to the acceptance of these indicators but as we have indicated already, we would prefer not to fetter judicial discretion by attempting to make and exhaustive enumeration one way or the other.

202. In Rajendra Prasad, the majority said: "It is constitutionally permissible to swing a criminal out of corporeal existence only if the security of State and Society, public order and the interests of the general public compel that course as provided in Article 19(2) to (6)." Our objection is only to the word "only." While it may be conceded that a murder which directly threatens, or has an extreme potentiality to harm or endanger the security of State and Society, public order and the interests of the general public, may provide "special reasons" to justify the imposition of the extreme penalty on the person convicted of such a heinous murder, it is not possible to agree that imposition of death penalty or murderers who do not fall within this narrow category is constitutionally impermissible. We have discussed and held above that the impugned provisions in Section 302, Penal Code, being reasonable and in the general public interest, do not offend Article 19, or its "ethos"; nor do they in any manner violate Articles 21 and 14.... No exhaustive enumeration of aggravating circumstances is possible. But this much can be said that in order to qualify for inclusion in the category of "aggravating circumstances" which may form the basis of "special reasons" in Section 354(3), circumstance found on the facts of a particular case, must evidence aggravation of an abnormal or special degree.

204. Dr. Chitale has suggested these mitigating factors:

Mitigating circumstances:—In the exercise of its discretion in the above cases, the court shall take into account the following circumstances:—

(1) That the offence was committed under the influence of extreme mental or emotional disturbance.

(2) The age of the accused. If the accused is young or old, he shall not be sentenced to death.

(3) The probability that the accused would not commit criminal acts of violence as would constitute a continuing threat to society.

(4) The probability that the accused can be reformed and rehabilitated. The state shall by evidence prove that the accused does not satisfy the conditions (3) and (4) above.

(5) That in the facts and circumstances of the case the accused believed that he was morally justified in committing the offence.

(6) That the accused acted under the duress or domination of another person.

(7) That the condition of the accused showed that he was mentally defective and that the said defect impaired his capacity to appreciate the criminality of his conduct.

205. We will do no more than to say that these are undoubtedly relevant circumstances and must be given great weight in the determination of sentence. Some of these factors like extreme youth can instead be of compelling importance....

206. According to some Indian decisions, the post-murder remorse, penitence or repentance by the murderer is not a factor which may induce the court to pass the lesser penalty.... But those decisions can no longer be held to be good law in view of the current penological trends and the sentencing policy outlined in sections 235(2) and 354(3)....

207. There are numerous other circumstances justifying the passing of the lighter sentence; as there are countervailing circumstances of aggravation. "We cannot obviously feed into a judicial computer all such situations since they are astrological imponderables in an imperfect and undulating society."

Nonetheless, it cannot be over-emphasised that the scope and concept of mitigating factors in the area of death penalty must receive a liberal and expansive construction by the courts in accord with the sentencing policy writ large in Section 354(3). Judges should never be bloodthirsty. Hanging of murderers has never been too good for them. Facts and figures, albeit incomplete, furnished by the Union of India, show that in the past, courts have inflicted the extreme penalty with extreme infrequency—a fact which attests to the caution and compassion which they have always brought to bear on the exercise of their sentencing discretion in so grave a matter. It is, therefore, imperative to voice the concern that courts, aided by the broad illustrative guide-lines indicated by us, will discharge the onerous function with evermore scrupulous care and humane concern, directed along the highroad of legislative policy outlined in Section 354(3), viz., that for persons convicted of murder, life imprisonment is the rule and death sentence an exception. A real and abiding concern for the dignity of human life postulates resistance to taking a life through law's instrumentality. That ought not to be done save in the rarest of rare cases when the alternative option is unquestionably foreclosed.

208. For all the forgoing reasons, we reject the challenge to the constitutionality of the impugned provisions contained in Sections 302, Penal Code, and 354(3) of the code of Criminal Procedure, 1973.

209. The writ petitions and the connected petitions can now be heard and disposed of, on their individual merits, in the light of the broad guidelines and principles enunciated in this judgment.

D. The United States

1. Gregg v. Georgia, 428 U.S. 153, 96 S.Ct. 2909, 49 L.Ed.2d 859 (1976)

Judgment of the Court, and opinion of Mr. Justice Stewart, Mr. Justice Powell, and Mr. Justice Stevens, announced by Mr. Justice Stewart.

The issue in this case is whether the imposition of the sentence of death for the crime of murder under the law of Georgia violates the Eighth and Fourteenth Amendments.

I

The petitioner, Troy Gregg, was charged with committing armed robbery and murder. In accordance with Georgia procedure in capital cases, the trial was in two stages, a guilt stage and a sentencing stage. [At the guilt stage, he was convicted by a jury of the murders of two men who had picked him up while he was hitchhiking.]

At the penalty stage, which took place before the same jury, neither the prosecutor nor the petitioner's lawyer offered any additional evidence. Both counsel, however, made lengthy arguments dealing generally with the propriety of capital punishment under the circumstances and with the weight of the evidence of guilt. The trial judge instructed the jury that it could recommend either a death sentence or a life prison sentence on each count. The judge further charged the jury that in determining what sentence was appropriate the jury was free to consider the facts and circumstances, if any, presented by the parties in mitigation or aggravation.

Finally, the judge instructed the jury that it "would not be authorized to consider [imposing] the penalty of death" unless it first found beyond a reasonable doubt one of these aggravating circumstances:

> One—That the offense of murder was committed while the offender was engaged in the commission of two other capital felonies, to-wit the armed robbery of [the two victims].

> Two—That the offender committed the offense of murder for the purpose of receiving money and the automobile described in the indictment.

> Three—The offense of murder was outrageously and wantonly vile, horrible and inhuman, in that they [sic] involved the depravity of [the] mind of the defendant.

Finding the first and second of these circumstances, the jury returned verdicts of death on each count.

The Supreme Court of Georgia affirmed the convictions and the imposition of the death sentences for murder. After reviewing the trial transcript and the record, including the evidence, and comparing the evidence and sentence in similar cases in accordance with the requirements of Georgia law, the court concluded that, considering the nature of the crime and the defendant, the sentences of death had not resulted from prejudice or any other arbitrary factor and were not excessive or disproportionate to the penalty applied in similar cases. The death sentences imposed for armed robbery, however, were vacated on the grounds that the death penalty had rarely been imposed in Georgia for that offense and that the jury improperly considered the murders as aggravating circumstances for the robberies after having considered the armed robberies as aggravating circumstances for the murders.

We granted the petitioner's application for a writ of certiorari limited to his challenge to the imposition of the death sentences in this case as "cruel and unusual" punishment in violation of the Eighth and the Fourteenth Amendments.

II

Before considering the issues presented it is necessary to understand the Georgia statutory scheme for the imposition of the death penalty. The Georgia statute … retains the death penalty for six categories of crime: murder, kidnaping for ransom or where the victim is harmed, armed robbery, rape, treason, and aircraft hijacking. The capital defendant's guilt or innocence is determined in the traditional manner, either by a trial judge or a jury, in the first stage of a bifurcated trial.

If trial is by jury, the trial judge is required to charge lesser included offenses when they are supported by any view of the evidence. After a verdict, finding, or plea of guilty to a capital crime, a presentence hearing is conducted before whoever made the determination of guilt. The sentencing procedures are essentially the same in both bench and jury trials. At the hearing:

> [T]he judge [or jury] shall hear additional evidence in extenuation, mitigation, and aggravation of punishment, including the record of any prior criminal convictions and pleas of guilty or pleas of nolo contendere of the defendant, or the absence of any prior conviction and pleas: Provided, however, that only such evidence in aggravation as the State has made known to the defendant prior to his trial shall be admissible. The judge [or jury] shall also hear argument by the defendant or his counsel and the prosecuting attorney … regarding the punishment to be imposed.).

The defendant is accorded substantial latitude as to the types of evidence that he may introduce. Evidence considered during the guilt stage may be considered during the sentencing stage without being resubmitted.

In the assessment of the appropriate sentence to be imposed the judge is also required to consider or to include in his instructions to the jury "any mitigating circumstances or aggravating circumstances otherwise authorized by law and any of [10] statutory aggravating circumstances which may be supported by the evidence....". The scope of the nonstatutory aggravating or mitigating circumstances is not delineated in the statute. Before a convicted defendant may be sentenced to death, however, except in cases of treason or aircraft hijacking, the jury, or the trial judge in cases tried without a jury, must find beyond a reasonable doubt one of the 10 aggravating circumstances specified in the statute. The sentence of death may be imposed only if the jury (or judge) finds one of the statutory aggravating circumstances and then elects to impose that sentence. If the verdict is death, the jury or judge must specify the aggravating circumstance(s) found. In jury cases, the trial judge is bound by the jury's recommended sentence.

In addition to the conventional appellate process available in all criminal cases, provision is made for special expedited direct review by the Supreme Court of Georgia of the appropriateness of imposing the sentence of death in the particular case. The court is directed to consider "the punishment as well as any errors enumerated by way of appeal," and to determine:

(1) Whether the sentence of death was imposed under the influence of passion, prejudice, or any other arbitrary factor, and

(2) Whether, in cases other than treason or aircraft hijacking, the evidence supports the jury's or judge's finding of a statutory aggravating circumstance ... and

(3) Whether the sentence of death is excessive or disproportionate to the penalty imposed in similar cases, considering both the crime and the defendant.

If the court affirms a death sentence, it is required to include in its decision reference to similar cases that it has taken into consideration.

A transcript and complete record of the trial, as well as a separate report by the trial judge, are transmitted to the court for its use in reviewing the sentence. The report is in the form of a 6 1/2-page questionnaire, designed to elicit information about the defendant, the crime, and the circumstances of the trial. It requires the trial judge to characterize the trial in several ways designed to test for arbitrariness and disproportionality of sentence. Included in the report are responses to detailed questions concerning the quality of the defendant's representation, whether race played a role in the trial, and, whether, in the trial court's judgment, there was any doubt about the defendant's guilt or the appropriateness of the sentence. A copy of the report is served upon defense counsel. Under its special review authority, the court may either affirm the death sentence or remand the case for resentencing. In cases in which the death sentence is affirmed there remains the possibility of executive clemency.

III

We address initially the basic contention that the punishment of death for the crime of murder is, under all circumstances, "cruel and unusual" in violation of the Eighth and Fourteenth Amendments of the Constitution. In Part IV of this opinion, we will consider the sentence of death imposed under the Georgia statutes at issue in this case.

The Court on a number of occasions has both assumed and asserted the constitutionality of capital punishment. In several cases that assumption provided a necessary foundation for the decision, as the Court was asked to decide whether a particular method of carrying out a capital sentence would be allowed to stand under the Eighth Amendment. But until Furman v. Georgia, 408 U.S. 238, 92 S.Ct. 2726, 33 L.Ed.2d 346 (1972), the Court never confronted squarely the fundamental claim that the punishment of death always, regardless of the enormity of the offense or the procedure followed in imposing the sentence, is cruel and unusual punishment in violation of the Constitution. Although this issue was presented and addressed in Furman, it was not resolved by the Court. Four Justices would have held that capital punishment is not unconstitutional per se; two Justices would have reached the opposite conclusion; and three Justices, while agreeing that the statutes then before the Court were invalid as applied, left open the question whether such punishment may ever be imposed. We now hold that the punishment of death does not invariably violate the Constitution.

A

....

In the earliest cases raising Eighth Amendment claims, the Court focused on particular methods of execution to determine whether they were too cruel to pass constitutional muster. The constitutionality of the sentence of death itself was not at issue, and the criterion used to evaluate the mode of execution was its similarity to "torture" and other "barbarous" methods....

But the Court has not confined the prohibition embodied in the Eighth Amendment to "barbarous" methods that were generally outlawed in the 18th century. Instead, the Amendment has been interpreted in a flexible and dynamic manner. The Court early recognized that "a principle to be vital must be capable of wider application than the mischief which gave it birth." Weems v. United States, 217 U.S. 349, 373 (1910). Thus the Clause forbidding "cruel and unusual" punishments "is not fastened to the obsolete but may acquire meaning as public opinion becomes enlightened by a humane justice." Id., at 378....

In Weems the Court addressed the constitutionality of the Philippine punishment of cadena temporal for the crime of falsifying an official document. That punishment included imprisonment for at least 12 years and one day, in chains, at hard and painful labor; the loss of many basic civil rights; and subjection to lifetime surveillance. Although the Court acknowledged the possibility that "the cruelty of pain" may be present in the challenged punishment, 217 U.S., at 366, it did not rely on that factor, for it rejected the proposition that the Eighth Amendment reaches only punishments that are "inhuman and barbarous, torture and the like." Id., at 368. Rather, the Court focused on the lack of proportion between the crime and the offense ...

Later, in Trop v. Dulles, [356 U.S. 86, 78 S.Ct. 590, 2 L.Ed.2d 630 (1958)] the Court reviewed the constitutionality of the punishment of denationalization imposed upon a soldier who escaped from an Army stockade and became a deserter for one day. Although the concept of proportionality was not the basis of the holding, the plurality observed in dicta that "[fines], imprisonment and even execution may be imposed depending upon the enormity of the crime." 356 U.S., at 100.

The substantive limits imposed by the Eighth Amendment on what can be made criminal and punished were discussed in Robinson v. California, 370 U.S. 660, 82 S.Ct. 1417, 8 L.Ed.2d 758 (1962) ... It held, in effect, that it is "cruel and unusual" to impose any punishment at all for the mere status of addiction. The cruelty in the abstract of the actual sentence imposed was irrelevant: "Even one day in prison would be a cruel and unusual punishment for the "crime" of having a common cold." Id., at 667. Most recently, in Furman v. Georgia, supra, three Justices in separate concurring opinions found the Eighth Amendment applicable to procedures employed to select convicted defendants for the sentence of death.

It is clear from the foregoing precedents that the Eighth Amendment has not been regarded as a static concept ... Thus, an assessment of contemporary values concerning the infliction of a challenged sanction is relevant to the application of the Eighth Amendment. As we develop below more fully ... this assessment does not call for a subjective judgment. It requires, rather, that we look to objective indicia that reflect the public attitude toward a given sanction.

But our cases also make clear that public perceptions of standards of decency with respect to criminal sanctions are not conclusive. A penalty also must accord with "the dignity of man," which is the "basic concept underlying the Eighth Amendment." Trop v. Dulles, supra, at 100 (plurality opinion). This means, at least, that the punishment not be "excessive." When a form of punishment in the abstract (in this case, whether capital punishment may ever be imposed as a sanction for murder) rather than in the particular (the propriety of death as a penalty to be applied to a specific defendant for a specific crime) is under consideration, the inquiry into "excessiveness" has two aspects. First, the punishment must not involve the unnecessary and wanton infliction of pain ... Second, the punishment must not be grossly out of proportion to the severity of the crime ...

B

Of course, the requirements of the Eighth Amendment must be applied with an awareness of the limited role to be played by the courts. This does not mean that judges have no role to play, for the Eighth Amendment is a restraint upon the exercise of legislative power ...

But, while we have an obligation to insure that constitutional bounds are not overreached, we may not act as judges as we might as legislators ...

Therefore, in assessing a punishment selected by a democratically elected legislature against the constitutional measure, we presume its validity. We may not require the legislature to select the least severe penalty possible so long as the penalty selected is not cruelly inhumane or disproportionate to the crime involved. And a heavy burden rests on those who would attack the judgment of the representatives of the people.

This is true in part because the constitutional test is intertwined with an assessment of contemporary standards and the legislative judgment weighs heavily in ascertaining such standards ... The deference we owe to the decisions of the state legislatures under our federal system ... is enhanced where the specification of punishments is concerned, for "these are peculiarly questions of legislative policy." Gore v. United States, 357 U.S. 386, 393, 78 S.Ct. 1280, 2 L.Ed.2d 1405 (1958).... A decision that a given punishment is impermissible under the Eighth Amendment cannot be reversed short of a constitutional amendment. The ability of the people to express their preference through the normal democratic processes, as well as through ballot referenda, is shut off. Revisions cannot be made in the light of further experience....

C

In the discussion to this point we have sought to identify the principles and considerations that guide a court in addressing an Eighth Amendment claim. We now consider specifically whether the sentence of death for the crime of murder is a per se violation of the Eighth and Fourteenth Amendments to the Constitution. We note first that history and precedent strongly support a negative answer to this question.

The imposition of the death penalty for the crime of murder has a long history of acceptance both in the United States and in England....

It is apparent from the text of the Constitution itself that the existence of capital punishment was accepted by the Framers. At the time the Eighth Amendment was ratified, capital punishment was a common sanction in every

State.... The Fifth Amendment, adopted at the same time as the Eighth, contemplated the continued existence of the capital sanction by imposing certain limits on the prosecution of capital cases ...

And the Fourteenth Amendment, adopted over three-quarters of a century later, similarly contemplates the existence of the capital sanction in providing that no State shall deprive any person of "life, liberty, or property" without due process of law.

For nearly two centuries, this Court, repeatedly and often expressly, has recognized that capital punishment is not invalid per se ...

Four years ago, the petitioners in Furman and its companion cases predicated their argument primarily upon the asserted proposition that standards of decency had evolved to the point where capital punishment no longer could be tolerated.... This view was accepted by two Justices. Three other Justices were unwilling to go so far; focusing on the procedures by which convicted defendants were selected for the death penalty rather than on the actual punishment inflicted, they joined in the conclusion that the statutes before the Court were constitutionally invalid.

The petitioners in the capital cases before the Court today renew the "standards of decency" argument, but developments during the four years since Furman have undercut substantially the assumptions upon which their argument rested. Despite the continuing debate, dating back to the 19th century, over the morality and utility of capital punishment, it is now evident that a large proportion of American society continues to regard it as an appropriate and necessary criminal sanction.

The most marked indication of society's endorsement of the death penalty for murder is the legislative response to Furman. The legislatures of at least 35 States have enacted new statutes that provide for the death penalty for at least some crimes that result in the death of another person. And the Congress of the United States, in 1974, enacted a statute providing the death penalty for aircraft piracy that results in death. These recently adopted statutes have attempted to address the concerns expressed by the Court in Furman primarily (i) by specifying the factors to be weighed and the procedures to be followed in deciding when to impose a capital sentence, or (ii) by making the death penalty mandatory for specified crimes. But all of the post-Furman statutes make clear that capital punishment itself has not been rejected by the elected representatives of the people.

In the only statewide referendum occurring since Furman and brought to our attention, the people of California adopted a constitutional amendment that authorized capital punishment, in effect negating a prior ruling by the Supreme Court of California ... that the death penalty violated the California Constitution.

The jury also is a significant and reliable objective index of contemporary values because it is so directly involved.... It may be true that evolving standards have influenced juries in recent decades to be more discriminating in imposing the sentence of death. But the relative infrequency of jury verdicts imposing the death sentence does not indicate rejection of capital punishment per se. Rather, the reluctance of juries in many cases to impose the sentence may well reflect the humane feeling that this most irrevocable of sanctions should be reserved for a small number of extreme cases.... Indeed, the actions of juries in many States since Furman are fully compatible with the legislative judgments, reflected in the new statutes, as to the continued utility and necessity of capital punishment in appropriate cases. At the close of 1974 at least 254 persons had been sentenced to death since Furman, and by the end of March 1976, more than 460 persons were subject to death sentences.

As we have seen, however, the Eighth Amendment demands more than that a challenged punishment be acceptable to contemporary society. The Court also must ask whether it comports with the basic concept of human dignity at the core of the Amendment ... Although we cannot "invalidate a category of penalties because we deem less severe penalties adequate to serve the ends of penology," Furman v. Georgia, supra, at 451 (Powell, J., dissenting), the sanction imposed cannot be so totally without penological justification that it results in the gratuitous infliction of suffering.

The death penalty is said to serve two principal social purposes: retribution and deterrence of capital crimes by prospective offenders.[1]

In part, capital punishment is an expression of society's moral outrage at particularly offensive conduct. This function may be unappealing to many, but it is essential in an ordered society that asks its citizens to rely on legal processes rather than self-help to vindicate their wrongs ...

"Retribution is no longer the dominant objective of the criminal law," Williams v. New York, 337 U.S. 241, 248, 69 S.Ct. 1079, 93 L.Ed. 1337 (1949), but neither is it a forbidden objective nor one inconsistent with our respect for the dignity of men ... Indeed, the decision that capital punishment may be the appropriate sanction in extreme cases is an expression of the community's belief that certain crimes are themselves so grievous an affront to humanity that the only adequate response may be the penalty of death.

---

1. Another purpose that has been discussed is the incapacitation of dangerous criminals and the consequent prevention of crimes that they may otherwise commit in the future. See People v. Anderson, 6 Cal. 3d 628, 651, 493 P. 2d 880, 896, cert. denied, 406 U.S. 958 (1972); Commonwealth v. O'Neal, [369 Mass. 242, 339 N.E.2d 676] at 685–686 (1975).

Statistical attempts to evaluate the worth of the death penalty as a deterrent to crimes by potential offenders have occasioned a great deal of debate. The results simply have been inconclusive ...

Although some of the studies suggest that the death penalty may not function as a significantly greater deterrent than lesser penalties, there is no convincing empirical evidence either supporting or refuting this view. We may nevertheless assume safely that there are murderers, such as those who act in passion, for whom the threat of death has little or no deterrent effect. But for many others, the death penalty undoubtedly is a significant deterrent. There are carefully contemplated murders, such as murder for hire, where the possible penalty of death may well enter into the cold calculus that precedes the decision to act. And there are some categories of murder, such as murder by a life prisoner, where other sanctions may not be adequate.

The value of capital punishment as a deterrent of crime is a complex factual issue the resolution of which properly rests with the legislatures, which can evaluate the results of statistical studies in terms of their own local conditions and with a flexibility of approach that is not available to the courts ... Indeed, many of the post-Furman statutes reflect just such a responsible effort to define those crimes and those criminals for which capital punishment is most probably an effective deterrent.

In sum, we cannot say that the judgment of the Georgia Legislature that capital punishment may be necessary in some cases is clearly wrong. Considerations of federalism, as well as respect for the ability of a legislature to evaluate, in terms of its particular State, the moral consensus concerning the death penalty and its social utility as a sanction, require us to conclude, in the absence of more convincing evidence, that the infliction of death as a punishment for murder is not without justification and thus is not unconstitutionally severe.

Finally, we must consider whether the punishment of death is disproportionate in relation to the crime for which it is imposed. There is no question that death as a punishment is unique in its severity and irrevocability ... When a defendant's life is at stake, the Court has been particularly sensitive to insure that every safeguard is observed ... But we are concerned here only with the imposition of capital punishment for the crime of murder, and when a life has been taken deliberately by the offender, we cannot say that the punishment is invariably disproportionate to the crime. It is an extreme sanction, suitable to the most extreme of crimes.

We hold that the death penalty is not a form of punishment that may never be imposed, regardless of the circumstances of the offense, regardless of the character of the offender, and regardless of the procedure followed in reaching the decision to impose it.

IV

We now consider whether Georgia may impose the death penalty on the petitioner in this case.

A

While Furman did not hold that the infliction of the death penalty per se violates the Constitution's ban on cruel and unusual punishments, it did recognize that the penalty of death is different in kind from any other punishment imposed under our system of criminal justice. Because of the uniqueness of the death penalty, Furman held that it could not be imposed under sentencing procedures that created a substantial risk that it would be inflicted in an arbitrary and capricious manner.... Indeed, the death sentences examined by the Court in Furman were "cruel and unusual in the same way that being struck by lightning is cruel and unusual. For, of all the people convicted of [capital crimes], many just as reprehensible as these, the petitioners [in Furman were] among a capriciously selected random handful upon whom the sentence of death has in fact been imposed ... [T]he Eighth and Fourteenth Amendments cannot tolerate the infliction of a sentence of death under legal systems that permit this unique penalty to be so wantonly and so freakishly imposed." Id., at 309–310 (Stewart, J., concurring).

Furman mandates that, where discretion is afforded a sentencing body on a matter so grave as the determination of whether a human life should be taken or spared, that discretion must be suitably directed and limited so as to minimize the risk of wholly arbitrary and capricious action.... .

In summary, the concerns expressed in Furman that the penalty of death not be imposed in an arbitrary or capricious manner can be met by a carefully drafted statute that ensures that the sentencing authority is given adequate information and guidance. As a general proposition these concerns are best met by a system that provides for a bifurcated proceeding at which the sentencing authority is apprised of the information relevant to the imposition of sentence and provided with standards to guide its use of the information.

We do not intend to suggest that only the above described procedures would be permissible under Furman or that any sentencing system constructed along these general lines would inevitably satisfy the concerns of Furman, for each distinct system must be examined on an individual basis. Rather, we have embarked upon this general exposition to make clear that it is possible to construct capital-sentencing systems capable of meeting Furman's constitutional concerns.

B

We now turn to consideration of the constitutionality of Georgia's capital-sentencing procedures. In the wake of Furman, Georgia amended its capital punishment statute, but chose not to narrow the scope of its murder provisions....

Georgia did act, however, to narrow the class of murderers subject to capital punishment by specifying 10 statutory aggravating circumstances, one of which must be found by the jury to exist beyond a reasonable doubt before a death sentence can ever be imposed. In addition, the jury is authorized to consider any other appropriate aggravating or mitigating circumstances. The jury is not required to find any mitigating circumstance in order to make a recommendation of mercy that is binding on the trial court ... but it must find a statutory aggravating circumstance before recommending a sentence of death.

These procedures require the jury to consider the circumstances of the crime and the criminal before it recommends sentence. No longer can a Georgia jury do as Furman's jury did: reach a finding of the defendant's guilt and then, without guidance or direction, decide whether he should live or die. Instead, the jury's attention is directed to the specific circumstances of the crime: Was it committed in the course of another capital felony? Was it committed for money? Was it committed upon a peace officer or judicial officer? Was it committed in a particularly heinous way or in a manner that endangered the lives of many persons? In addition, the jury's attention is focused on the characteristics of the person who committed the crime: Does he have a record of prior convictions for capital offenses? Are there any special facts about this defendant that mitigate against imposing capital punishment (e.g., his youth, the extent of his cooperation with the police, his emotional state at the time of the crime). As a result, while some jury discretion still exists, "the discretion to be exercised is controlled by clear and objective standards so as to produce nondiscriminatory application." Coley v. State, 231 Ga. 829, 834, 204 S.E. 2d 612, 615 (1974).

As an important additional safeguard against arbitrariness and caprice, the Georgia statutory scheme provides for automatic appeal of all death sentences to the State's Supreme Court. That court is required by statute to review each sentence of death and determine whether it was imposed under the influence of passion or prejudice, whether the evidence supports the jury's finding of a statutory aggravating circumstance, and whether the sentence is disproportionate compared to those sentences imposed in similar cases.

In short, Georgia's new sentencing procedures require as a prerequisite to the imposition of the death penalty, specific jury findings as to the circumstances of the crime or the character of the defendant. Moreover, to guard further against a situation comparable to that presented in Furman, the Supreme Court of Georgia compares each death sentence with the sentences imposed on similarly situated defendants to ensure that the sentence of death in a particular case is not disproportionate. On their face these procedures seem to satisfy the concerns of Furman....

The petitioner contends, however, that the changes in the Georgia sentencing procedures are only cosmetic, that the arbitrariness and capriciousness condemned by Furman continue to exist in Georgia—both in traditional practices that still remain and in the new sentencing procedures adopted in response to Furman.

1

First, the petitioner focuses on the opportunities for discretionary action that are inherent in the processing of any murder case under Georgia law. He notes that the state prosecutor has unfettered authority to select those persons whom he wishes to prosecute for a capital offense and to plea bargain with them. Further, at the trial the jury may choose to convict a defendant of a lesser included offense rather than find him guilty of a crime punishable by death, even if the evidence would support a capital verdict. And finally, a defendant who is convicted and sentenced to die may have his sentence commuted by the Governor of the State and the Georgia Board of Pardons and Paroles.

The existence of these discretionary stages is not determinative of the issues before us. At each of these stages an actor in the criminal justice system makes a decision which may remove a defendant from consideration as a candidate for the death penalty. Furman, in contrast, dealt with the decision to impose the death sentence on a specific individual who had been convicted of a capital offense. Nothing in any of our cases suggests that the decision to afford an individual defendant mercy violates the Constitution. Furman held only that, in order to minimize the risk that the death penalty would be imposed on a capriciously selected group of offenders, the decision to impose it had to be guided by standards so that the sentencing authority would focus on the particularized circumstances of the crime and the defendant.

2

The petitioner further contends that the capital sentencing procedures adopted by Georgia in response to Furman do not eliminate the dangers of arbitrariness and caprice in jury sentencing that were held in Furman to be violative of the Eighth and Fourteenth Amendments. He claims that the statute is so broad and vague as to leave juries free to act as arbitrarily and capriciously as they wish in deciding whether to impose the death penalty. While there is no claim that the jury in this case relied upon a vague or overbroad provision to establish the existence of a statutory aggravating circumstance, the petitioner looks to the sentencing system as a whole (as the Court did in Furman and we do today) and argues that it fails to reduce sufficiently the risk of arbitrary infliction of death sentences. Specifically, Gregg urges that the statutory aggravating circumstances are too broad and too vague, that the sentencing procedure allows for arbitrary grants of mercy, and that the scope of the evidence and argument that can be considered at the presentence hearing is too wide.

The petitioner attacks the seventh statutory aggravating circumstance, which authorizes imposition of the death penalty if the murder was "outrageously or wantonly vile, horrible or inhuman in that it involved torture, depravity of mind, or an aggravated battery to the victim," contending that it is so broad that capital punishment could be imposed in any murder case. It is, of course, arguable that any murder involves depravity of mind or an aggravated battery. But this language need not be construed in this way, and there is no reason to assume that the Supreme Court of Georgia will adopt such an open-ended construction. In only one case has it upheld a jury's decision to sentence a defendant to death when the only statutory aggravating circumstance found was that of the seventh … and that homicide was a horrifying torture-murder.

The petitioner also argues that two of the statutory aggravating circumstances are vague and therefore susceptible of widely differing interpretations, thus creating a substantial risk that the death penalty will be arbitrarily inflicted by Georgia juries. In light of the decisions of the Supreme Court of Georgia we must disagree. First, the petitioner attacks that part of § 27-2534.1 (b)(1)* that authorizes a jury to consider whether a defendant has a "substantial history of serious assaultive criminal convictions." The Supreme Court of Georgia, however, has demonstrated a concern that the new sentencing procedures provide guidance to juries. It held this provision to be impermissibly vague … because it did not provide the jury with "sufficiently 'clear and objective standards.' " Second, the petitioner points to § 27-2534.1(b)(3)* which speaks of creating a "great risk of death to more than one person." While such a phrase might be susceptible of an overly broad interpretation, the Supreme Court of Georgia has not so construed it. The only case in which the court upheld a conviction in reliance on this aggravating circumstance involved a man who stood up in a church and fired a gun indiscriminately into the audience … On the other hand, the court expressly reversed a finding of great risk when the victim was simply kidnaped in a parking lot.

The petitioner next argues that the requirements of Furman are not met here because the jury has the power to decline to impose the death penalty even if it finds that one or more statutory aggravating circumstances are present in the case. This contention misinterprets Furman. Moreover, it ignores the role of the Supreme Court of Georgia which reviews each death sentence to determine whether it is proportional to other sentences imposed for similar crimes. Since the proportionality requirement on review is intended to prevent caprice in the decision to inflict the penalty, the isolated decision of a jury to afford mercy does not render unconstitutional death sentences imposed on defendants who were sentenced under a system that does not create a substantial risk of arbitrariness or caprice.

The petitioner objects, finally, to the wide scope of evidence and argument allowed at presentence hearings. We think that the Georgia court wisely has chosen not to impose unnecessary restrictions on the evidence that can be offered at such a hearing and to approve open and far-ranging argument ... So long as the evidence introduced and the arguments made at the presentence hearing do not prejudice a defendant, it is preferable not to impose restrictions. We think it desirable for the jury to have as much information before it as possible when it makes the sentencing decision.

3

Finally, the Georgia statute has an additional provision designed to assure that the death penalty will not be imposed on a capriciously selected group of convicted defendants. The new sentencing procedures require that the State Supreme Court review every death sentence to determine whether it was imposed under the influence of passion, prejudice, or any other arbitrary factor, whether the evidence supports the findings of a statutory aggravating circumstance, and "[w]hether the sentence of death is excessive or disproportionate to the penalty imposed in similar cases, considering both the crime and the defendant." ... In performing its sentence-review function, the Georgia court has held that "if the death penalty is only rarely imposed for an act or it is substantially out of line with sentences imposed for other acts it will be set aside as excessive." Coley v. State, 231 Ga., at 834, 204 S.E. 2d, at 616. The court on another occasion stated that "we view it to be our duty under the similarity standard to assure that no death sentence is affirmed unless in similar cases throughout the state the death penalty has been imposed generally...." Moore v. State, 233 Ga. 861, 864, 213 S.E. 2d 829, 832 (1975)....

It is apparent that the Supreme Court of Georgia has taken its review responsibilities seriously. In Coley, it held that "[the] prior cases indicate that the past practice among juries faced with similar factual situations and like aggravating circumstances has been to impose only the sentence of life imprisonment for the offense of rape, rather than death." 231 Ga., at 835, 204 S.E. 2d, at 617. It thereupon reduced Coley's sentence from death to life imprisonment. Similarly, although armed robbery is a capital offense under Georgia law ... the Georgia court concluded that the death sentences imposed in this case for that crime were "unusual in that they are rarely imposed for [armed robbery]. Thus, under the test provided by statute, ... they must be considered to be excessive or disproportionate to the penalties imposed in similar cases." 233 Ga., at 127, 210 S.E. 2d, at 667. The court therefore vacated Gregg's death sentences for armed robbery and has followed a similar course in every other armed robbery death penalty case to come before it.

The provision for appellate review in the Georgia capital-sentencing system serves as a check against the random or arbitrary imposition of the death penalty. In particular, the proportionality review substantially eliminates the possibility that a person will be sentenced to die by the action of an aberrant jury. If a time comes when juries generally do not impose the death sentence in a certain kind of murder case, the appellate review procedures assure that no defendant convicted under such circumstances will suffer a sentence of death.

V

The basic concern of Furman centered on those defendants who were being condemned to death capriciously and arbitrarily. Under the procedures before the Court in that case, sentencing authorities were not directed to give attention to the nature or circumstances of the crime committed or to the character or record of the defendant. Left unguided, juries imposed the death sentence in a way that could only be called freakish. The new Georgia sentencing procedures, by contrast, focus the jury's attention on the particularized nature of the crime and the particularized characteristics of the individual defendant. While the jury is permitted to consider any aggravating or mitigating circumstances, it must find and identify at least one statutory aggravating factor before it may impose a penalty of death. In this way the jury's discretion is channeled. No longer can a jury wantonly and freakishly impose the death sentence; it is always circumscribed by the legislative guidelines. In addition, the review function of the Supreme Court of Georgia affords additional assurance that the concerns that prompted our decision in Furman are not present to any significant degree in the Georgia procedure applied here.

For the reasons expressed in this opinion, we hold that the statutory system under which Gregg was sentenced to death does not violate the Constitution. Accordingly, the judgment of the Georgia Supreme Court is affirmed.

It is so ordered.

[Although this opinion represents the views of only three of the seven justices who voted to affirm the judgment, it is reproduced as the more thorough of the two opinions written, and because Justice Stewart was one of the five justices who held the statute at issue in Furman unconstitutional, while Justice Stevens had taken the seat of Justice Douglas, who had also voted with the majority in Furman.]

(concurrences and dissents omitted)

Appendix

Relevant Provisions of Applicable Legal Instruments

A. Japan

1. Constituion

Article 13

All of the people shall be respected as individuals. Their right to life, liberty, and the pursuit of happiness shall, to the extent that it does not interfere with the public welfare, be the supreme consideration in legislation and in other governmental affairs.

Article 31

No person shall be deprived of life or liberty, nor shall any other criminal penalty be imposed, except according to procedure established by law.

Article 33

No person shall be apprehended except upon warrant issued by a competent judicial officer which specifies the offense with which the person is charged, unless he is apprehended, the offense being committed.

Article 34

No person shall be arrested or detained without being at once informed of the charges against him or without the immediate privilege of counsel; nor shall he be detained without adequate cause; and upon demand of any person such cause must be immediately shown in open court in his presence and the presence of his counsel.

Article 37

(1) In all criminal cases the accused shall enjoy the right to a speedy and public trial by an impartial tribunal.

(2) He shall be permitted full opportunity to examine all witnesses, and he shall have the right of compulsory process for obtaining witnesses on his behalf at public expense.

(3) At all times the accused shall have the assistance of competent counsel who shall, if the accused is unable to secure the same by his own efforts, be assigned to his use by the State.

Article 38

(1) No person shall be compelled to testify against himself.

(2) Confession made under compulsion, torture or threat, or after prolonged arrest or detention shall not be admitted in evidence.

(3) No person shall be convicted or punished in cases where the only proof against him is his own confession.

2. Statutes

a. *Code of Criminal Procedure*

Article 1

The purpose of this Code is to make the facts of the case clear as well as to apply and enforce properly and speedily the punitive laws and orders with respect to criminal cases, while taking into full consideration the maintenance of public welfare and the guarantee of the fundamental human rights of an individual.

Article 39

(1) A suspect or defendant in custody is entitled to meet the defence counsel, or a person who is to be a defence counsel upon request of a person who is empowered to appoint a counsel (if this person is not a qualified attorney, this is limited to cases where the permission as provided by Article 31, paragraph 2 has been granted) without the presence of any person, or receive documents and other things.

...

(3) Public prosecutors, clerks of the Public Prosecutors' Office, or police officers (i.e. police officers and sergeants) may, when it is needed for investigation, and provided that it is before indictment, designate the place and time of the consultation and the reception of documents; however, this designation shall not be of a nature that unreasonably restricts the right of the suspect in preparing the defence.

Article 197

(1) Necessary questioning may be performed to fulfill the objective of an investigation. However, compulsory measures may not be performed unless there exists a special provision in this law....

Article 198

(1) Public prosecutors, assistant officers of public prosecutors, and judicial police officials may, as required during the investigation of a crime, request the attendance of and interrogate the suspect. However, unless placed under arrest or held in custody, the suspect may reject a request to attend or withdraw from the interrogation at any time ...

Article 319

(1) Confession that is made under compulsion, torture or threat, or is made after unreasonably long arrest or detention, or that is doubtful of having been not made voluntarily, may not be made as evidence....

Article 411

Appeals court may still quash second instance court decisions in its judgment when the court finds one of the following causes and finds that there will be serious injustice if second instance court decisions are not quashed, in the event the court does not find any of the causes set forth in Article 405 ...

(2) In the event the weight of the sentence is improper.

b. Habeas Corpus Law

Article 2

A person who is subjected to physical restraint other than by a lawful and proper procedure may apply for relief as provided in this law.

Such application may be made by any person on behalf of the person under restraint.

c. Habeas Corpus Rules

Article 4

An application under Article 2 of the Habeas Corpus Law may be made only where the restraint, or the judgment or administrative decision relating to the restraint, is either patently without authority or patently and seriously violates a form or procedure established by law. Provided that such application may not be made where other suitable means are available for obtaining the objects of the writ, unless it is clear that the objects of the writ cannot be achieved by such other means within a reasonable period of time.

d. Penal Code

Article 11

The death penalty shall be performed in prison by hanging. The person who receives the death penalty shall be detained in this prison until such time of execution.

Article 230-2

If the act [of injuring the reputation of another by publicly alleging facts] involves the public interest, and if the act can be acknowledged to have solely been intended for the promotion of the public interest, the truthfulness of the fact shall be examined, and if it is proved that it was true, the act shall not be punishable.

Article 240

If a robber injures a person, he shall be punished with penal servitude for life or a period of not less than six years; if he causes the death of another, he shall be punished with death or penal servitude for life.

B. European Human Rights System

1. European Convention on Human Rights and Fundamental Freedoms, November 4, 1950, Council of Europe Treaty Series No. 5, as amended by Protocol No. 11 to the Convention for the Protection of Human Rights and Fundamental Freedoms, Restructuring the Control Machinery Established Thereby, Council of Europe Treaty Series No. 155, May 11, 1994

Article 3—Prohibition of torture

No one shall be subjected to torture or to inhuman or degrading treatment or punishment.

Article 5—Right to liberty and security

1. Everyone has the right to liberty and security of person. No one shall be deprived of his liberty save in the following cases and in accordance with a procedure prescribed by law:

    a. the lawful detention of a person after conviction by a competent court;

b. the lawful arrest or detention of a person for non-compliance with the lawful order of a court or in order to secure the fulfilment of any obligation prescribed by law;

c. the lawful arrest or detention of a person effected for the purpose of bringing him before the competent legal authority on reasonable suspicion of having committed an offence or when it is reasonably considered necessary to prevent his committing an offence or fleeing after having done so;

d. the detention of a minor by lawful order for the purpose of educational supervision or his lawful detention for the purpose of bringing him before the competent legal authority;

e. the lawful detention of persons for the prevention of the spreading of infectious diseases, of persons of unsound mind, alcoholics or drug addicts or vagrants;

f. the lawful arrest or detention of a person to prevent his effecting an unauthorised entry into the country or of a person against whom action is being taken with a view to deportation or extradition.

2. Everyone who is arrested shall be informed promptly, in a language which he understands, of the reasons for his arrest and of any charge against him.

3. Everyone arrested or detained in accordance with the provisions of paragraph 1.c of this article shall be brought promptly before a judge or other officer authorised by law to exercise judicial power and shall be entitled to trial within a reasonable time or to release pending trial. Release may be conditioned by guarantees to appear for trial.

4. Everyone who is deprived of his liberty by arrest or detention shall be entitled to take proceedings by which the lawfulness of his detention shall be decided speedily by a court and his release ordered if the detention is not lawful.

5. Everyone who has been the victim of arrest or detention in contravention of the provisions of this article shall have an enforceable right to compensation.

Article 6—Right to a fair trial

1. In the determination of his civil rights and obligations or of any criminal charge against him, everyone is entitled to a fair and public hearing within a reasonable time by an independent and impartial tribunal established by law. Judgment shall be pronounced publicly but the press and public may be excluded from all or part of the trial in the interests of morals, public order or national security in a democratic society, where the interests of juveniles or the protection of the private life of the parties so require, or to the extent strictly necessary in the opinion of the court in special circumstances where publicity would prejudice the interests of justice.

2. Everyone charged with a criminal offence shall be presumed innocent until proved guilty according to law.

3. Everyone charged with a criminal offence has the following minimum rights:

> 1. to be informed promptly, in a language which he understands and in detail, of the nature and cause of the accusation against him;
>
> 2. to have adequate time and facilities for the preparation of his defence;
>
> 3. to defend himself in person or through legal assistance of his own choosing or, if he has not sufficient means to pay for legal assistance, to be given it free when the interests of justice so require;
>
> 4. to examine or have examined witnesses against him and to obtain the attendance and examination of witnesses on his behalf under the same conditions as witnesses against him;
>
> 5. to have the free assistance of an interpreter if he cannot understand or speak the language used in court.

Article 8—Right to respect for private and family life

1. Everyone has the right to respect for his private and family life, his home and his correspondence.

2. There shall be no interference by a public authority with the exercise of this right except such as is in accordance with the law and is necessary in a democratic society in the interests of national security, public safety or the economic well-being of the country, for the prevention of disorder or crime, for the protection of health or morals, or for the protection of the rights and freedoms of others.

Article 14—Prohibition of discrimination

The enjoyment of the rights and freedoms set forth in this Convention shall be secured without discrimination on any ground such as sex, race, colour, language, religion, political or other opinion, national or social origin, association with a national minority, property, birth or other status.

Article 17—Prohibition of abuse of rights

Nothing in this Convention may be interpreted as implying for any State, group or person any right to engage in any activity or perform any act aimed at the destruction of any of the rights and freedoms set forth herein or at their limitation to a greater extent than is provided for in the Convention.

2. Protocol No. 6 to the Convention for the Protection of Human Rights and Fundamental Freedoms Concerning the Abolition of the Death Penalty, April 28, 1983, Council of Europe Treat Series No. 114, as Amended by Protocol No. 11 to the Convention for the Protection of Human Rights and Fundamental Freedoms, Restructuring the Control Machinery Established Thereby, May 11, 1994, Council of Europe Treaty Series No. 155

...

Article 1—Abolition of the death penalty

The death penalty shall be abolished. No-one shall be condemned to such penalty or executed.

Article 2—Death penalty in time of war

A State may make provision in its law for the death penalty in respect of acts committed in time of war or of imminent threat of war; such penalty shall be applied only in the instances laid down in the law and in accordance with its provisions. The State shall communicate to the Secretary General of the Council of Europe the relevant provisions of that law.

Article 3—Prohibition of derogations

No derogation from the provisions of this Protocol shall be made under Article 15 of the Convention.

Article 4—Prohibition of reservations[1]

No reservation may be made ... in respect of the provisions of this Protocol....

---

1. Text amended according to the provisions of Protocol No. 11 (ETS No. 155).

C. India

1. Constitution

....

PART III—FUNDAMENTAL RIGHTS—GENERAL

Article13 . Laws inconsistent with or in derogation of the fundamental rights.

(1) All laws in force in the territory of India immediately before the commencement of this Constitution, in so far as they are inconsistent with the provisions of this Part, shall, to the extent of such inconsistency, be void.

(2) The State shall not make any law which takes away or abridges the rights conferred by this Part and any law made in contravention of this clause shall, to the extent of the contravention, be void....

Article 14. Equality before law.

The State shall not deny to any person equality before the law or the equal protection of the laws within the territory of India.

Article 19. Protection of certain rights regarding freedom of speech, etc.

(1) All citizens shall have the right—

> (a) to freedom of speech and expression;
>
> (b) to assemble peaceably and without arms;
>
> (c) to form associations or unions;
>
> (d) to move freely throughout the territory of India;
>
> (e) to reside and settle in any part of the territory of India; and
>
> (f) to practice any profession, or to carry on any occupation, trade or business.

(2) Nothing in sub-clause (a) of clause (1) shall affect the operation of any existing law, or prevent the State from making any law, in so far as such law imposes reasonable restrictions on the exercise of the right conferred by the said sub-clause in the interests of the sovereignty and integrity of India, the security of the State, friendly relations with foreign States, public order, decency or morality, or in relation to contempt of court, defamation or incitement to an offence.

(3) Nothing in sub-clause (b) of the said clause shall affect the operation of any existing law in so far as it imposes, or prevent the State from making any law imposing, in the interest of the sovereignty and integrity of India or public order, reasonable restrictions on the right conferred by the said sub-clause.

(4) Nothing in sub-clause (c) of the said clause shall affect the operation of any existing law in so far as it imposes, or prevent the State from making any law

imposing, in the interests of the the sovereignty and integrity of India or public order or morality, reasonable restrictions on the exercise of the right conferred by the said sub-clause.

(5) Nothing in sub-clause (d) and (e) of the said clause shall affect the operation of any existing law in so far as it imposes, or prevent the State from making any law imposing, reasonable restrictions on the exercise of any of the rights conferred by the said sub-clauses either in the interests of the general public or for the protection of the interests of any Schedule Tribe.

(6) Nothing in sub-clause (g) of the said clause shall affect the operation of any existing law in so far as it imposes, or prevent the State from making any law imposing, in the interests of the general public, reasonable restrictions on the exercise of the right conferred by the said sub-clause, and, in particular, nothing in the said sub-clause shall affect the operation of any existing law in so far as it relates to, or prevent the State from making any law relating to,—

(i) the professional or technical qualifications necessary for practicing any profession or carrying on any occupation, trade or business, or

(ii) the carrying on by the State, or by a corporation owned or controlled by the State, of any trade, business, industry or service, whether to the exclusion, complete or partial, of citizens or otherwise.

Article 20. Protection in respect of conviction for offences.

(1) No person shall be convicted of any offence except for violation of a law in force at the time of the commission of the Act charged as an offence, nor be subjected to a penalty greater than that which might have been inflicted under the law in force at the time of the commission of the offence.

(2) No person shall be prosecuted and punished for the same offence more than once.

(3) No person accused of any offence shall be compelled to be a witness against himself.

Article 21. Protection of life and personal liberty.

No person shall be deprived of his life or personal liberty except according to procedure established by law.

Article 22. Protection against arrest and detention in certain cases.

(1) No person who is arrested shall be detained in custody without being informed, as soon as may be, of the grounds for such arrest nor shall he be denied the right to consult, and to be defended by, a legal practitioner of his choice.

(2) Every person who is arrested and detained in custody shall be produced before the nearest magistrate within a period of twenty-four hours of such arrest excluding the time necessary for the journey from the place of arrest to the

court of the magistrate and no such person shall be detained in custody beyond the said period without the authority of a magistrate.

(3) Nothing in clauses (1) and (2) shall apply—

(a) to any person who for the time being is an enemy alien; or

(b) to any person who is arrested or detained under any law providing for preventive detention.

(4) No law providing for preventive detention shall authorise the detention of a person for a longer period than three months unless—

(a) an Advisory Board consisting of persons who are, or have been, or are qualified to be appointed as, Judges of a High Court has reported before the expiration of the said period of three months that there is in its opinion sufficient cause for such detention:

Provided that nothing in this sub-clause shall authorise the detention of any person beyond the maximum period prescribed by any law made by Parliament under sub-clause (b) of clause (7); or

(b) such person is detained in accordance with the provisions of any law made by Parliament under sub-clauses (a) and (b) of clause (7).

(5) When any person is detained in pursuance of an order made under any law providing for preventive detention, the authority making the order shall, as soon as may be, communicate to such person the grounds on which the order has been made and shall afford him the earliest opportunity of making a representation against the order.

(6) Nothing in clause (5) shall require the authority making any such order as is referred to in that clause to disclose facts which such authority considers to be against the public interest to disclose.

(7) Parliament may by law prescribe—

(a) the circumstances under which, and the class or classes of cases in which, a person may be detained for a period longer than three months under any law providing for preventive detention without obtaining the opinion of an Advisory Board in accordance with the provisions of sub-clause (a) of clause (4);

(b) the maximum period for which any person may in any class or classes of cases be detained under any law providing for preventive detention; and

(c) the procedure to be followed by an Advisory Board in an inquiry under sub-clause (a) of clause (4).

Article 31C. Saving of laws giving effect to certain directive principles.

Notwithstanding anything contained in article 13, no law giving effect to the policy of the State towards securing all or any of the principles laid down in

Part IV shall be deemed to be void on the ground that it is inconsistent with, or takes away or abridges any of the rights conferred by article 14 or article 19;

Provided that where such law is made by the Legislature of a State, the provisions of this article shall not apply thereto unless such law, having been reserved for the consideration of the President, has received his assent.

Article 32. Remedies for enforcement of rights conferred by this Part.

(1) The right to move the Supreme Court by appropriate proceedings for the enforcement of the rights conferred by this Part is guaranteed.

(2) The Supreme Court shall have power to issue directions or orders or writs, including writs in the nature of habeas corpus, mandamus, prohibition, quo warranto and certiorari, whichever may be appropriate, for the enforcement of any of the rights conferred by this Part.

(3) Without prejudice to the powers conferred on the Supreme Court by clauses (1) and (2), Parliament may by law empower any other court to exercise within the local limits of its jurisdiction all or any of the powers exercisable by the Supreme Court under clause (2).

(4) The right guaranteed by this article shall not be suspended except as otherwise provided for by this Constitution.

PART IV—DIRECTIVE PRINCIPLES OF STATE POLICY

Article 37. Application of the principles contained in this Part.

The provisions contained in this Part shall not be enforceable by any court, but the principles therein laid down are nevertheless fundamental in the governance of the country and it shall be the duty of the State to apply these principles in making laws.

Article 39A. Equal justice and free legal aid.

The State shall secure that the operation of the legal system promotes justice, on a basis of equal opportunity, and shall, in particular, provide free legal aid, by suitable legislation or schemes or in any other way, to ensure that opportunities for securing justice are not denied to any citizen by reason of economic or other disabilities.

Article 51. Promotion of international peace and security.

The State shall endeavour to

(a) promote international peace and security;

(b) maintain just and honourable relations between nations;

(c) foster respect for international law and treaty obligations in the dealings of organised peoples with one another; and

(d) encourage settlement of international disputes by arbitration.

Article 51A. Fundamental Duties.—It shall be the duty of every citizens of India

(a) to abide by the Constitution and respect its ideals and institutions, the National Flag and the National Anthem;

...

PART XI. RELATIONS BETWEEN THE UNION AND THE STATES—CHAPTER I.—LEGISLATIVE RELATIONS

Article 246. Subject-matter of laws made by Parliament and by the Legislatures of States.

(1) Notwithstanding anything in clauses (2) and (3), Parliament has exclusive power to make laws with respect to any of the matters enumerated in List I in the Seventh Schedule (in this Constitution referred to as the "Union List").

(2) Notwithstanding anything in clause (3), Parliament, and, subject to clause (1), the Legislature of any State also, have power to make laws with respect to any of the matters enumerated in List III in the Seventh Schedule (in this Constitution referred to as the "Concurrent List")....

SEVENTH SCHEDULE

List I—Union List

...

9. Preventive detention for reasons connected with Defence, Foreign Affairs, or the security of India; persons subjected to such detention.

...

List III—Concurrent List

...

3. Preventive detention for reasons connected with the security of a State, the maintenance of public order, or the maintenance of supplies and services essential to the community; persons subjected to such detention.

...

2. Statutes

a. Code of Criminal Procedure

162. Statements to police not to be signed: Use of statements in evidence.

(1) No statement made by any person to a police officer in the course of an investigation under this Chapter, shall, if reduced to writing, be signed by the person making it; nor shall any such statement or any record thereof, whether

in a police diary or otherwise, or any part of such statement or record, be used for any purpose, save as hereinafter provided, at any inquiry or trial in respect of any offence under investigation at the time when such statement was made:

Provided that when any witness is called for the prosecution in such inquiry or trial whose statement has been reduced into writing as aforesaid, any part of his statement, if duly proved, may be used by the accused, and with the permission of the Court, by the prosecution, to contradict such witness in the manner provided by section 145 of the Indian Evidence Act, 1872 (1 of 1872) ; and when any part of such statement is so used, any part thereof may also be used in the re-examination of such witness, but for the purpose only of explaining any matter referred to in his cross-examination.

(2) Nothing in this section shall be deemed to apply to any statement falling within the provisions of clause (1) of section 32 of the Indian Evidence Act, 1872 (1 of 1872), or to affect the provisions of section 27 of that Act.

Explanation.—An omission to state a fact or circumstance in the statement referred to in sub-section (1) may amount to contradiction if the same appears to be significant and otherwise relevant having regard to the context in which such omission occurs and whether any omission amounts to a contradiction in the particular context shall be a question of fact.

164. Recording of confessions and statements.

(1) Any Metropolitan Magistrate or Judicial Magistrate may, whether or not he has jurisdiction in the case, record any confession or statement made to him in the course of an investigation under this Chapter or under any other law for the time being in force, or at any time afterwards before the commencement of the inquiry or trial:

Provided that no confession shall be recorded by a police officer on whom any power of a Magistrate has been conferred under any law for the time being in force.

(2) The Magistrate shall, before recording any such confession, explain to the person making it that he is not bound to make a confession and that, if he does so, it may be used as evidence against him; and the Magistrate shall not record any such confession unless, upon questioning the person making it, he has reason to believe that it is being made voluntarily.

(3) If at any time before the confession is recorded, the person appearing before the Magistrate states that he is not willing to make the confession, the Magistrate shall not authorise the detention of such person in police custody.

(4) Any such confession shall be recorded ... and shall be signed by the person making the confession; and the Magistrate shall make a memorandum at the foot of such record to the following effect::

I have explained to (name) that he is not bound to make a confession and that, if he does so, any confession he may make may be used as evidence against him and I believe that this confession was voluntarily made. It was taken in my presence and hearing, and was read over to the person making it and admitted by him to be correct, and it contains a full and true account of the statement made by him.

(Signed) A.B. Magistrate

(5) Any statement (other than a confession) made under sub-section (1) shall be recorded in such manner hereinafter provided for the recording of evidence as is, in the opinion of the Magistrate, best fitted to the circumstances of the case; and the Magistrate shall have power to administer oath to the person whose statement is so recorded.

(6) The Magistrate recording a confession or statement under this section shall forward it to the Magistrate by whom the case is to be inquired into or tried.

235. Judgment of acquittal or conviction.

(1) After hearing arguments and points of law (if any), the Judge shall give a judgment in the case.

(2) If the accused is convicted, the Judge shall, unless he proceeds in accordance with the provisions of section 360, hear the accused on the question of sentence, and then pass sentence on him according to law.

Section 354. Language and contents of judgment.

....

(3) When the conviction is for an offence punishable with death or, in the alternative, with imprisonment for life or imprisonment for a term of years, the judgment shall state the reasons for the sentence awarded, and, in the case of sentence of death, the special reasons for such sentence.

....

(5) When any person is sentenced to death, the sentence shall direct that he be hanged by the neck till he is dead.

b. Evidence Act, 1872

25. Confession to police officer not to be proved.

No confession made to a police officer shall be proved as against a person accused of any offence.

26. Confession by accused while in custody of police not to be proved against him.

No confession made by any person whilst he is in the custody of a police-officer, unless it be made in the immediate presence of a Magistrate, shall be proved as against such person.

27. How much of information received from accused may be proved.

Provided that, when any fact is deposed to as discovered in consequence of information received from a person accused of any offence, in the custody of a police officer, so much of such information, whether it amounts to a confession or not, as relates distinctly to the fact thereby discovered, may be proved.

29. Confession otherwise relevant not to become irrelevant because of promise of secrecy, etc.

If such a confession is otherwise relevant, it does not become irrelevant because it was made under a promise of secrecy, or in consequence of a deception practiced on the accused person for the purpose of obtaining it, or when he was drunk, or because it was made in answer to questions which he need not have answered, whatever may have been the form of those questions, or because he was not warned that he was not bound to make such confession, and that the evidence of it might be given against him.

30. Consideration of proved confession affecting person making it and others jointly under trail for same offence.

When more persons than one are being tried jointly for the same offence, and a confession made by one of such persons affecting himself and some other of such persons is proved, the Court may take into consideration such confession as against such other person as well as against the person who makes such confession.

c. Penal Code

Section 299. Culpable homicide.

Whoever causes death by doing an act with the intention of causing death, or with the intention of causing such bodily injury as is likely to cause death, or with the knowledge that he is likely by such act to cause death, commits the offence of culpable homicide.

[exceptions, illustrations, and explanations omitted.]

Section 300. Murder.

Except in the cases hereinafter excepted, culpable homicide is murder, if the act by which the death is caused is done with the intention of causing death, or

2ndly.—If it is done with the intention of causing such bodily injury as the offender knows to be likely to cause the death of the person to whom the harm is caused, or

3rdly.—If it is done with the intention of causing bodily injury to any person and the bodily injury intended to be inflicted is sufficient in the ordinary course of nature to cause death, or

4thly.—If the person committing the act knows that it is so imminently dangerous that it must, in all probability, cause death, or such bodily injury as is likely to cause death, and commits such act without any excuse for incurring the risk of causing death or such injury as aforesaid.

[exceptions, illustrations, and explanations omitted.]

Section 302. Punishment for murder

Whoever commits murder shall be punished with death, or imprisonment for life, and shall also be liable to fine.

Section 303. Punishment for murder by life-convict.

Whoever, being under sentence of imprisonment for life, commits murder, shall be punished with death.

d. *Preventive Detention Act, 1950*

1. Short title, extent and duration.

(1) This Act may be called the Preventive Detention Act, 1950.

...

(3) It shall cease to have effect on the 1st day of April, 1951, save as respects things done or omitted to be done before that date.

...

3. Power to make orders detaining certain persons.

(1) The Central Government or the State Government may—

(a) if satisfied with respect to any person that with a view to preventing him from acting in any manner prejudicial to —

(i) the defence of India, the relations of India with foreign powers, or the security of India, or

(ii) the security of the State or the maintenance of public order, or

(iii) the maintenance of supplies and services essential to the community, or

(b) if satisfied with respect to any person who is a foreigner within the meaning of the Foreigners Act, 1946 (XXXI of 1946), that with a view to regulating his continued presence in India or with a view to making arrangements for his expulsion from India, it is necessary so to do, make an order directing that such person be detained.

(2) Any district magistrate or sub-divisional magistrate, or, in a presidency-town, the commissioner of police, may, if satisfied as provided in sub-clauses

(ii) and (iii) of clause (a) of sub-section (1), exercise the power conferred by the said sub-section.

...

4. Power to regulate place and conditions of detention.

So long as a detention order is in force in respect of any person, he shall be liable to be removed to and detained in, such place and under such conditions, including conditions as to maintenance, discipline, and punishment for breaches of discipline as the Central Government or, as the case may be, the State Government may from time to time by general or special order specify.

...

7. Grounds of order of detention to be disclosed to persons affected by the order.

(1) When a person is detained in pursuance of a detention order, the authority making the order shall, as soon as may be, communicate to him the grounds on which the order has been made, and shall afford him the earlier opportunity of making a representation against the order, in a case where such order has been made by the Central Government, to that Government, and in a case where it has been made by a State Government or an officer subordinate thereto, to the State Government.

(2) Nothing in sub-section (1) shall require the authority to disclose facts which it considers to be against the public interest to disclose.

8. Constitution of Advisory Boards.

(1) The Central Government and each State Government shall, whenever necessary, constitute one or more Advisory Boards for the purposes of this Act.

(2) Every such Board shall consist of two persons who are, or have been, or are qualified to be appointed as, Judges of a High Court, and such persons shall be appointed by the Central Government or the State Government, as the case may be.

9. Reference to Advisory Boards.

In every case where a detention order has been made under sub-clause (iii) of clause (a), or clause (b), of sub-section (1) of section 3, the Government making the order, or if the order has been made by an officer specified in sub-section (2) of section 3, the State Government to which such officer in subordinate, shall, within six weeks from the date of detention under the order, place before the Advisory Board constituted by it under section 8 the grounds on which the order has been made and the representation, if any, made by the person affected by the order, and in case where the order has been made by an officer, also the report made by such officer under sub-section (3) of section 3.

10 . Procedure by Advisory Boards.

(1) The Advisory Board shall, after considering the materials placed before it and, if necessary, after calling for such further information from the Central Government or the State Government or from the person concerned, as it may deem necessary, submit its report to the Central Government or the State Government, as the case may be, within ten weeks from the date of detention under the detention order.

(2) The report of the Advisory Board shall specify in a separate part thereof the opinion of the Advisory Board as to whether or not there is sufficient cause for the detention of the person concerned.

(3) Nothing in this section shall entitle any person against whom a detention order has been made to attend in person or to appear by any legal representative in any matter connected with the reference to the Advisory Board, and the proceedings of the Advisory Board and its report, excepting that part of the report in which the opinion of the Advisory Board is specified, shall be confidential.

11 . Confirmation of detention order.

In any case where the Advisory Board has reported that there is in its opinion sufficient cause for the detention of the person concerned, the Central Government or the State Government, as the case may be, may confirm the detention order and continue the detention of the person concerned for such period as it thinks fit.

12 . Duration of detention in certain cases.

(1) Any person detained in any of the following classes of cases or under any of the following circumstances may be detained without obtaining the opinion of an Advisory Board for a period longer than three months, but not exceeding one year from the date of his detention, namely, where such person has been detained with a view to preventing him from acting in any manner prejudicial to—

   (a) the defence of India, relations of India with foreign powers or the security of India; or

   (b) the security of a State or the maintenance of public order.

(2) The case of every person detained under a detention order to which the provisions of sub-section (1) apply shall, within a period of six months from the date of his detention, be reviewed where the order was made by the Central Government or a State Government, by such Government, and where the order was made by any officer specified in sub-section (2) of section 3, by the State Government to which such officer is subordinate, in consultation with a person who is, or has been, or is qualified to be appointed as, a Judge of a High Court nominated in that behalf by the Central Government or the State Government, as the case may be.

13 . Revocation of detention orders.

(1) Without prejudice to the provisions of section 21 of the General Clauses Act, 1897 (X of 1897), a detention order may at any time be revoked or modified—

(a) notwithstanding that the order has been made by an officer mentioned in sub-section (2) of section 3, by the State Government to which that officer is subordinate or by the Central Government ;

(b) notwithstanding that the order has been made by a State Government, by the Central Government.

(2) The revocation of a detention order shall not bar the making of a fresh detention order under section 3 against the same person.

14. Disclosure of grounds of detention, etc.

(1) No court shall, except for the purposes of a prosecution for an offence punishable under sub-section (2), allow any statement to be made, or any evidence to be given, before it of the substance of any communication made under section 7 of the grounds on which a detention order has been made against any person or of any representation made by him against such order; and, notwithstanding anything contained in any other law, no court shall be entitled to require any public officer to produce before it, or to disclose the substance of, any such communication or representation made, or the proceedings of an Advisory Board or that part of the report of an Advisory Board which is confidential.

(2) It shall be an offence punishable with imprisonment for a term which may extend to one year, or with fine, or with both, for any person to disclose State Government, as the case may be, any contents or matter purporting to be contents of any such communication or representation as is referred to in sub-section (1):

Provided that nothing in this sub-section shall apply to a disclosure made to his legal adviser by a person who is the subject of a detention order.

...

e. Terrorists and Disruptive Activities (Prevention) Act, 1987

3. Punishment for terrorist acts.

(1) Whoever with intent to overawe the Government as by law established or to strike terror in the people or any section of the people or to alienate any section of the people or to adversely affect the harmony amongst different sections of the people does any act or thing by using bombs, dynamite or other explosive substances or inflammable substances or fire-arms or other lethal

weapons or poisons or noxious gases or other chemicals or by any other substances (whether biological or otherwise) of a hazardous nature in such a manner as to cause, or as is likely to cause, death of, or injuries to, any person or persons or loss, of, or damage to, or destruction of, property or disruption of any supplies or services essential to the life of the community, or detains any person and threatens to kill or injure such person in order to compel the Government or any other person to do or abstain from doing any act, commits a terrorist act.

(2) Whoever commits a terrorist act, shall,

> (i) if such act has resulted in the death of any person, be punishable with death or imprisonment for life and shall also be liable to fine;

> (ii) in any other case, be punishable with imprisonment for a term which shall not be less than five years but which may extend to imprisonment for life and shall also be liable to fine.

(3) Whoever conspires or attempts to commit, or advocates, abets, advises or incites or knowingly facilitates the commission of, a terrorist act or any act preparatory to a terrorist act, shall be punishable with imprisonment for a term which shall not be less than five years but which may extend to imprisonment for life and shall also be liable to fine.

(4) Whoever harbours or conceals, or attempts to harbour or conceal, any terrorist shall be punishable with imprisonment for a term which shall not be less than five years but which may extend to imprisonment for life and shall also be liable to fine.

15. Certain confessions made to police officers to be taken into consideration.

(1) Notwithstanding anything contained in the Code or in the Indian Evidence Act, 1872, (1 of 1872) but subject to the provisions of this section, a confession made by a person before a police office not lower in rank than a Superintendent of Police and recorded by such police officer either in writing or on any mechanical device like cassettes, tapes or sound tracks from out of which sounds or images can be reproduced, shall be admissible in the trial of such person for an offence under this Act or rules made thereunder.

(2) The police officer shall, before recording any confession under sub-section (1), explain to the person making it that he is not bound to make a confession and that, if he does so, it may be used as evidence against him and such police officer shall not record any such confession unless upon questioning the person making it, he has reason to believe that it is being made voluntarily.

16 . Protection of witnesses.

(1) Notwithstanding anything contained in the Code, all proceedings before a Designated Court shall be conducted in camera:

Provided that where the Public Prosecutor so applies, any proceedings or part thereof may be held in open court.

(2) A Designated Court may, on an application made by a witness in any proceedings before it or by the Public Prosecutor in relation to such witness or on its own motion, take such measures as it deems fit for keeping the identity and address of any witness secret.

(3) In particular, and without prejudice to the generality of the provisions of sub-section (2), the measures which a Designated Court may take under that sub-section may include—

(a) the holding of the proceedings at a place to be decided by the Designated Court;

(b) the avoiding of the mention of the names and addresses of the witnesses in its orders or judgments or in any records of the case accessible to public;

(c) the issuing of any directions for securing that the identity and addresses of the witnesses are not disclosed;

(d) that it is in the public interest to order that all or any of the proceedings pending before such a court shall not be published in any manner.

(4) Any person who contravenes any direction issued under subsection (3) shall be punishable with imprisonment for a term which may extend to one year and with fine which may extend to one thousand rupees.

21. Presumption as to offences under section 3.

(1) In a prosecution for an offence under sub-section (1) of section 3, if it is proved—

(a) that the arms or explosives or any other substances specified in section 3 were recovered from the possession of the accused and there is reason to believe that such arms or explosives or other substances of a similar nature, were used in the commission of such offence; or

(b) that by the evidence of an expert the finger prints of the accused were found at the site of the offence or on anything including arms and vehicles used in connection with the commission of such offence; or

(c) that a confession has been made by a co-accused that the accused had committed the offence; or

(d) that the accused had made a confession of the offence to any person other than a police officer, the Designated Court shall presume, unless the contrary is proved, that the accused had committed such offence.

(2) In a prosecution for an offence under sub-section (3) of section 3, if it is proved that the accused rendered any financial assistance to a person accused of, or reasonably suspected of, an offence under this section, the Designated Court shall presume, unless the contrary is proved, that such person has committed the offence under that sub-section.

D. The United States

1. Constitution of the United States

Art. I, §9, Clause 2.

The Privilege of the Writ of Habeas Corpus shall not be suspended, unless when in Cases of Rebellion or Invasion the public Safety may require it.

Fifth Amendment

No person shall be held to answer for a capital, or otherwise infamous crime, unless on a presentment or indictment of a Grand Jury, except in cases arising in the land or naval forces, or in the Militia, when in actual service in time of War or public danger; nor shall any person be subject for the same offence to be twice put in jeopardy of life or limb; nor shall be compelled in any criminal case to be a witness against himself, nor be deprived of life, liberty, or property, without due process of law; nor shall private property be taken for public use, without just compensation.

Sixth Amendment

In all criminal prosecutions, the accused shall enjoy the right to a speedy and public trial, by an impartial jury of the State and district wherein the crime shall have been committed, which district shall have been previously ascertained by law, and to be informed of the nature and cause of the accusation; to be confronted with the witnesses against him; to have compulsory process for obtaining witnesses in his favor, and to have the Assistance of Counsel for his defence.

Eighth Amendment

Excessive bail shall not be required, nor excessive fines imposed, nor cruel and unusual punishments inflicted.

Fourteenth Amendment, Section 1

All persons born or naturalized in the United States, and subject to the jurisdiction thereof, are citizens of the United States and of the

State wherein they reside. No State shall make or enforce any law which shall abridge the privileges or immunities of citizens of the United States; nor shall any State deprive any person of life, liberty, or property, without due process of law; nor deny to any person within its jurisdiction the equal protection of the laws.

2. United States Code

Title 10, section 801

[A note following this section codifies the following language, enacted by P.L. 109-148, Div A, Title X, § 1005, 119 Stat. 2739 (December 30, 2005) as amended by P.L. 109-366, § 10, 120 Stat. 2636 (October 17, 2006).]

Sec. 1005. Procedures for status review of detainees outside the United States.

(a) Submittal of procedures for status review of detainees at Guantanamo Bay, Cuba, and in Afghanistan and Iraq.

(1) In general. Not later than 180 days after the date of the enactment of this Act, the Secretary of Defense shall submit to the Committee on Armed Services and the Committee on the Judiciary of the Senate and the Committee on Armed Services and the Committee on the Judiciary of the House of Representatives a report setting forth—

(A) the procedures of the Combatant Status Review Tribunals and the Administrative Review Boards established by direction of the Secretary of Defense that are in operation at Guantanamo Bay, Cuba, for determining the status of the detainees held at Guantanamo Bay or to provide an annual review to determine the need to continue to detain an alien who is a detainee; and

(B) the procedures in operation in Afghanistan and Iraq for a determination of the status of aliens detained in the custody or under the physical control of the Department of Defense in those countries.

(2) Designated Civilian Official. The procedures submitted to Congress pursuant to paragraph (1)(A) shall ensure that the official of the Department of Defense who is designated by the President or Secretary of Defense to be the final review authority within the Department of Defense with respect to decisions of any such tribunal or board (referred to as the 'Designated Civilian Official') shall be a civilian officer of the Department of Defense holding an office to which appoint-

ments are required by law to be made by the President, by and with the advice and consent of the Senate.

(3) Consideration of new evidence. The procedures submitted under paragraph (1)(A) shall provide for periodic review of any new evidence that may become available relating to the enemy combatant status of a detainee.

....

(e) Judicial review of detention of enemy combatants.

....

(2) Review of decisions of combatant status review tribunals of propriety of detention.

(A) In general. Subject to subparagraphs (B), (C), and (D), the United States Court of Appeals for the District of Columbia Circuit shall have exclusive jurisdiction to determine the validity of any final decision of a Combatant Status Review Tribunal that an alien is properly detained as an enemy combatant.

(B) Limitation on claims. The jurisdiction of the United States Court of Appeals for the District of Columbia Circuit under this paragraph shall be limited to claims brought by or on behalf of an alien—

(i) who is, at the time a request for review by such court is filed, detained by the United States; and

(ii) for whom a Combatant Status Review Tribunal has been conducted, pursuant to applicable procedures specified by the Secretary of Defense.

(C) Scope of review. The jurisdiction of the United States Court of Appeals for the District of Columbia Circuit on any claims with respect to an alien under this paragraph shall be limited to the consideration of—

(i) whether the status determination of the Combatant Status Review Tribunal with regard to such alien was consistent with the standards and procedures specified by the Secretary of Defense for Combatant Status Review Tribunals (including the requirement that the conclusion of the Tribunal be supported by a preponderance of the evidence and allowing a rebuttable presumption in favor of the Government's evidence); and

(ii) to the extent the Constitution and laws of the United States are applicable, whether the use of such standards and procedures to make the determination is consistent with the Constitution and laws of the United States.

(D) Termination on release from custody. The jurisdiction of the United States Court of Appeals for the District of Columbia Circuit with respect to the claims of an alien under this paragraph shall cease upon the release of such alien from the custody of the Department of Defense.

Title 28, section 2241

(a) Writs of habeas corpus may be granted by the Supreme Court, any justice thereof, the district courts and any circuit judge within their respective jurisdictions. The order of a circuit judge shall be entered in the records of the district court of the district wherein the restraint complained of is had....

(c) The writ of habeas corpus shall not extend to a prisoner unless—

(1) He is in custody under or by color of the authority of the United States or is committed for trial before some court thereof; or

(2) He is in custody for an act done or omitted in pursuance of an Act of Congress, or an order, process, judgment or decree of a court or judge of the United States; or

(3) He is in custody in violation of the Constitution or laws or treaties of the United States; or

(4) He, being a citizen of a foreign state and domiciled therein is in custody for an act done or omitted under any alleged right, title, authority, privilege, protection, or exemption claimed under the commission, order or sanction of any foreign state, or under color thereof, the validity and effect of which depend upon the law of nations; or

(5) It is necessary to bring him into court to testify or for trial....

(e) (1) No court, justice, or judge shall have jurisdiction to hear or consider an application for a writ of habeas corpus filed by or on behalf of an alien detained by the United States who has been determined by the United States to have been properly detained as an enemy combatant or is awaiting such determination.

(2) Except as provided in paragraphs (2) and (3) of section 1005(e) of the Detainee Treatment Act of 2005 (10 U.S.C. 801 note), no court, justice, or judge shall have jurisdiction to hear or consider any other action against the United States or its agents relating to any aspect of the detention, transfer, treatment, trial, or conditions of confinement of an alien who is or was detained by the United States and has been determined by the United States to have been properly detained as an enemy combatant or is awaiting such determination.

Bibliography

Awasthi, S.K. and R.P. Kataria, *Law Relating to Protection of Human Rights* (New Delhi, Orient Publishing Company, 2000).

Beer, Lawrence W., "Constitutional Revolution in Japanese Law, Society and Politics", 16 *Modern Asian Studies* 33 (1982).

Council of Europe, website, http://www.coe.int/.

———, *Implementation of judgments of the European Court of Human Rights: Court Judgments Pending Before the Committee of Ministers for Control of Execution for More than Five Years, or Otherwise Raising Important Issues*, AS/Jur (2005) 32, 9 June 2005, ajdoc32 2005.

———, *Implementation of judgments of the European Court of Human Rights: Supplementary Introductory Memorandum (Revised)*, AS/Jur (2005), 20 December 2005, ajdoc55 2005rev.

Dean, Meryll, *Japanese Legal System* (London, Cavendish Publishing Ltd., 2d ed., 2002).

Eibu-Horeisha, Inc., *II EHS Law Bulletin Series* (Tokyo, Eibu-Horeisha, Inc. 1988).

European Court of Human Rights, website, http://www.echr.coe.int/echr.

LaFave, Wayne R., Jerold H. Israel, Nancy J. King, *Criminal Procedure* (St. Paul, MN., Thomson-West, 4th ed., 2004).

Merrills, J.G. and A.H. Robertson, *Human Rights in Europe: A Study of the European Convention on Human Rights* (Manchester, Manchester University Press, 4th ed., 2001).

Maki, John M., *Court and Constitution in Japan: Selected Supreme Court Decisions, 1948–1960*, with translations by Ikeda Masaaki, David C.S. Sissons, and Kurt Steiner (Seattle, University of Washington Press, 1964).

Ovey, Clare and Robin C.A. White, *Jacobs and White, The European Convention on Human Rights* (Oxford, Oxford University Press, 3d ed., 2002).

Reynolds, Thomas H. and Arturo A. Flores, "Foreign Law Guide: Current Sources of Codes and Basic Legislation in Jurisdictions of the World", http://www.foreignlawguide.com/ip.

Rotunda, Ronald D. and John E. Nowak, *Treatise on Constitutional Law: Substance and Procedure* (St. Paul, MN.; The West Group; 3d Ed., 1999).

Seervai, H.M., *Constitutional Law of India* (Vols. 1 and 2, Delhi, Universal Book Traders, 4th ed., 1999; Vol. 3, Bombay, N.M. Tripathi Private, Ltd., 4th ed., 1996).

Index